Berry College

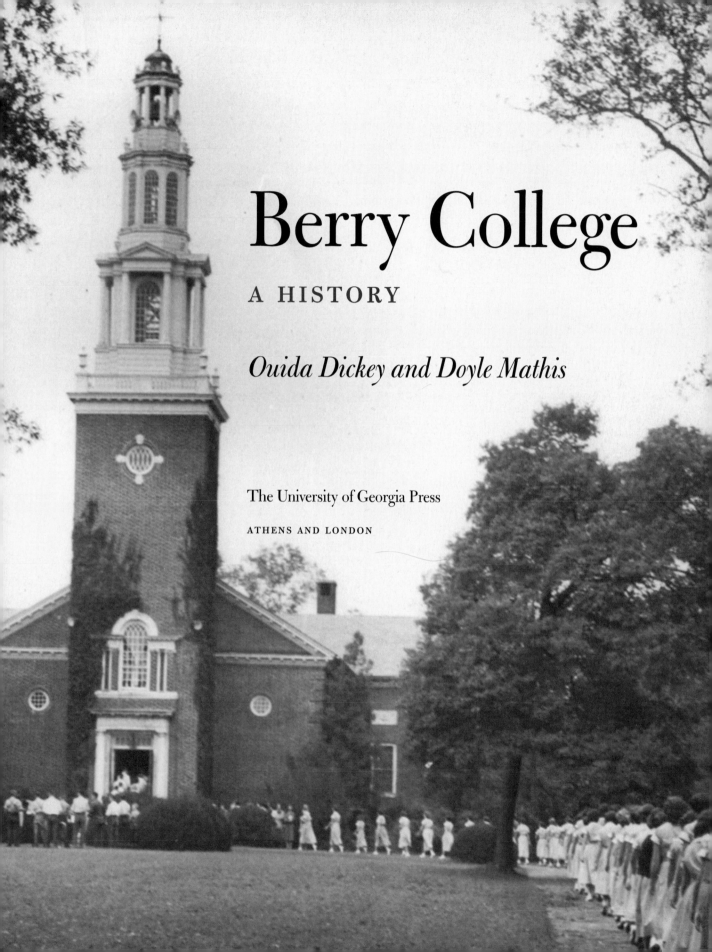

Berry College

A HISTORY

Ouida Dickey and Doyle Mathis

The University of Georgia Press

ATHENS AND LONDON

© 2005 by The University of Georgia Press

Athens, Georgia 30602

All rights reserved

Designed by Kathi Dailey Morgan

Set in Bulmer by Bookcomp

Printed and bound by Maple-Vail

The paper in this book meets the guidelines for

permanence and durability of the Committee on

Production Guidelines for Book Longevity of the

Council on Library Resources.

Printed in the United States of America

09 08 07 06 05 C 5 4 3 2 1

Library of Congress Cataloging-in-Publication Data

Dickey, Ouida.

Berry College : a history / Ouida Dickey and Doyle Mathis.

   p. cm.

Includes bibliographical references and index.

ISBN 0-8203-2758-1 (hardcover : alk. paper)

1. Berry College—History.   I. Mathis, Doyle.   II. Title.

LD405.B22D53 2005

378.758'35—dc22   2005008516

ISBN-13 978-0-8203-2758-7 (hardcover : alk. paper)

British Library Cataloging-in-Publication Data available

All photographs appear courtesy of Berry College.

This book is dedicated to all—trustees, presidents, faculty, staff, alumni, and friends—who devoted years and resources to the development and betterment of Berry College.

Contents

Foreword

The history of Berry College has long been considered the story of its founder, Martha Berry. For many of us, it is hard to separate Martha Berry and her remarkable career from the story of the institution that bears her name. I have told alumni audiences that Martha Berry floats through my office and often looks over my shoulder as I carry out the business of the day. People usually laugh, even as they recognize the ways in which an extraordinary figure can make her presence felt more than sixty years after death. A great leader should inspire those who follow, and my colleagues and I strongly feel such inspiration early in the twenty-first century.

Of course, one can appropriate Martha Berry's vision to support both approval and opposition to current policies. For example, it is possible to cite written statements from 1925 to debate twenty-first-century college practices. For a dozen or more years after Martha Berry's death, "Miss Berry's wishes" certainly became the justification for resisting necessary changes. Conversely, several Berry College presidents have invoked the founder's example to justify departures from tradition. Berry was a whirlwind who introduced more changes in her forty years at the helm than most institutions face during eighty to one hundred years.

Berry's educational experiment has lived on without her only because others took up her cause. This book tells the story of Martha Berry and her successors and shows how her vision has evolved over subsequent generations. Although the authors' firsthand experience spans more than half the history recounted here, the book is no memoir. The narrative rests on documentary evidence. Familiar and beloved old stories that cannot be verified have not found their way into the story.

Ouida Word Dickey came to Berry as a college freshman in 1946. Doyle Mathis began his studies here in 1954. They both pursued graduate studies after their college years. Dr. Dickey began her service to Berry as a faculty member in the business program and served many years as associate dean and later as dean of academic services. Dr. Mathis returned to his alma mater in 1975 to become academic dean, a position that subsequently became vice president for academic affairs and then provost. After his retirement, Dr. Mathis taught in the Department of Government and International Studies. As the college centennial approached, I asked my two colleagues to begin work on a history of Berry's first one hundred years. This volume represents a product of their fine efforts. Not only have Drs. Dickey and Mathis given us this history, they have also prepared the way for other students of college history to follow. Their careful archival work will guide others in the years to come.

Berry College is known for the beauty of its campus and buildings and for its parklike twenty-eight thousand acres. The real distinction of the college, however, is its mission, which is to educate the head, the heart, and the hands, and its motto, "Not to be ministered unto, but to minister." Linking the Berry of 1902 and the Berry of the twenty-first century are our commitment to the intellectual, moral, and spiritual growth of our students; our conviction that important lessons are gained from worthwhile work done well; and our belief that serving one's community is a primary end of higher education. In its second century, Berry proudly remains, as our charter states, "Christian in spirit," even as we offer our students an environment that is open, friendly, and welcoming to persons of diverse backgrounds.

Our institutional history is critical to us. More important, however, is our mission to prepare today's students for a world that they—not their teachers—will inhabit. Undergraduates will live well beyond those who instruct them. In such a sense, Berry College has always been about tomorrow. In 1902, Martha Berry dreamed of giving her first pupils a future to which they could look forward. All these years later, that dream continues.

SCOTT COLLEY
President of Berry College

Acknowledgments

The authors thank many individuals for their assistance with the development of this book. Scott Colley, president of Berry College, encouraged us from the beginning of the project and prepared the foreword. Evelyn Pendley, Berry associate professor of English emerita, and John Lipscomb, Berry vice president for development emeritus, provided valuable information to supplement their earlier writings on Berry history.

Others who have been especially helpful in various offices and divisions at Berry include Susan Asbury-Newsome, former curator of Oak Hill and the Martha Berry Museum; Jonathan Harwell, Laquieda Joiner, Martha Reynolds, Judy Thompson, and Jeremy Worsham, Memorial Library; Shannon Biggers and Stacy Cates, public relations; Judy Hopper, Angie Reynolds, and Alan Storey, president's office; Thomas Dasher, Kathy McKee, and Elizabeth Shamblin, provost's office; Cathy Simpson and Linda Tennant, registrar's office; Maria Popham, institutional research; Carol Willis, student affairs; John Heneisen, student work opportunity; Scott Breithaupt and Kathleen Ray, alumni and constituent relations; Frank George, advancement and land management; Beverly Cornett, Penny Evans-Plants, and Timothy Farnham, information technology; Mike King and Bob Pearson, health and physical education; and Bob Skelton, Win-Shape Centre. In addition, Herman Higgins, Donald Jones, and Ollie Scoggins, former faculty and staff, provided useful information, as did Robert E. Lee, former Berry dean; John R. Bertrand, former Berry president; and Joe Walton, former vice president for finance.

Pat Millican of the Northwest Georgia Genealogical Society assisted with the Berry ancestral search. Richard Stobaeus, graduate of the Northfield Mount Hermon School in Massachusetts, brought insights into that school's relationship to Berry. Nancy Berry, widow of Henry Berry, Martha Berry's nephew, provided important letters from her collection of Berry family memorabilia.

This work would not have been possible without the excellent service provided by the staff of the Berry College Archives, Memorial Library. We offer special thanks to archivist Rebecca Roberts, archives technical assistant Amy Summerlin, and former archivist Ruth Ash as well as to Tyler Womack of the Oak Hill staff.

Alisa Ray of Berry's office of faculty research and sponsored programs provided the essential service of preparing the manuscript. Alumnae Jennifer Dickey and Rheba Mathis read the entire manuscript and contributed many important improvements, and Susan Bandy provided much of the sports history. Kathy Knapp also read the manuscript and made helpful suggestions. Jonathan Atkins of the Berry faculty read the manuscript and proposed very valuable editorial enhancements. We also thank readers Gordon McKinney, professor of history and director of the Appalachian Center at Berea College, and John R. Thelin, university research professor in educational policy studies at the University of Kentucky; indexer Diane Land; copyeditor Ellen Goldlust-Gingrich; and project editor Jon Davies and editor-in-chief Nancy Grayson, both at the University of Georgia Press. All of these colleagues and friends have helped to make this book much better than it would have been, but the authors are responsible for any remaining errors.

Introduction

Although not yet allowed to vote in the United States, women received new opportunities for public life as a consequence of the Progressive spirit that began sweeping the nation in the 1890s. Pioneers such as Jane Addams and Florence Kelley initiated a settlement-house movement to alleviate the suffering of the poor masses in the nation's cities. A decade later, near the small town of Rome in northwest Georgia, Martha Berry was equally moved by the plight of the poor, and despite her friends' and family's admonitions not to become involved, Berry embarked on a quest to provide opportunities for a largely forgotten segment of the population.

A young woman such as Berry, with little formal education and no prior business or educational experience, would seem to have had little chance of success establishing an educational institution at the beginning of the twentieth century, much less developing it into a four-year college, yet that is what Martha Berry accomplished. Having grown up as part of the landed gentry in the southern Appalachian foothills, surrounded by the destitution of rural areas, she recognized that lack of education kept much of the population trapped in a cycle of poverty. Berry's vision was to break that cycle by making education available and affordable for the region's children, and she turned that vision into reality by devoting her resources and time to the fulfillment of her dream.

Berry's initial efforts were straightforward—moving small numbers of students from illiteracy to high-school diplomas. She gained momentum through wealthy family and friends in the East, and those friendships and connections helped her expand her following even more. Unlike her contemporary, Mary McLeod Bethune, the daughter of a former slave who worked her way through college and later founded Bethune-Cookman College in Daytona Beach, Florida, Martha Berry knew little of the meaning of work until she envisioned a school to "free" mountain children from the bonds of poverty and improve their quality of life on the homestead. And although she was well read, Berry's formal education consisted of little more than a few years of home tutoring and a few months of finishing school.

The expected path for a woman of Martha Berry's social standing was marriage and motherhood, but she instead chose to claim her students as her children. Berry devoted her efforts toward school fundraising and the daily direction of her institution. Her efforts helped her acquire the resources to turn her institution from a small, whitewashed day school into a residential campus of three institutions with a combined enrollment of more than one thousand students at the time of her death in 1942.

Berry's legacy extended well beyond her schools, however. Susan Asbury, a researcher and former curator of the Martha Berry Museum, noted in her foreword to the 2002 reprinting of *Miracle in the Mountains* that Martha Berry's involvement in social movements extended to such concerns and ideologies as "home economics, colonial revival, scientific management, cultural preservation, and educational reform. . . . She was an avid social reformer . . . who undertook a role as 'moral housekeeper' to a particular region."[1]

Visitors from as far away as India and Japan came to inspect Berry's schools, which focused on the education of the head, the heart, and the hands, and other institutions were created with characteristics fashioned after Berry's or designed to fill another void. After visiting Berry's schools, the Georgia commissioner of education, W. B. Merritt, stated in 1906 that Martha Berry had "blazed the way for the establishment of the district agricultural schools throughout the state." These schools were the forerunners of such institutions of public higher education as Georgia Southern University, Georgia Southwestern State University, State University of West Georgia, Abraham Baldwin Agricultural College, Middle Georgia College, and South Georgia College. Virginia and Tennessee educators also studied Berry's efforts before embarking on their own. At Berry's death, J. R. McCain, president of Agnes Scott College in Atlanta, wrote, "One of the great accomplishments of her life was influencing other schools to put on work programs and personalized training. I happen to know of her influence on Nacoochee Institute and Rabun Gap School, upon Lees-McRae College, upon Highland Institute and Stuart Robinson School, and upon a great many others for both whites and blacks."[2]

For their accomplishments and influence on others, the Berry Schools received wide recognition, and Berry herself received eight honorary doctorates: a doctorate in pedagogy from the University of Georgia in 1920, a doctorate of laws from the University of North Carolina in 1930, a doctorate of laws from Bates College and a doctorate in humanities

from Berry College in 1933, a doctorate in public service from Oglethorpe University and a doctorate of laws from Duke University in 1935, a doctorate of letters from Oberlin College in 1936, and a doctorate of laws from the University of Wisconsin in 1937. Martha Berry also received other significant honors. In 1924 the Georgia General Assembly voted her Distinguished Citizen of the State. In 1930 Ida Tarbell included Martha Berry on a list of "America's 50 Greatest Women," and in 1931 the readers of *Good Housekeeping* magazine voted her one of "America's Twelve Greatest Women."

Perhaps the most notable recognition came with Martha Berry's reception in 1934 by King George V and Queen Mary at the Court of St. James's. Other honors and awards Martha Berry received include the Roosevelt Medal (1925), *Pictorial Review*'s annual Achievement Award (1927), appointment to the national committee for observance of the four hundredth anniversary of the English Bible (1935), appointment to the Georgia State Planning Board (1937), an American Institute of Social Sciences Medal (1939), the annual Humanitarian Award from the Variety Clubs of America (1940), and the key to the city of Chattanooga, Tennessee (1940).

Honors continued to come after her death. The *Martha Berry,* a liberty ship, was christened in her honor in Savannah in 1944; the *Berry,* a victory ship, was christened in San Francisco in honor of her school in 1945. In 1966 the Atlanta Gas Light Company placed its Shining Light Award at Berry's grave near the Berry College Chapel. During the 1950s, the Georgia Legislature designated U.S. Highway 27 from Tennessee to Florida the Martha Berry Highway, and in 1981 the legislature again recognized Berry by hanging her portrait in the State Capitol Gallery. Reflecting on the preceding hundred years, *Georgia Trend* magazine in 2000 named Martha Berry one of "100 Georgians of the Century." Hall of fame inductions for Martha Berry include Georgia Women of Achievement Hall of Fame in 1992 and the University of Georgia's Agriculture Hall of Fame in 2002. Despite the widespread recognition and accolades that Berry received throughout her life, however, her posthumous fame has been limited primarily to her native state. Indeed, she was so idolized and enshrined in the Rome area that her successors had difficulty moving on as needed, and failure to make noticeable progress for a decade after her death proved a serious setback for the college.

Berry's success has not been without criticism. Some critics felt that her concern for training students to return to their rural environments and upgrade the quality of life there interfered with the need to prepare students for life elsewhere. A few former students questioned her requirement that all students should work and accused her of "slave labor." Later, the John M. Olin Foundation questioned whether the work program might be limited only to those needing the financial support.

Berry's southern upbringing no doubt influenced her concentration on land acquisition rather than securities as the best investment for endowment. The result of this focus was a beautiful and expansive domain as well as separated campuses and increased expenses to maintain infrastructure, such as roads and grounds. It cost Berry in other ways as well. The Olin Foundation declined to sponsor a building, at least partially because of the schools' extensive landholdings.

Martha Berry might have fixed her place in history more prominently had she established her college somewhat earlier and more strongly emphasized its development in relation to her other schools. She enjoyed great fame and success through the 1920s, but the Great Depression and her recurring illnesses seriously hampered her efforts over the last decade of her life. Despite her infirmities, she continued to direct as much of the institution as she could until her death. Had she delegated more responsibility to carefully selected college administrators, her successors would have been better prepared to carry on her mission. The failure adequately to prepare her successors and the later reluctance of those in charge to make the changes necessary for appropriate development adversely affected the advancement of the college until William McChesney Martin's accession to the chairmanship of the board of trustees and the arrival of John R. Bertrand in 1956.

Yet despite such shortcomings, Martha Berry was a long-range planner, particularly with regard to buildings and campus development, and she has often been cited as a visionary and an agent of change. She made drastic changes over her forty years. However, her final letter to alumni admonishing them "to hold the Schools to the original plan," letters to others carrying basically the same message, and her comments that she would rather see Berry closed than changed to just another school were often cited as reasons not to make changes and undoubtedly at times deterred progress.[3] The letters, though opened only after Martha Berry's death in 1942, were written in 1925. Without question, those messages have been greatly misinterpreted through the years. As later administrators would demonstrate, carrying out Martha Berry's mission could best be accomplished by making policy, procedural, and programmatic changes in keeping with the times, as she had done in the schools' early days.

In *Half Century at Berry*, S. H. Cook articulated his belief in change by quoting Harry Golden: "Reverence for the past is important, but the past must not lay too heavy a hand on the future."[4] Heeding the admonishments of both Cook and Berry, the college's leaders have continued its commitment to provide opportunity and affordable education for qualified students with emphasis on high academic standards, practical work experience, community service, and values based on Christian principles. While continuing to pursue the mission of educating the head, the heart, and the hands, the college has expanded its reach to a wide range of cultural, economic, and social backgrounds. Although Martha Berry's death was traumatic for the school she created, the foundation she laid proved so strong that it sustained the school through the years of transition.

Berry College

Descriptions of the educational and socioeconomic conditions
of the southern highlanders in the latter part of the nineteenth
century and the early years of the twentieth century provide
the historical setting for the founding of the Berry School.
As Martha Berry, a daughter of privilege, learned about the lack
of education and the poor economic circumstances of people
in rural areas of the South, she became interested in efforts to
improve their opportunities for a better life, thereby forever
changing the direction of her life.

CHAPTER ONE

Origin of a Vision

The Rise of Public and Private Schools

The Georgia Constitution of 1777, written just a
year after the adoption of the Declaration of Independence, called for the building of schools in each
county to be supported by the state, and six years
later the state legislature authorized the first of these
schools, which came to be known as academies. By
1800, almost all of the state's schools, including the
county academies, were private, requiring the payment of tuition. These academies provided a classi-
cal education as well as more practical courses and
prepared some students for college. For most students, however, attendance at the academies, which
offered both elementary and secondary, or high-
school, education, represented the extent of their
education. Other private elementary schools soon
came into existence. These old-field schools de-
rived their name from the fact that they were often
built in fields no longer suitable for agriculture, and

they typically offered arithmetic, English, geography, reading, spelling, and writing. Most Georgia
children, however, received little or no education.[1]

In 1817, the Georgia legislature provided for a
free-school fund, but before any schools were established, the fund was restricted to the children
of the poor, with money apportioned to counties
for the education solely of children of families willing essentially to declare themselves paupers. The
schools for children of those classified as poor provided limited educational opportunities in counties
across the state. In 1837, the legislature passed a
measure providing for a common-school system, but
an economic depression began that year, and the
law was rescinded in 1840. The children of Georgia's middle- and upper-class families continued to
receive education in the private old-field schools
and academies, while the children of the indigent
attended the public poor schools. In the late 1850s,
the state legislature enacted another plan to establish

a broad system of public schools, but the Civil War soon brought an end to this effort.[2]

In 1870, the state legislature authorized a public-school system, which soon was established at the primary level. The school terms initially lasted three months per year and increased only to four months by 1890. High schools remained private, since the 1877 Constitution provided only for elementary education and the state university. In 1903, the state had just seven four-year high schools, which graduated a total of ninety-four students.[3]

For more than a century in various parts of the world, interest in education for the practical needs of life had stimulated a movement for manual-labor education. Johann Heinrich Pestalozzi was one of the earliest adherents of the combination of manual and industrial activities with education. As early as 1775, he operated a school in Zurich, Switzerland, that included in its curriculum farm production and other manual activities. Over the next three decades he worked unsuccessfully to establish a system of such schools, but Phillip Emanuel von Fellenberg and others had better results establishing manual-labor schools in Switzerland during the first half of the nineteenth century. These institutions combined literary instruction, science education related to agriculture, and farm labor.[4]

In 1797, John De le Howe established the first U.S. manual-labor school, at Lithe, South Carolina. He sought to prepare boys to be farmers and girls to be farmers' wives. By 1830, manual-labor schools operated in numerous states, most of them different from Howe's school in that the primary focus was not teaching manual arts but rather connecting education and labor. While student labor was expected to assist in reducing educational expenses and economic class distinctions, it would also improve students' health. The idea was that the mind and the body were so interconnected that both would benefit from being "educated" in tandem. Some educators

and religious leaders saw manual-labor schools as a means of financing education, in particular for those preparing for the ministry, while others viewed the schools as providing a more democratic education because every student worked as part of his or her education.[5] Many U.S. institutions of higher education, including Centre, Furman, Richmond, and Wake Forest as well as Georgia's Emory, Mercer, and Oglethorpe Universities, either were founded as part of or were associated with the manual-labor movement. Blackburn College in Illinois, founded in 1837, has the longest U.S. tradition of a mandatory on-campus work program, while Kentucky's Berea College, founded in 1855, is often considered the nation's most widely recognized work-study college. Other well-known work colleges include North Carolina's Warren Wilson, founded in 1894, and Missouri's College of the Ozarks, founded in 1906.[6] By 1840, Georgia had ten Protestant denominational manual-labor schools.

However, Georgia's manual-labor movement faded as quickly as it had arisen, essentially disappearing by the early 1840s. The problem arose in part because too many schools had been established too quickly and with inadequate planning; in addition, many people gradually realized that the idea was not very practical. The movement probably did lead to the post–Civil War creation of agricultural and industrial schools and may also have led to a continuing desire for vocational education, which was incorporated into the high schools, particularly in rural areas, from the early twentieth century through the federal Smith-Hughes Act of 1917. The manual-labor schools also constituted forerunners of the agricultural and mechanical-arts high schools authorized in each of Georgia's congressional districts by a 1906 state law.[7]

In the late 1800s, a variety of other schools were established across the nation, including institutions serving African Americans. The Normal

School for Negroes was founded in 1881 in Alabama. Booker T. Washington served as the first principal of this school, which became famous as Tuskegee Institute. Mary McLeod Bethune, an African American woman, founded Daytona Normal and Industrial Institute for Negro Girls at Daytona Beach, Florida, in 1904, and after merging with Cookman Institute, the school became Bethune-Cookman College. In 1915, a woman from New England, Alice Lloyd, established a school in the mountains of eastern Kentucky, and she served as its head for forty-seven years until her death, when the school took on her name.[8] In 1911, the superintendent of the public school system of Rowan County, Kentucky, Cora Wilson Stewart, began a night-school program to teach adults to read and write, with volunteers from the public schools for children serving as instructors. Known as Moonlight Schools because they were open on nights when the moon was sufficiently bright to allow people to make their way to the schools, these programs enrolled approximately twelve hundred people the first year, and by 1915 an estimated forty thousand Kentucky adults had learned basic literacy from the schools. This model soon spread to more than a dozen other states.[9]

As a result of her travels and contacts with donors and educators, Martha Berry would certainly have known of Berea and Warren Wilson, but no evidence suggests that she borrowed ideas from either of these institutions. The early primary influence on Berry was the Mount Hermon School for Boys, where several early members of Berry's faculty and staff were educated or had previously worked. Martha Berry and members of her staff visited the Massachusetts school several times, and Berry's school was sometimes known at both institutions as the Mount Hermon of the South.[10] Prominent evangelist Dwight L. Moody had founded the Northfield Seminary for Girls in Massachusetts in the late 1870s, and in

1881 he followed with the Mount Hermon School for Boys, also located in Northfield. Mount Hermon offered education to young men of limited financial means and required each student to engage in manual labor for two hours each day, thereby instilling in them the dignity of labor. Although the school was not influenced or controlled by any particular denomination, it was thoroughly Christian, demanding of its students the highest standards of personal character and requiring Bible study. Mount Hermon purported to "educate the Head, the Hand, and the Heart."[11]

Also developing in the late 1800s was the Sunday school movement, and it reached the Rome area around 1895, when both Martha Berry and Mary F. "Mamie" McHenry started Sunday schools in the region. At that time, Floyd County had many small elementary schools established or already operating, some founded without public support but later funded by the Floyd County Board of Education, others promised county support before they opened. These schools generally lacked good facilities and supplies, the teachers often were not well educated, and many of the schools charged tuition and fees.

The highlanders of northwest Georgia and other rural areas of the South desperately needed education. Under these circumstances, a single school like that established by Martha Berry could have a substantial impact on education in the surrounding community and even the state.

Martha Berry's Roots and Early Life

Martha Berry inherited her pioneering spirit from her Scots-Irish ancestors and from her parents. Her Berry ancestors had come to the British colonies in North America from Northern Ireland during the first half of the eighteenth century.[12] Thomas Berry, Martha's great-grandfather, fought in the American

Captain Thomas Berry, father of Martha Berry, c. 1868.

Frances Rhea Berry, mother of Martha Berry, c. 1910.

Oak Hill, home of Martha Berry, purchased by her father in 1871, 1916.

Revolution in Virginia. He died in Blount County, Tennessee, in 1805. James Enfield Berry, Martha's grandfather, a merchant, was born in Washington County, Virginia, on April 15, 1790. He served as postmaster in Maryville, Tennessee, where Martha's father, Thomas, was born on September 21, 1821. The family moved to Chattanooga in the late 1830s, and James served as the city's first mayor in 1840 before moving his family to Summerville, Chattooga County, Georgia, about twenty-five miles north of Rome, in the early 1840s. He later moved to Jacksonville, Alabama, where he died on January 26, 1857.[13]

In 1846, Martha's father bought his first land (160 acres) with a brother-in-law.[14] Ready for new challenges and opportunities, Thomas joined the military for the Mexican War and served as a first lieutenant in Company D of the Battalion of Georgia Mounted Volunteers from September 1847 until his discharge in July 1848.[15] He soon joined a group of about fifteen people from Floyd County who left Rome on March 6, 1849, to join the California gold rush. It is not known how long Thomas Berry remained in California, but according to family tradition, he returned without large amounts of gold or money.[16]

Thomas Berry married Frances Margaret Rhea, the daughter of Lewis L. Rhea, a wealthy plantation owner, and Martha Holloway Rhea, in Cherokee County, Alabama, on April 11, 1860.[17] Thomas and Frances lived on a plantation in the Turkeytown area, a few miles east of Gadsden in Cherokee County

Berry siblings and friends on an outing at the Oostanaula River, 1890s.

(later Etowah County). The 1860 Census reported the Berry real estate as worth $5,200 and their personal estate as $10,000 (approximately $203,000 in 2003), including at least one slave.[18]

Less than a year after his marriage, Berry rejoined the military, enlisting in Company A, Thirty-first Regiment, Alabama Infantry, on March 3, 1861. He was initially a first lieutenant, but after appointment as assistant quartermaster on May 7, 1862, he was promoted to the rank of captain on October 14 of that year. He was with his unit when it surrendered at Vicksburg on July 4, 1863, following the Union siege. After his parole a few days later, Berry appears to have spent most of the remainder of the war in or near Alabama, procuring supplies needed by the army.[19]

In July 1866, Thomas Berry bought his first property in Floyd County, Georgia, a home on Howard Street (now east Rome's Second Avenue)

that he purchased from John R. Freeman for $7,750 ($96,980 in 2003).[20] According to family legend, he was able to borrow $50,000 in the North because, unlike many of his fellow southerners, he had paid all his northern debts at the beginning of the war, and he used that money to buy other properties, including space for a business on the "cotton block," the southernmost block of Broad Street in downtown Rome. In July 1871, Thomas bought the Berry family home property, later called Oak Hill, from Andrew M. Sloan for $9,000.[21] A Rome newspaper advertisement for this property described it as "one and a half miles north of Rome, on the Summerville Road, 116 acres mostly fine river bottom—elegant improvements—beautiful situation—the former residence of Maj. C. H. Smith (Bill Arp, so called.)"[22]

Thomas Berry, his younger brothers, James and John, and several others were partners in Berrys and

Company, a wholesale and retail grocery distributor and buyer and seller of cotton. The company made high-interest loans to farmers in both Georgia and Alabama, securing the loans with liens on crops and mortgages.[23] The business was quite successful from the late 1860s to the early 1880s, when Thomas Berry had a stroke and began to drop out of the business. In 1882 the name of the business changed to Montgomery, McLaurin, and Company, although Thomas Berry seems to have continued to participate to some extent.[24]

Thomas and Frances Berry had eight children between 1861 and 1878: Eugenia (Jennie), Martha, Isaac (Ike), Rebecca (Bessie), Thomas, Lila, Laura, and Frances. Following the death of his brother, James, Thomas Berry raised three of James's children, Charlie, Mary, and Sarah. Martha was born in Cherokee County, Alabama, and gave her birth date as October 7, 1866.[25]

As a young girl, Martha Berry enjoyed horseback riding with her father in the hill and mountain areas near their home. Sometimes they talked with people they met along the roads and trails; at other times, Martha and her father visited in the log-cabin homes of the poor people of the highlands. Captain Berry, a comparatively wealthy merchant, cotton buyer, and plantation owner, was well known by the people living in the surrounding areas; he often received requests for assistance and seems to have had a genuine desire to help his poorer neighbors. Martha got to know many of the hill people and continued to travel the trails and roads on horseback or in a carriage and to visit with the people for decades after the death of her father.

Martha wrote that "The greatest influence in my life was having a father who praised and encouraged me whenever I did anything well and who taught me to love animals, birds and flowers and take care of every living thing. He never allowed me to waste even an apple peeling, and I had to save the bread crumbs

Martha Berry, c. 1883.

for the birds. He made me feel that if I wasted anything that a living creature could use it was sinful." In 1882, Thomas Berry wrote some of his other ideas in the back of the Berry family Bible under the heading "Free Labor": "The Retired Merchant Farmer with no income is growing poorer. Must make his children go to work. Teach them the value of time and economy with work while it is day work in the seed time. Work in the harvest. Master work. Be brave. Don't be afraid of work or of tools." Martha Berry was also influenced by her governess and teacher, Ida McCullough, writing, "I had for ten years a governess who had a strong Christian character and a great love for nature. . . . She always read stories of heroes and heroines and of people whose lives were brave and true, and she had the power of kindling my imagination and making them live again. I felt that I also could and MUST do something worthwhile with my life."[26]

Martha Berry and Frances Rhea Berry, on vacation in Tennessee, c. 1888.

Her sister, Frances, described Martha as a slender girl with gray-blue eyes, very fair skin, very black hair, a lovely smile, and a good personality. Elizabeth Brewster, who helped Martha Berry with her early schools, described Martha as being of medium height with a rounded figure, a little inclined to stoutness, and as energetic and youthful; she had a quick, elastic step; dark hair; gray eyes; regular features; a mouth that combined firmness with gentleness; a southern accent; a soft, cultured voice; a gracious manner; a quick wit; irresistible charm; and a face that lit up when she spoke. Brewster also mentioned Martha's tact, insight, business integrity, keen sense of humor, courage, and poise.[27]

When Martha was about sixteen, a young man a few years her senior came from Virginia to Rome to learn the cotton business from Thomas Berry. The man, whose name no longer survives, began to court Martha, but her parents urged her to complete her education before marrying. Like all of her sisters except Jennie, Martha attended Madame LeFevre's Edgeworth School in Baltimore. Martha did not like the school and threatened to return home, but her father said he would send her right back if she did. Her father learned that she was displeased with her clothes, which apparently did not appear in style to the wealthy girls from other areas of the country, so he sent money so that Madame LeFevre could take his daughter shopping. Although Martha subsequently seemed happier, she took advantage of the opportunity to come home before the end of the year when her father suffered his stroke. She did not return to school but instead spent time with her father and helped her mother with the additional responsibilities brought on by Thomas Berry's illness.[28]

Thomas Berry died on January 18, 1887, leaving Martha two tracts of land across the Summerville Road from their home. Her mother received the use of and profits from Oak Hill and the interest on fifteen thousand dollars in bonds during her lifetime.[29] Very little is known of Martha's life during the following decade. She helped her mother with business and family matters and assisted with her younger sisters. She had continued to see the man from Virginia after her return from Baltimore; her parents approved of the relationship and bought a house in east Rome that was apparently intended to be the couple's home following their marriage. Martha, however, would not consider marriage while her father was so ill, and although the romance continued for a time following Thomas Berry's death, she subsequently announced the end of the engagement. During this time, various other young men of the area sought her attention, and she often played tennis on the two courts at her home. She played jokes on her younger brothers and sisters or their governess. She read and studied in a retreat she made for herself in a small log cabin that had been built as a playhouse and had sometimes been used as a school for the Berry children. She also liked to travel and eventually made several trips to Europe.[30]

By the mid-1890s, Martha was thirty years old and had probably decided that she likely would not marry. She was thinking of becoming a writer. She enjoyed being with her family and friends but also spent time by herself reading and writing. The Berry family was affluent, enjoying many benefits not available to most families of the time, including servants; a governess; private schools; trips to other parts of the country and Europe; a summer mountain home at Mentone, Alabama; hundreds of acres of land; horses for riding; and tennis courts. Yet Martha Berry chose to give up this life of relative leisure as well as marriage and a traditional family to assume a life of service to others. She either inherited or learned from her mother the characteristics of graciousness and hospitality, courage, and determination. From her father, she inherited or learned genuine concern for the needs of others, a spirit of adventure, a sense for meeting challenges and seizing opportunities, some business skills, and the ability to interact with people of all stations in life. Although lacking the education and experience that would have been beneficial in the work ahead, Martha Berry gradually assumed the challenge of helping to bring greater opportunities for a better life to the people of the southern highlands and rural areas.

Life in the Southern Highlands

Most of the people living in northwestern Georgia in the latter part of the nineteenth century were descendants of those who had migrated south and west from Virginia, North Carolina, South Carolina, and Ten-

nessee or had come from older sections of Georgia as a result of the 1832 lotteries that distributed former Cherokee Indian lands to whites. The new owners could then settle on the land or sell it to others. Lots that might be expected to contain gold included 40 acres; other lots—the majority—contained 160 acres.[31] Those fortunate enough to acquire sufficient land in the good soil areas of the valleys and river bottoms usually prospered, but such was not the case for those living on mountains and hilly lands.

In 1860, the per capita wealth of Georgia's whites was double that of New York or Pennsylvania residents. The average farm in Georgia was twice the size of the average midwestern farm, and the value of the property owned by the average Georgia slaveholder was five times that of the property of the average person in the North. Many of Georgia's poor whites lived in the mountains and hills in the northern part of the state, areas that were home to relatively few blacks.[32] Yeoman and tenant farmers in the hill country north of Rome did not experience the same prewar success as the South's large farm and plantation owners. These small farmers usually did not own slaves, generally did not use the best agricultural practices, and often were relegated to small plots of poor-quality land. These farmers usually had large families—good for the supply of labor but bad for the expenses of food, clothing, and other necessities. The farms shrank as they were divided among the numerous children, most of whom had neither the time nor the opportunity to attend school.

The Civil War severely disrupted the South's economy, leaving it in a shambles by the end of the conflict. Working even the most meager farm operation became extremely difficult without young adult or middle-aged males, and many families became even poorer. Even men who survived the war and returned able bodied had great difficulty getting their lives and those of their families in order. A decade of

Reconstruction brought more economic and political disruptions, which were exacerbated by national depressions beginning in 1873 and 1882.

During the 1870s and 1880s, Georgia's government operated largely on behalf of business and industrial interests rather than on behalf of the agricultural interests that represented the majority of the state's population. In the mid-1880s, as the plight of the farmers in the South and across the nation worsened, farmers began to organize for self-support, setting up buying and selling co-ops and distributing information about better farming methods. Georgia's primary agricultural organization was the Farmers' Alliance, and by 1890 it numbered well over one hundred thousand members. The group's interests shifted from purely economic to more political, a shift that accelerated when cotton prices dropped by half during that year. Even though the Farmers' Alliance won a large majority in both houses of the Georgia legislature in the 1890 elections, few of the group's proposals for improving farmers' futures became law. Finding the Democratic Party unresponsive, many debt-ridden farmers then turned to the new Populist Party, led in Georgia by Thomas Watson, but the Populists accomplished no more than the Farmers' Alliance had.

The period from 1864 to 1896 represented a time of agricultural hardship throughout most of the United States, with the South faring even worse than the remainder of the country. In 1860, the output per farm in the South was slightly above the U.S. average, but by 1910, southern farms' output averaged only 43 percent of that for the nation as a whole.[33] Despite the bad times for agriculture and the extremely poor performance of southern farms, the vast majority of the region's native whites as well as its black males remained engaged in agriculture through the early twentieth century.

Although some owned large farms and more owned small farms, most southern farmers of both races became tenants or sharecroppers. Those who could afford to do so rented land and usually a house for cash, a set amount of farm produce, or a percentage of farm production. These renters usually provided their own animals, tools, seeds, and fertilizers. A growing majority could not afford to provide their own supplies and consequently became sharecroppers. The landowners supplied land, a house, and equipment, while the sharecroppers provided labor. The landowners and sharecroppers usually divided the crops equally.[34]

The sharecropping system frequently led to an inescapable cycle of debt. Most sharecroppers and renters as well as many landowners lacked money to buy food and other necessities. These people became dependent on the country stores and other merchants (including Berrys and Company) for credit because few banks existed to provide loans. In exchange, liens were usually placed on the expected crops; in bad years, however, the crops did not cover the debt, and it had to be carried over until the sale of the next year's crop. The result was an often crushing spiral of debt. Merchants who extended credit usually insisted on cotton crops, which were expected to sell for the best prices, but the resulting increase in production instead caused cotton prices to decline.[35]

Southern highlanders often knew little about hygiene and sanitation and suffered from a variety of diseases linked to their poor conditions. Very large families often lived in perhaps two or three rooms in poorly built cabins. Residents would sleep together even when ill; one person's contagious disease would spread quickly among family members. Prevalent diseases included pellagra, typhoid, tuberculosis, scarlet fever, diphtheria, and smallpox. Because there were few physicians, numerous health-care needs went unattended.

Furthermore, the people of the southern highlands often received insufficient nourishment that

Laundry day for a rural Georgia family, c. 1925.

Children at a mountain cabin, c. 1925.

exacerbated their health problems. Corn and pork were staples of the region's generally poor diets, which were supplemented by wild creatures that could be hunted, such as rabbits, squirrels, and opossums; "sallets" of such wild plants as bear's lettuce, cress, and poke; wild blackberries, strawberries, and huckleberries; and grapes. Gardens produced beans, Irish potatoes, and onions and perhaps beets, cabbages, sweet potatoes, and turnips. Apples and peaches grew wild or in orchards. Fruits and vegetables, which were dried outdoors, were often covered with flies. Canning was a common practice, and foods were usually prepared by frying or boiling. A large percentage of the people, both men and women, dipped snuff, chewed tobacco, or did both.

The highlanders made their own liquor and drank it as they wished. The health, hygiene, and sanitation of the hill people generally left much to be desired.[36]

The southern highlanders generally had a strong interest in religion. Even those who were illiterate or very poor readers often had extensive knowledge of the Bible, and they enjoyed theological debates. The earliest European settlers had been largely Calvinists, particularly Scots-Irish Presbyterians who were prominent supporters of American independence and strongly believed in freedom of religion from government control. Their insistence on an educated clergy sometimes resulted in a lack of sufficient ministers and slower growth of the numbers of congregations and total membership than might have been the case otherwise. To fill this void, Presbyterians established academies and colleges to educate their ministers and the people generally.

In the second half of the eighteenth century, the number of Baptists grew rapidly in North Carolina and Virginia, and their influence soon spread throughout those states as well as the broader South. Fundamental democracy was a major principle that guided their practices. They believed that each man, regardless of economic circumstances or education, had the right to think for himself and to develop individual religious beliefs. Baptist religious services were very emotional and quite dramatic, stressing sin and repentance. Baptists encouraged only adult believers and insisted on baptism by immersion. They believed that their ministers were divinely called, and they usually had very limited education and served for little or no pay.

While Baptists were persecuted in some southern areas during the colonial era, they played an important role in achieving freedom of religion and separation of church and state in the new nation. Many people came to view the Baptists as fighting the common people's battles and as protesting political, social, and religious privilege associated with the upper classes. These views sometimes discouraged education, which was not considered important even for ministers. The Baptists became the South's largest religious group, followed by the Methodists and then the Presbyterians.[37]

A higher level of illiteracy than in other areas of the United States and fewer opportunities for good or even marginal education marked the lives of the highlanders, who usually lived in isolated areas. Even when schools were available, teachers were difficult to obtain. Most teachers were inadequately trained, young, and inexperienced. In fact, many teachers had only a rudimentary education obtained in elementary schools like those in which they were teaching. Even when better-trained teachers were available, less competent, local teachers often were employed. The people of the highlands in particular did not want teachers who were too progressive and preferred teachers well acquainted with and accepting of local customs and beliefs. Furthermore, a lack of attendance laws and lax enforcement of those that did exist resulted in low attendance rates, even when school was in session, which was usually only a few months each year. School facilities and supplies, usually of very poor quality and quantity, did not help students observe cleanliness and order or develop other beneficial characteristics. Unless the students were quite fortunate and determined, they received very little education.[38]

Such were the conditions endured by the rather poor people in the hill country north of Rome, from which Martha Berry's first students came. In 1902, a Massachusetts man observed that these were "a poor, ignorant, neglected people and God alone knows the greatness of their need." He also thought that the area's poor whites were in a "degraded condition" and that in another generation their apathy could put them on "a much lower scale of humanity" than even the blacks. The poor whites, he said, generally lacked ambition and did not desire education, while most blacks had ambition and wanted education.[39] While such problems certainly existed across the country, the people of the highlands and other areas of the rural South needed educational opportunities and other assistance.

Martha Berry's passion for educating the economically deprived youth of the rural South developed gradually from the late 1890s through her founding of Sunday schools, day schools, and, in 1902, a boarding school for boys. She established a board of trustees, incorporated the Boys Industrial School, and donated land she had inherited to the school. She established an appreciation for academics, religion, work, and simplicity. The institution awarded its first high-school diploma in 1904 and changed its name to the Berry School in 1908.

CHAPTER TWO

Sharpening the Focus

Early Sunday and Day Schools

In 1904, Martha Berry related her initial contact with the children she would later teach:

The poor people of the neighboring hills and piney woods had often appealed to my sympathy, but I had never thought seriously of their condition, or really tried to do anything for them, until one Sunday afternoon in the spring, about six years ago. On this particular Sunday afternoon, I was in a little cabin which I had fitted up as my "den," enjoying, all alone, the freshness and delight of the spring beauty and blossoms by which I was surrounded. I suddenly became aware of three little faces peering in at me from the window. They were bright faces, and the unspoken longing that I saw in them caused me to throw aside my book, to go forward, and to speak to them. But they were very shy, these three little "poor white" children, and it was only

by tempting them with apples that I could coax them to come into the cabin and talk to me. After I had gained their confidence, I remembered that it was Sunday, and I began to tell some Bible stories. They had never heard any of these stories before, and they listened with an almost pathetic eagerness. Their bright faces, their keen interest, and their need of knowledge so touched my heart that I told them to come back again the next Sunday, and to bring all brothers and sisters, and I would tell them more stories out of the Bible.[1]

In 1953, W. W. Phillips, one of those three boys, recalled a slightly different version of the story. He and two brothers, Tom and Albert Carter, were returning from their regular Sunday afternoon swim in the Oostanaula River when Martha and her two youngest sisters, Frances and Laura, called out for the boys to come over to where the women were standing under some trees in the Berry yard. The

Martha Berry at the Original Cabin, c. 1902.

Berrys asked the boys' names, where they lived, and whether they attended Sunday school. After the boys indicated that they did not, the Berry sisters led them to the log cabin and talked to them about the Bible and then asked them to come back the next Sunday and bring others. As Phillips recalled, seven or so children came the next week, and the number soon grew to eighteen and beyond. The log cabin where Martha Berry met the children is now called the Original Cabin, and that event marks the beginning of the Berry Schools and Berry College. [2]

The gatherings soon grew to include more than thirty people, not just children but also fathers, mothers, and babies, and the little cabin could barely hold them all. People sat on chairs as well as boxes, mats, and whatever else was available. Martha Berry continued to tell stories from the Bible and played a small, antiquated melodeon (a reed organ) while leading the group in singing hymns. Because many of the people could not read, Berry would say a line of a hymn before the group would sing it.

Berry was interested primarily in the children. She found them eager to learn anything she presented. Many of them proved quite capable and learned quickly. They studied nature while taking walks through the nearby woods, and the children began collecting leaves, plants, and stones to decorate the cabin. Demonstrating under an old microscope the difference in their hands before and after washing, Berry taught them the importance of cleanliness.

After the Sunday gatherings had been going on for a time, Berry began to visit the people in their homes, which were often isolated log cabins. The children particularly welcomed her visits, sometimes showing that they remembered her lessons on cleanliness by presenting themselves to her with still dripping and shining faces and hands. Berry came to be known in the area as the Sunday Lady or Miss Mattie.

Most of the people lived in poverty, and families were often large. The cabins were built of rough logs, sometimes with large cracks all the way through the walls. The cabins might be crowded, cluttered, and not especially clean, with dogs all around. Many parents had forgotten skills possessed by their families in earlier generations and thus could not pass these basics on to their children, and fewer still had money to pay for training or education for their children.

As a result of the Sunday sessions in the little cabin and visits to the homes, Martha Berry recalled, she "seemed to realize, more forcibly than ever, the great possibilities lying dormant in their bright minds, and loving, intelligent little souls; and that which had been at first but a simple desire to do something for their betterment—I hardly knew what—became at once a determined resolve to devote my entire time and means in teaching them the way to help themselves. I saw that they needed only opportunities and a guiding hand to make them useful and successful men and women whose lives would be a blessing to humanity. I saw that these people needed . . . to know how . . . to do the practical things of life in the best possible way."[3]

As the Original Cabin became too crowded, Martha Berry decided to construct a one-room building approximately half a mile away, across the Summerville Road from the Berry family home on some land she had inherited from her father. The rough lumber cost her approximately one hundred dollars, and the men and boys she was teaching did most of the construction work. She moved her Sunday school for families into the little whitewashed building and before long added a day school for the children. The county school board provided a teacher for the school for five months each year,

and Berry paid the teacher for an additional month. The teacher's responsibilities included visiting the pupils' homes and investigating conditions there as well as lending books to the families. Martha's youngest sister, Frances, assisted with singing and sewing classes for the girls and with a debating class for the boys. The small one-room building soon had to be enlarged to hold everyone, and Berry received requests from people in outlying areas for other Sunday schools and day schools.

The first of the additional Sunday school locations was in an old church at Possum Trot, several miles from the existing school. Mary Ruth Beams Camp recalled beginning attendance at Possum Trot in 1897, when she was four and a half. Her parents, William Thomas Beams and Ann Mary Cockrill Beams, had previously taught in several Floyd County communities and assisted Berry in organizing the Possum Trot school, where they taught for two years before moving to the whitewashed school, which Mary Ruth Beams referred to as the "Little White Chapel School."[4]

Rain fell on the first Sunday at Possum Trot, and the building's roof leaked so badly that it became obvious that it had to be repaired. Those in attendance were somewhat reluctant to participate, but Martha Berry finally persuaded the men to provide boards while she provided nails and lemonade, and the job was completed before the next Sunday. Martha started another day school at Possum Trot, again supplementing the county's five-month pay for the teacher by an additional month. She also provided an organ and some books for a library. She required the teacher to meet with the families on Saturdays to familiarize them with the use of the books. The Possum Trot school added classrooms in the early 1930s and continued to operate until 1954.

The two Sunday and day schools proved quite popular and successful, so Berry agreed to extend the work to Mount Alto, a few miles southwest of

The Whitewashed Schoolhouse, the first classroom building
for the Boys Industrial School, c. 1902.

her first location. She had an old house repaired, whitewashed, and furnished with pictures, an organ, and books. At times, she had to sweep the floors, bring in wood for the stove, and do other common chores unless she could persuade those attending to help. One early student recalled many years later that Martha, Laura, and Frances each conducted one of the three Sunday schools. After Elizabeth Brewster, a graduate of Stanford University in California, came to help Martha Berry with her work in 1901, Berry would go on Sunday mornings either to the Possum Trot or the Mount Alto school, while Brewster would go to the other one.[5] The Sunday school at the original location met in the afternoon, with several people, including Martha and Frances Berry, teaching more than a hundred students.

With the additional help, Martha Berry opened another school at Foster's Bend, approximately twenty miles away. On February 27, 1899, the county board of education provided one hundred dollars for a schoolhouse at Foster's Bend, although the records do not mention Martha Berry at that time. In February 1901, however, the county board provided money to the Foster's Bend school through Berry.[6] This was a more isolated area, and the people's needs seem to have been even greater than those of the students at the other three schools; nevertheless, the school soon served many more students than had initially been expected. The county board of education obviously was not satisfying the need for basic public education.

On February 14, 1900, Martha Berry formally requested that the school board establish a permanent school at the whitewashed schoolhouse. The board agreed, resolving, "Miss Mattie Berry has built a schoolhouse near her residence and within the limit prescribed by this Board, and by her personal interest in the children has now a flourishing school, and expects to continue the same, therefore, Be it resolved . . . That this Board recognizes the said

Elizabeth Brewster, the first teacher at the Boys Industrial School, c. 1910.

school as permanently on the payroll of the board as long as Miss Berry or any appointee of her shall show interest in the school comparable to that at present shown." The board then set the attendance boundaries for the school.[7]

Martha Berry had now organized and was overseeing operations for four Sunday schools and four day schools, some of them in rural Floyd County as far as twenty miles away from her home. But she was not satisfied. In early 1901, she asked the county board of education for the loan of eighteen desks and two blackboards for use in the "Summer Hill School," offering to take personal responsibility for the items. The board approved the request, but no information regarding this facility has been found in the records of the Berry Schools.[8]

*Possum Trot students with teacher Jessie Ross Morris,
late 1910s.*

Berry kept very busy coordinating the teachers' efforts. She was pleased with what had already been accomplished, but she wanted more. Children often missed school because of bad weather, the long distances they had to walk to get to school, or the need to work at home, and for six months each year when the day schools were not in session, contact with most children occurred only through the Sunday schools. Poverty and the hard work required of the children resulted in poor conditions for them when they were at home. She sought ways to keep children in school for longer periods of time to provide both a better environment and a better opportunity to retain what they had learned, and she began to explore with family and friends how best to accomplish these changes.

Working with the schools also familiarized Berry with other problems faced by the poorer people of the surrounding countryside and highland areas. Decades of planting the same crops had seriously depleted and eroded the soil. As a result, the farmers became poorer and poorer over the years, and home conditions deteriorated. Berry concluded that an industrial school could improve these people's lot in life and that it would have to be a boarding school to ensure attendance and discipline and to provide the opportunity to teach by association and example. The boarding school would be for either boys or girls, but not both, at least in the beginning. She was inclined to start with girls but after careful consideration decided that beginning with boys would be more practical because they could better endure the initial hardships of the simple, rustic life at the school while accomplishing the rugged work necessary to clear and develop the campus. Also, she was planning a farm school, and the boys' work would be important to support the institution. Teaching the boys improved farming methods would make them better farmers and would help improve their communities when they returned home.

The Boys Industrial School

As Berry developed her vision, she became convinced that greater educational opportunities would lead to brighter futures for the most capable of the poor children growing up in ignorance around her. She also expected that others would sympathize with these efforts and would be willing to offer financial support. She wrote letters to some of her friends and traveled to Atlanta but was unable to raise the needed funds. She then realized that she would have to provide the school's primary support, at least in the beginning, and that she was committing herself to a lifetime of service. Some members of her family and friends tried to discourage her from further involvement. Berry talked with Moses Wright, a Rome attorney and husband of Martha's sister, Rebecca, about the proper legal structure for establishing a boarding school and about donating some of her land. At her family's request, he initially discouraged her. Establishing and operating a boarding school would bring even more headaches than the day schools and would essentially end the social life that she enjoyed. Eventually, however, he gave his support, helping her to create a corporation and to donate eighty-three acres of land for the project.

In late 1901, Berry arranged for the construction of a two-story, ten-room dormitory near the little whitewashed schoolhouse, often directing the workers herself. She provided a thousand dollars (approximately $22,000 in 2003) for the building and named it Brewster Hall in honor of her assistant. Brewster Hall at first included a kitchen and a dining hall as well as student rooms, although several additions were constructed before it burned on November 6, 1920. The campus had no entrance from the Summerville Road; entry was from the road to Possum Trot, Redmond Gap Road, by the whitewashed schoolhouse. Paths led from the schoolhouse to the dormitory and to the nearby site where other build-

Brewster Hall, the first dormitory, built by students in 1901, c. 1905.

ings were soon to be constructed in what had been a dense oak grove.[9]

Berry had little money to furnish the dormitory, but some friends donated a small cooking stove, a few utensils and dishes, a rag carpet, an old piano, and some furniture. Students constructed additional furniture and washstands from rough lumber and wooden boxes. Berry purchased, at very low cost, cots that the army was discarding, although many of them were too short for the older boys. Martha's sister, Frances, took a sewing machine to the dormitory and made sheets, pillowcases, and curtains. The little whitewashed school had a stove for heat in the middle of the room and wooden benches for

the students. The benches were not attached to the floor, and they were often moved out of place or turned over, spilling everything. In a corner were a water bucket and a gourd dipper. The paths to the schoolhouse were muddy on rainy days, and the floor became covered with red clay.

While preparing to open the boarding school, Berry visited Mount Hermon School for boys in Massachusetts. In October 1901, she inquired about teachers at Mount Hermon, and Richard L. Watson, an 1891 graduate of Mount Hermon, wrote to indicate his interest in working at her school. She accepted his offer a few days later and was ready to open in January 1902. She prepared a prospectus with the name Industrial School for Boys, listing the teachers as Prof. R. L. Watson, Miss Mildred Morton, Miss Elizabeth Brewster, and Mrs. Mary Cornelius, matron. Watson would be responsible for the business department and the manual work, and Martha Berry would live at the school and provide personal supervision. The day school would continue to operate in conjunction with the boarding school, serving approximately seventy-five boys and girls. Board and tuition for the industrial school were ten dollars a month, while students at the day school were expected to pay two dollars a month. The prospectus stated the school's goal as "to place the pupils under the most refining home influences, and to fit them to be useful citizens." The school would provide business, literary, and industrial training and a Christian education, although it was "undenominational." The initial plan was to begin the boarding school on January 2, 1902, but the opening date was later changed to January 13, subsequently celebrated as the date of the school's founding. The *Rome Tribune* continued to run an advertisement for the new school for more than a week after its official opening.[10]

Watson may have changed his mind about coming to Georgia, and on January 10, Berry wrote to Henry F. Cutler, principal at Mount Hermon, stating that she had Watson's correspondence, including his proposal to work for her and his acceptance of her offer, and had relied on his promise in opening the school. The boys were coming in, and she was counting on Watson to supervise the practical work. Watson did not arrive in time for the opening of the boarding school but was there before the end of February.[11] When he arrived, he insisted that the prospectus giving him the title "Prof." be corrected, and a four-page "catalog" listing him as "Mr." was prepared. That brief document referred to the institution as the "Boys' Industrial School."

The boarding school opened with only five students: Pinkney Dean, Henry Dearing, Clarence Gould, Ott Manning, and Allard Russell.[12] Berry preferred to begin with only a few boys to allow the gradual development of methods and procedures. Three of the boys came from the outlying Sunday schools—one each from Foster's Bend, Mount Alto, and Possum Trot. Students could pay their fees in cash, could work for their tuition, or could pay in kind. All students were required to work two hours per day, seven days a week, even if they had paid their fees in cash. Two of the first five boys paid, but the other three worked extra to cover their attendance. (A few years later, Emory Alexander paid his fees with a team of oxen, which became a very valuable asset on the farm. Alexander graduated from the Berry boys' high school in 1912 and later served as a member of the agriculture faculty of the University of Georgia.) Money was scarce in most students' families, but some of them had sizable farms and rather good homes. The amount received from students for board and tuition payments for the year ending May 14, 1904, was $2,557.85, almost half as much as the donations received that year.[13]

The number of boarding students grew to eighteen before the end of the first spring term. Under the immediate supervision of Watson and the direction of Berry, the students cleared the underbrush; built paths and then roads; constructed small buildings for a workshop, a laundry, barns, a dairy, a poultry house, a bathhouse, and a woodshed; and soon began to grow vegetables for their own consumption. The boys were delighted to have Watson, the first man on the staff, direct their labor, believing that the women never knew when the boys had worked enough.[14]

Watson thought Berry was doing truly wonderful work, but he did not consider her a good manager and told her so. He thought her "impulsive and easily influenced by a few tears." However, he considered her "unexcelled as a promoter of this particular work and among this peculiar people." After just a month, Watson told Berry that he wanted to go back to Mount Hermon, but she wanted him to stay and tried to make him happy.[15] Nevertheless, he remained for just one term. Berry visited Mount Hermon during the summer of 1902, spending at least part of her time studying and attending lectures in an effort to prepare herself better for the work she was undertaking.[16] While there, she recruited Mount Hermon's Albert S. McClain to replace Watson in the fall of 1902, with responsibility for directing the work program and performing a wide variety of other tasks. According to Brewster, McClain took off his coat and went to work before he even entered the school buildings. He took over preparation of the noon meal, while Brewster cooked breakfast and Morton cooked the evening meal. Before long, the students were sufficiently trained to assume most of the responsibility for preparing meals.[17]

McClain at first was very pleased with the school's development, saying in 1904 that things had greatly improved since his arrival and indicating that Martha Berry did not interfere and left everything to him. The school's board of trustees created an industrial department in 1905 and appointed McClain its manager, and he remained in that role for six years.[18] In 1910, however, he wrote to Henry Cutler that Berry had become "a hard place to work." It was difficult for him to know just what he was expected to do because Martha Berry was continually changing her mind. "I wish Miss Berry knew how to treat people," he lamented. By the following January, McClain had decided to leave at the end of the school year.[19]

When the boarding school began, it had one horse—Roany the Sunday school horse—along with a small plow, one or two hoes, rakes, axes, and

Albert McClain, the first manager of Berry's industrial department, c. 1905.

mattocks. Martha Berry often directed the boys' "work hour" and sometimes joined in the work herself. The boys washed the dishes, cleaned their rooms, chopped wood, and dug up stumps. They soon were growing cotton, corn, sorghum, peas, sweet and Irish potatoes, garden vegetables, peaches, melons, figs, and a great variety of other crops. They ate some of the produce fresh, sold some, and canned much of it for later use. A few of the boys stayed during the summer for full-time work on the farms or in the gardens and orchards. They were initially reluctant to do tasks they considered women's work, such as washing clothes.[20] After supper, the teachers directed the boys in the preparation of their lessons for the next day. Following the study time, teachers and students played games, sang songs, or read stories for a short time to help the boys feel at home and love the school. Before bedtime the students read a chapter from the Bible, with each person reading a verse, and offered a prayer. Between 9:00 and 9:30, everyone went to bed, lights were turned out, and the building became quiet.

In the fall of 1902, the school nearly ran out of dishes because of extra students enrolling, but a shipment of more than nineteen hundred arrived from a generous donor. The school had to sell some of the dishes to pay the freight and had to borrow a wagon to haul the dishes to the school. When the well went dry in the fall of 1903, the boys had to haul water from a creek and from neighbors' wells. Berry decided it was time to seek a connection to the Rome water system. Convicts dug a ditch for about two miles, Berry bought the pipe, and the students filled in the part of the ditch on the school property. The students did not complain about the extra work because they were pleased to have a regular supply of water. No telephone connection to the campus existed until the spring 1904 term, and not until the summer of 1908 did telephones connect the vari-

ous offices and dormitories and some of the other buildings.[21]

Martha Berry's day schools taught their students the practical things in life, and the boarding school initially took a similar approach. Although the students received a basic literary education, they spent a great deal of time learning how to improve agriculture and carpentry and gaining industrial and work experience. They were expected to go back to their communities and become better farmers or perhaps to minister to or teach their own people. Some of the boys had opportunities to secure clerkships or positions in banks before earning diplomas, but John Eagan, president of the board of trustees, suggested that Berry tell them that their places in the school would be filled with other students should they choose to accept such positions.[22]

Berry planned to promote "Moral, Mental and Physical Education for the Young." The school would provide the basis on which boys or young men could formulate high and noble aims and offer a useful education, unavailable elsewhere, at low cost. As the school's catalog put it, "We aim to make of the boy a workman as well as a student by giving dignity to manual labor. We believe that the study of the Word of God is the central element in the development of manly character, and an aid in assuming the responsibilities of life. The Bible will therefore be made an important feature in all courses of study." Although most of the boys were expected to return and farm or do other work in rural areas, special attention would be given to students wishing to go on to college. Country teachers often had only an elementary education, and the school claimed to have designed the curriculum with such teachers in mind.[23]

The school required students to be at least fourteen years old and to have good moral character and reputation. According to the catalog, "Man is a trinity. He has body, mind, and soul. We seek to develop all three phases of man's nature as one har-monious whole." Therefore, the school had three departments: industrial, literary, and religious. Students, faculty, and staff went together to church in Rome on Sunday mornings, rotating among different denominations. Sunday school was held in the afternoon, and Sunday night services were the responsibility of the school's chapter of the Young Men's Christian Association, which was established during the 1902–3 school year. The best education, Berry believed, trained the head, the heart, and the hands.[24]

School rules forbade students to leave the grounds without permission, to go to Rome (except for church) more than once a month, or to go home more than once each term. Students could not smoke or consume intoxicating drinks. Everyone was to rise at 5:45 a.m., to be in bed by 9:30 p.m., and to attend study hall at night and church services on Sunday mornings. Lack of interest or falling behind in one's studies could result in denial of privileges or suspension from school. The school also sought "to help every student to realize the value of work well done, and to inspire each boy with the idea of the dignity of labor."[25]

The early school seal included the major elements of the college seal of today, although they were displayed in a somewhat different manner. The four quarters of the seal then and now include a cabin for simplicity, a Bible for religious emphasis, a lamp for learning, and a plow for work. The early motto, "Be a lifter, not a leaner," was later replaced with "Not to be ministered unto, but to minister," the original motto of the girls' school. An early alma mater was "Dear Foster Mother of Our Youth," and an early school song was "There's a Glory That Hovers o'er Georgia's Fair Hills." Literary and debating societies became active in the earliest days of the Boys Industrial School, with one literary society named for Watson, who continued to send prizes for winning speak-ers after his departure. The three primary literary societies during those early years were the Cicero-nian, the Oostanaula, and the Philomathean. The school library apparently began with about a dozen books, but under the leadership of Clayton Henson, a student, contributions increased the number to a thousand volumes in just a year.[26] In January 1904, students began to produce a monthly publication, the *Boys Industrial School Advance,* which was replaced in January 1907 by a joint faculty-student publication, the *Southern Highlander.* The school's administration continued to put out that publication until 1966.

In its early days, the Boys Industrial School had a primary department, an intermediate department, and an academic department. The primary department taught students how to study and do math because many of them had previously had very little opportunity for education. Even though some of the students were above the traditional high-school age, they had to begin with the basics. The intermediate department consisted of two years of preparatory study for high school and included courses in arithmetic, geography, history, English, and the Bible. The academic department initially provided a three-year high-school program of study and offered courses in algebra, botany, chemistry, geometry, Greek, history, Latin, and physics. When it became clear that some of the students wanted to go on to college, the high-school program was divided into a college-preparatory course of study and a practical course of study. The boys at first received training in agriculture through supervision of their practical work experience, but after a few years the curriculum came to include agriculture courses. Students in all grades studied the Bible.

The high-school program became a four-year course of study in 1905, while the school continued to offer a three-year high-school preparatory program. Students received grades in conduct as well

Clayton Henson, Berry's first graduate, c. 1904.

as in their courses, and poor conduct grades would result in probation or dismissal from the school.[27] The program began to gain respect from colleges and universities, and by 1908 the University of Georgia, the University of Alabama, Alabama Polytechnic Institute (Auburn), and North Carolina's Davidson College had indicated that they welcomed graduates of the Boys Industrial School.[28] Some colleges accepted Berry graduates as sophomores, and several specified that they did not require examinations before enrolling Berry alumni.

Seven boys graduated from the Boys Industrial School before the name was changed to the Berry School in January 1908. Of the original five boarders, only Pinkney Dean graduated. Two of the eighteen others enrolled by the end of the first term, Clayton Henson and Roland Selman, continued at the school until they earned their high-school diplomas. The first graduate was Henson, who finished in April 1904 and went on to the University of Georgia. He became an attorney and had a long career in law in Cartersville. Five students graduated in the spring of 1905, including Gordon Keown, who worked at Berry for most of the remainder of his life, serving as postmaster, alumni trustee, and acting director of the institution for two years immediately following Martha Berry's death. Because of the added fourth year of high school, no students graduated in 1906 and only one graduated in 1907. All of the first seven graduates were from Floyd County or the adjacent counties of Chattooga, Gordon, and Walker. The first graduate from outside Georgia, Bernie Levine Frost, came from Montevallo, Alabama, and received his diploma in 1908. A few other students of the Boys Industrial School later received high-school diplomas from the Berry School, but most of the early students dropped out before graduation. The average age of the early students was about nineteen. By 1906, students enrolled from five different states, and the number of students attending the Boys Industrial School exceeded 150.

The first principal of the Boys Industrial School was Gaylord W. Douglass, a Mount Hermon graduate who had resigned his position as head of the history department there to come to Georgia. Although he served at Berry for only two years, he helped to put the school on a stronger academic path. He attracted others from the Mount Hermon School and its sister institution for girls, the Northfield Seminary, and in the spring of 1906 the industrial school had six teachers, three with college degrees.[29] With Douglass's departure, Robert H. Adams became the school's next principal, in January 1908, and he remained in that position until 1914. Adams had come to the Boys Industrial School as a teacher in 1904, having completed most of his work for a degree at Davidson College, although he did not graduate until later. The Boys Industrial School, its successor Berry School, and the Martha Berry School for Girls were fortunate to engage from across the country self-sacrificing teachers and workers willing to accept meager salaries and humble living conditions.

John Eagan, first chairman of Berry's board of trustees, c. 1918.

Organizing, Building, Financing

From its inception, the Boys Industrial School had a board of trustees.[30] The original board included Martha Berry; her brother-in-law and attorney, Moses Wright;[31] her brother, Thomas; Rome businessmen J. Paul Cooper and John H. Reynolds; and John J. Eagan, a wealthy Atlanta businessman. Wright, the first person Martha Berry asked to serve on the board, had grown up in a home located near where the chapel for the boys' campus (now Berry College Chapel) was built in 1915, was known as an outstanding speaker, and served as a superior court judge from about 1905 until 1920. He was a frequent visitor to the Berry campus and an active trustee until his death in 1925. Thomas Berry worked as director of the school farm shortly after the boarding school was created, later pursued a career in the railroad industry, and served as a trustee until 1929, when he resigned over a disagreement concerning water rights.[32] Cooper, who served as a Berry trustee until he resigned in 1921, owned the largest cotton brokerage firm in Boston as well as other business interests. Reynolds, president of the First National Bank of Rome and an administrator of Martha's father's estate, served as the Berry board's first treasurer and remained a trustee until he resigned in 1911.

Eagan, the only original trustee who lived outside of Rome, was the first chairman of the board of trustees, serving from 1902 until his death in 1924.[33] His mother had lived in Rome, and her sister was the first wife of John M. Berry, brother of Martha's father. Eagan sometimes referred to Martha Berry as "cousin" in letters to her, although numerous people at the time and subsequently believed that he had a romantic interest in Martha Berry. When Eagan died, Martha Berry wrote of his importance to the school,

> When I organized the Berry Schools and decided to deed the property my father had given me to a board of trustees, I asked John J. Eagan, of Atlanta, to become chairman of this board. His acceptance meant that he would not only give generously of his means but that he would consider this a sacred trust—an opportunity for Christian service. During the early years of the school he came to see us at least once a month, and spent days organizing our splendid business system. Sometimes he would come and spend ten days or two weeks with us, and while there he always came to the office in the morning when the office force began work at eight o'clock and remained there until they quit work at five o'clock in the afternoon. He visited not only the business department, but every department

of the school. I can see him now, standing talking earnestly with the boys in the shop, in the dairy, in the classroom, in the kitchen—his life has been woven into every department of Berry Schools and into the hearts and lives of thousands of boys and girls at Berry. Everyone looks forward to the morning and evening prayer service at Berry, and John J. Eagan with his Bible in his hand would lead the boys in their morning and evening devotions—it is a picture that will never be forgotten at Berry. We always looked forward to his visits, and when he was on the campus we felt stronger, safer, more secure, because we knew that we had as chairman of our Board of Trustees a man whose life was given for others and devoted to the service of the Master. His recreation was driving our old Sunday school horse through the piney woods, visiting the humblest homes, and bringing to them hope and good cheer. One old lady who lived all alone in her cabin home [and] was unable to read because of blindness said to me that she always looked forward to Mr. Eagan's visits, because he seemed to give her back her sight and filled the room with sunshine. How many trips he made all over this countryside, traveling across hills and valleys, always with a helping hand and message of cheer.[34]

On January 10, 1903, the six original trustees filed a petition for a charter to incorporate the Boys Industrial School. The petition stated that Martha Berry had erected buildings on her land and was operating an industrial school for boys there and that she was donating eighty-three acres of land to the corporation.[35] The charter, approved on April 6, 1903, for twenty years with the right of renewal, authorized the new corporation "to have and use a common seal, to sue and to be sued, to buy and to sell and to otherwise dispose of real estate and rights therein, to receive gifts, donations and bequests of realty and personalty, to enforce good order for the management of said School, to erect buildings, to employ teachers, to grant scholarships and to carry on a School to meet the needs of poor boys from the rural districts." The "School shall forever remain undenominational, except that the Bible shall be taught; the teachers shall be members of some protestant Church, and the training of scholars shall be with the view to aid in their moral, industrial, and educational uplifting." The incorporators would be a perpetual board for the management of the school, and the board could fill its vacancies. Martha Berry would be consulted in filling such vacancies and would be the active manager of the school with the right to name her successor in her will. On January 31, 1908, the charter was amended to change the name of the institution to the Berry School.[36]

The first official meeting of the Berry trustees was held on April 3, 1903. At that meeting, the group formally adopted the charter and bylaws and decided to hold only one regular meeting each year unless special circumstances required additional sessions.[37] The initial bylaws gave Berry the title of general manager, which she used for about five years until she received the title of director, which she used until her death. At the board's 1907 meeting, she was authorized to employ a cashier and an auditor and was asked to present the expenditures from her private funds for school travel expenses. A year later, the auditor reported Berry had used $840 from her personal funds for school expenses, but she declined to be reimbursed.[38]

In 1906, Hoke Smith of Atlanta joined the board of trustees, serving until 1910. Smith was a lawyer and owner and editor of the *Atlanta Journal*, had previously served as U.S. secretary of the interior under President Grover Cleveland, and had spoken at the 1904 ceremony at which Henson became the industrial school's first graduate. Smith went on to serve as governor of Georgia (1907–9, 1911) and as a U.S. senator (1911–21), in which capacity he

coauthored the Smith-Hughes Act, supporting vocational education in public high schools nationwide.[39]

By 1908, the school had purchased an additional 457 acres of land for a total cost of $33,540, or slightly less than $75 per acre (about $1,586 an acre in 2003).[40] The little whitewashed schoolhouse was enlarged several times but burned in April 1905. A larger and much more impressive replacement was completed before the end of the year and was dedicated on January 13, 1906, the fourth anniversary of the industrial school's founding. In addition to classrooms, the building housed an auditorium and the school library. Originally called the Recitation Hall, this building later came to be known as the Administration Building and is now named the Hoge Building.[41] At the same time, a new campus entrance from Summerville Road was added.

Other buildings were added to the campus during this time. A log cabin was built in the summer and fall of 1902, with plans drawn up by John Gibbs Barnwell, an architect who also designed several other early campus structures. Originally called simply the Cabin, the building was simple and inexpensive yet also very attractive. The Cabin served as a guesthouse and social center, and Martha Berry and Elizabeth Brewster lived there for a time. The second floor served as an office for Berry and her secretary. The Cabin was eventually used as a school for children of campus employees, and in later years it served as the alumni office.[42] Behind or west of the Cabin was an open-air place of worship used before the Mount Berry Chapel (now Berry College Chapel) was constructed in 1915. The outdoor chapel was located in a dogwood grove with benches and a lectern made of dogwood, giving it the name the Dogwood Chapel.

Rhea Cottage was built in 1903, Smith Cottage in 1904, and Inman Hall in the summer of 1905.[43] Rhea Cottage was named for Martha Berry's mother,

The Recitation Hall (later the Hoge Building), c. 1910.

Dogwood Chapel, where early church services were held, c. 1914.

Frances Rhea, and served first as a dormitory, although by 1910 the first floor contained offices for Berry and others while the second floor was used as living quarters for the principal and the comptroller. Berry's office was later moved to the upper floor. An addition to the building served as the Mount Berry post office. Starting in the early 1920s and continuing until the present, the building has served as a staff residence, although the name was changed to Boxwood Cottage when a larger Rhea Hall was built in 1922. Smith Cottage served as the school infirmary. Inman was first a dormitory, then a science laboratory, later the school store, and then a dormitory again. It now provides apartments for faculty and staff.

Located near the later site of the Berry College Chapel, Glenwood House, which had previously belonged to Moses Wright's father, Augustus, was purchased in 1906. The house was taken down in 1915 when the chapel was built, and the materials were used to construct Glenwood Cottage, which has since served as a staff residence. New dairy barns and a steam laundry were constructed in 1906. Martha Berry took a fund-raising trip to the resort town of Poland Springs, Maine, and the residents of the guesthouse where she stayed contributed funds for the 1907 construction of Poland Hall, which served as a dormitory until the 1930s, when it became staff residence apartments. An enlarged dairy barn to accommodate thirty-two cows was constructed during the same year. All of these buildings were located at the south end of the present college campus.

Neither Martha Berry's personal resources nor those contributed by her family and friends provided sufficient financial support for the operation and development of her boarding school. At first she sought additional support from the county board of education, which had provided funds for her day school at the same location. On February 4, 1902, the board noted in its minutes that Berry had received twenty additional desks, which would remain the property of the board. In May of that year, the board loaned six blackboards for use at the "Martha Berry Industrial School." The county school board provided $650 to support the school for the 1902–3 year, $600 in each of the next three years, and $300 for each of the following two years, ending its funding in 1910. The board minutes indicate that Berry made all of these requests, some of them during personal appearances before the board. The board denied a request from Principal Robert Adams for a 1911 appropriation, and no further record of county funding for the school has been found.[44]

The county board and commissioner of schools visited the Berry School by invitation on October 11, 1902, and May 4, 1903. In the fall of 1902, the county school commissioner stated that he thought the Berry teachers should attend the monthly county teachers' meetings. Martha Berry was present and stated that one of her teachers had attended the previous spring but that her teachers would no longer be able to do so because they would be teaching on Saturdays, when the meetings apparently were held. The county board agreed in March 1903 to support a school a few hundred yards from the Boys Industrial School at the intersection of Summerville Road and O'Brian Gap Road, where the current Berry service road meets Martha Berry Highway and just across the road from the college president's home. The petitioners explained that their school was necessary because Berry's school would not accept girls and because the boys were required to pay tuition.[45] The available records do not provide a response from Martha Berry to the petitioners' complaint, although she did establish a separate school for girls a few years later. Her schools continued to charge tuition, although many of her students paid their way by working on the campus.

Facing these difficulties, Martha Berry decided in the fall of 1902 that she needed to go to the northern part of the United States to attempt to raise funds. She appeared before the county board of education on her birthday, October 7, and stated that she was often asked whether her county board was giving assistance to the school, and she wanted to be able to answer in the affirmative. In response, the board agreed to provide the $650 for the 1902–3 school year mentioned earlier as well as a letter of endorsement signed by the board members. The minutes reported "That she had at great expense to herself established and up to date maintained the school, That she had become impressed with the fact that our country boys were neglected and many of them were growing up in ignorance and many without proper moral training and with no means of earning a living, That she had decided to devote the school especially to the boys and had excluded all girls, That she had an expensive corps of three teachers well qualified for the work."[46]

In October and November 1902, Berry obtained letters of introduction for her northern trip from the pastors of Rome's First Baptist, First Methodist, and First Presbyterian Churches and from the editor of the *Atlanta News*. One of these letters stated that "the moral and religious training is most admirable. It richly deserves the sympathy and support of all interested in the uplift of our boys." A second letter stated that anyone interested in the education of poor boys of the South should help to enlarge the physical plant and give scholarships. Another letter indicated that Berry had given the full limit of her income and beyond.[47]

Berry was reluctant to travel far away to ask for aid from strangers, but her teachers and the students gave her encouragement, telling her that they were expecting and praying for large gifts as well as providing her with lists of things the school needed. Elizabeth Brewster had a sealskin coat, which she insisted that Berry take to protect her from the cold. Martha and Frances Berry reached New York by the middle of November 1902, staying for several weeks in a boardinghouse.[48] Martha Berry contacted two or three people with whom she had attended school in Baltimore, but they were not encouraging. However, one put Berry in contact with a Brooklyn church pastor who agreed to have her speak of her work at a prayer meeting. She had never before made a public presentation and dreaded the thought of talking to the group, and the night of the meeting was stormy and she had difficulty getting to the church. Although she arrived when the group was almost ready to depart, the pastor gave her a few minutes to speak. The group was so impressed that they promised to send a box to her school at Christmastime and gave fifty dollars, the amount she requested to help one boy stay in school for a year.

A few of those in the audience also gave her names and addresses of other people to contact for support. From the list she obtained an appointment with R. Fulton Cutting, a prominent multimillionaire businessman known in some circles as the First Citizen of New York. She told him the story of her school and the boys' needs, and in response, he asked what she got from the school. Nothing, she informed him—she received no salary, paid her own expenses, and had even donated land to the school. She then quickly added that she experienced the joy of seeing untaught boys find opportunities for transformed lives. He wrote her a check, and when she left his office and unfolded it, she discovered to her delight that he had given her five hundred dollars. Her first "begging trip," as she put it, portended well for her future fund-raising success.[49]

Indeed, fund-raising became one of Berry's chief responsibilities. She wrote many letters and made numerous trips throughout both the North and the South, becoming quite adept at describing her school and its students' needs. And her efforts soon bore fruit. Contributions for the year ending on May 4, 1904, totaled $5,201.96 ($106,081 in 2003) and rose rather quickly to $41,327.68 ($842,779 in 2003) for the year ending March 31, 1908.[50] In addition to Cutting, early contributors included Andrew Carnegie and George Foster Peabody.

Berry had little success in establishing an endowment for the Boys Industrial School, however. While she had hoped that a visit from a representative of the Southern Education Board would result in a contribution toward an endowment, the board declined. Peabody also refused to fund an endowment, writing that they were only for colleges, not for high schools. In his view, shared by some other philanthropists, high schools should seek funds only for current expenses because taxpayers should eventually assume responsibility for supporting such institutions. Peabody even stated that if offered fifty thousand dollars for an endowment, a high school should decline the money.[51]

The Berry School's close relationship with the Mount Hermon School continued through these early years. Berry visited the Massachusetts school several more times, and William R. Moody, son of Dwight L. Moody and president of the Mount Hermon trustees, visited the Boys Industrial School at least twice. The Georgia school relied on Mount Hermon for advice on such mundane matters as where to obtain diplomas and how to arrange information on them. J. Andrew Bird, a 1905 graduate of the Boys Industrial School, studied at Mount Hermon for a year before returning to teach at Berry's school.[52]

After its inception, the Boys Industrial School developed rapidly into a successful, growing institution with a good reputation. A solid foundation existed on which Martha Berry would continue to build, changing the school's name to the Berry School and adding a school for girls, a foundation school, and later a college.

Between 1909 and 1925, Martha Berry established foundation schools for boys and girls not ready for high school. Enrollment increased significantly. New buildings and greatly expanded landholdings facilitated this growth, but the schools also faced their first serious political and legal problems. The fame of the schools and their founder spread across much of the nation, and with the assistance of prominent benefactors such as Andrew Carnegie, Theodore Roosevelt, and Henry Ford, the schools advanced greatly.

CHAPTER THREE

Growing Pains

Expansion

According to a school catalog, "From the time [Martha Berry] began the little Sunday school in the old pine-pole cabin she had it in her heart to have a school for girls, for she realized how narrow and shut-in their lives are, and how much harder it is for the country girl to get an education than it is for her brothers."[1] She felt a need to provide opportunities for the sisters and future wives of her boys.

Soon after the boarding school for boys opened, Berry began efforts to meet with President Theodore Roosevelt. He planned a southern trip in 1905 but advised Berry that he could not visit her school at that time. She then sent him pictures of the school.[2] In early 1907, Berry traveled to Washington, D.C., where she requested an appointment with First Lady Edith Roosevelt, who declined because her son was ill but said that perhaps the two women could meet on Berry's next trip to the city. Later that year, Berry

invited the president to attend the end-of-school-year activities, but he again declined. In the fall of 1907, however, Edith Roosevelt sent Berry a letter and a fifty-dollar donation, and when Berry was in Washington the following April, she was invited to have lunch at the White House.[3]

President Roosevelt received Martha Berry on April 21. She told him the story of her school, so impressing him that he arranged a dinner for her with him and some of his wealthy and influential friends, although he also expressed regret that she did not also have a school for girls. He subsequently wrote to Berry that he would come see her school following a trip to Africa after leaving the presidency. He made good on his promise, visiting on October 8, 1910, delivering a speech to the students, and having a meal in the Cabin, subsequently known as the Roosevelt Cabin.[4]

Between her 1908 meeting with Roosevelt at the White House and his visit to Georgia, Martha Berry

Roosevelt Cabin, c. 1905.

had decided to move ahead with a school for girls without the approval of her board of trustees. For the new school's recitation hall, Berry selected a cabin that she had used as a Sunday school about three-quarters of a mile north of the boys' school. After cutting a supply of logs, the boys from her school began to build a dormitory for the girls on a small hill a short distance west of Sunshine Shanty, as the recitation hall was called. The boys were excited to work on this project and soon completed Louise Hall, which was named after Louise Inman, president of the Martha Berry Circle of Atlanta, the group that provided funding for the building. Louise Hall had a parlor, a dining room, a kitchen, an office and living quarters for the principal, and student rooms upstairs. A small laundry building was located behind Louise Hall. Although Sunshine Shanty was torn down after it was no longer needed, Louise Hall still stands on the Log Cabin Campus, as the original area of the girls' school is known, and serves as a staff residence.[5]

Martha Berry opened her new school for girls on Thanksgiving Day 1909. Like the school for boys,

the girls' school began with five students; by the spring term, however, enrollment had increased to thirteen. The boys' high school continued to be known as the Berry School even after the establishment of the girls' high school. The principal of the girls' school was Alberta Patterson, whose sister, Elizabeth Patterson, taught at the boys' school. Martha Berry had first shown Alberta Patterson a pile of logs for the planned construction of Louise Hall but presented her idea as if a glorious school were already in operation. In May 1910, the Berry trustees ratified all of Martha Berry's actions regarding the new school.[6]

In 1910 the Martha Berry Circle of Atlanta funded the construction of a second building, Atlanta Hall, located near Louise Hall. The new structure served as a dining hall and provided additional dormitory space. In 1911 Barnwell Chapel was constructed and named for Captain John Barnwell, the Rome architect who designed the early girls' school buildings as well as some of those at the boys' school. The chapel doubled as a student-assembly location and a study hall, and the small rooms on the sides of

Theodore Roosevelt at the Martha Berry School for Girls, 1910.

the building were used as classrooms. Several other log buildings were soon added, many of them still in use at the beginning of the twenty-first century.

By the early 1920s, Martha Berry envisioned a greater girls' school, built in a grand style far different from that of the Log Cabin Campus.[7] Berry was acquainted with Thomas A. and Mina Miller Edison and visited them at their New Jersey home, and the Edisons introduced her to Henry Ford, with whom Berry had for several years been attempting to establish a relationship.[8] On another occasion, she met Edison and Ford in Muscle Shoals, Alabama, and she and some of her students spent a brief time with Henry Ford and his wife, Clara, in Rome on March 21, 1922, as they were passing through on a train to Florida.[9] Ford soon provided tractors and a truck to the school, and Berry continued to try to persuade him to visit. She succeeded on April 7, 1923, as the Fords were traveling from Florida back to Michigan.[10] Berry entertained the Fords on the Log Cabin Campus, and they became especially interested in the girls' needs. The Fords first contributed the money for Clara Hall, a stone dormitory for slightly more than one hundred girls completed in 1925. Over the next six years, the Fords contributed funds for an entirely new girls' campus with impressive Gothic Revival buildings located on a small hill several hundred yards east of the Log Cabin Campus. Martha Berry's dream of a great girls'-school plant had been fulfilled.

Students weaving in the Sunshine Shanty, c. 1915.

Martha Berry School for Girls, c. 1913.

Henry and Clara Ford with Martha Berry, c. 1930.

The early curricula for the high schools emphasized practical courses teaching skills that could be used on farms and in rural communities. The boys studied agriculture and mechanics, while the girls took courses in various areas of home economics, dairying, and gardening. Both boys and girls studied the Bible and such basic high-school subjects as English, history, and science.[11] Numerous Berry students planned careers in teaching, primarily in rural schools, and some wanted to go to college, so the school offered some preparation for these goals.

The Southern Association of Colleges and Secondary Schools accredited the Berry high schools in 1922. Georgia's educational landscape had changed greatly in the preceding ten years, however. In 1912, the state constitution was amended to allow for a general system of high schools, and in 1917 Congress passed the Smith-Hughes Act, authored by Georgians Hoke Smith and Dudley Hughes, providing for vocational agriculture and home economics courses in public high schools. In 1921, the Carnegie Corporation conjectured that within a generation, private high schools such as Berry would no longer be needed.[12] And by the mid-1920s, Georgia was beginning to convert its district agricultural and mechanical high schools to other purposes; by 1933, that process was completed. Despite these changes, Martha Berry seems never to have considered the possibility that there might not be a need for her high schools. She and her staff continued to give significant, if not primary, emphasis to the high schools until after her death. Emphasis on the high schools consumed resources that might have been used to strengthen the college.

In addition to the high schools and the foundation schools, a four-grade primary school for children of campus employees and for those living nearby who had difficulty getting to other schools was begun in 1911 in a cabin on the campus of the boys' school.

Ford Dining Hall, the building for which Henry Ford was most involved in planning, 1930s.

Student milkmaids, early 1920s.

This school was apparently discontinued for a time, but it was located in the Roosevelt Cabin in 1921.[13]

In 1915, Berry initiated yet another project, a school for boys, some older than normal high-school age, who had received no opportunities for education and needed to learn reading, writing, arithmetic, and improved agricultural methods. Berry had acquired land at the foot of Lavender Mountain, and Grady Hamrick, a 1912 graduate of the Berry School, began constructing Pine Lodge with the help of six boys. The Mountain Farm School, as the new unit was first called, opened with eleven boys on January 4, 1916. They lived in an old cabin near the spring until Pine Lodge was completed, at which time the old cabin became the dining room and kitchen. The new school soon came to cater to boys too young for the high school (which had a

minimum age of sixteen by the 1920s), with some preference given to homeless boys. The students built roads and barns and operated a farm of several hundred acres during the day and received instruction at night. After a few months at the farm school, the boys had earned enough credit for tuition at the Berry School, and those who were prepared academically moved to the lower campus.[14]

More buildings were subsequently added to the mountain campus. Cherokee Lodge, constructed in 1920, provided a dining room and kitchen on the first floor and classroom space on the second floor. Meacham Hall was built in 1921 as a dormitory and apartment for Hamrick, who was appointed superintendent or headmaster. A dining hall (now Hill Dining Hall) and a classroom building or recitation hall (now Hamrick Hall) were completed in 1923.

Pine Lodge at the Foundation School, c. 1918.

In the fall of 1922, the school on the mountain campus became the foundation school for boys, with five teachers and ninety-five students. Thirty of the students were transferred from the grammar school that had operated on the boys' high-school campus; seventeen came from the former farm school on the mountain campus; and the remaining students were new to Berry. Ten boys received grammar-school diplomas the following spring. Separation from the high-school students worked well, resulting in stronger discipline among the grammar-school students, who also created their own Young Men's Christian Association and literary societies.[15] The small foundation school for girls was on the same campus as the girls' high school.

From the beginning of the schools, religion received special emphasis. Students regularly attended the Berry-operated Sunday school and churches in Rome, ministers or other speakers came to the cam-pus, and the Young Men's Christian Association and Young Women's Christian Association were founded shortly after the schools opened and conducted Sunday-evening programs.[16] Chapel programs (often not religious services) held during the week were compulsory for the students and expected for the faculty.[17] A nondenominational or interdenominational campus Christian congregation, the Mount Berry Church, was established on February 22, 1912, and held services conducted by ministers or chaplains from the major Protestant denominations.[18] After 1915, the church met in the Mount Berry Chapel, which also served as the site of many of the schools' ceremonial activities. When not on the platform, Martha Berry sat in the center of the first row of the back balcony.[19]

"Work hour" remained a very important component of the Berry program. The 14 hours per week of mandatory manual labor was increased to 17.5

Grady Hamrick, superintendent of the Foundation School, with students, c. 1918.

hours by 1910 (2.5 hours five days a week and 5 hours on Mondays, when no classes were held), and students who needed to earn their tuition put in extra hours, often working full time during the summer or for one of the two school terms each year. A summer or a fall or spring term of full-time work would earn two terms of tuition credit. Through 1954, the summer workday was usually nine or nine and a half hours. As the amount of land in the school domain increased, students needed more time to reach their work locations; consequently, on March 16, 1915, the student work program was changed to two consecutive eight-hour days for a total of sixteen hours per week, a schedule that continued until the 1960s. The stated purposes of the work program

were to assist worthy young people in their efforts to obtain an education and "to utilize the labor of the students for the necessary work of the institution."[20]

Uniforms—overalls for the boys and specially made dresses for the girls—were required, and the rules for personal conduct remained very strict. Students were not permitted to engage in card games, to use tobacco, or to leave campus without permission, among other things.[21] As is typical on school campuses, occasional outbreaks of disease occurred. In 1920 a student was diagnosed with smallpox, but a quarantine prevented any additional cases. Eugene Gunby, whose legs were paralyzed, graduated from the boys' high school in 1919, but by 1925, Martha

Kitchen crew students and supervisor outside Blackstone Dining Hall, 1918.

Boys working on a construction project, c. 1920.

Berry directed that Berry enroll no students who were "crippled, maimed, or deformed."[22]

Another typical facet of campus life, athletics, also existed at Berry. In 1925, Martha Berry directed that football was not to be played, although other intramural athletic contests frequently took place, usually pitting residence halls against each other.[23] Much less frequently athletic contests were held against outside teams, and at times school authorities entirely banned these activities. The Pentecost Gymnasium, named for a student who headed the effort to raise the necessary funds, was built on the boys' school campus in 1911. A decade later, a gymnasium was added to a dormitory on the Log Cabin Campus for the girls' school; the gymnasium remained in use until the completion of a new one on the Ford campus in the late 1920s. An annual field day involved many of the traditional track and field events as well as the crowning of a queen.[24]

Special end-of-school-year activities included debates in connection with baccalaureate and commencement services. Mountain Day, a celebration of Martha Berry's birthday, began in 1914. The Berry Alumni Association was established in 1908, and when the first twelve students graduated from the girls' high school in 1914, association members voted to admit girls. Clayton Henson, the first graduate, served as the association's president until 1915, when Gordon Keown, a graduate of the second class, took over, remaining in the position until 1923. The Berry Alumni Association began to hold a banquet and meeting in conjunction with spring commencement. Local alumni clubs were organized in 1922, first in Atlanta and soon thereafter in Blue Ridge and Dalton, Georgia; Birmingham, Alabama; and Chattanooga, Tennessee.[25]

In 1921 the Berry Alumni Association presented a proposal to the board of trustees for a campaign to raise twenty thousand dollars from former students to construct, as a present to Martha Berry, the House o' Dreams, a building on top of Lavender Mountain, the highest point on the school lands, with a view of three states. The trustees endorsed the proposal, and students performed most of the construction work. However, it was not done in secret and as a surprise to Martha Berry, as has sometimes been suggested.[26]

Many early teachers at the Berry Schools left after a short time, but others stayed for the remainder of their lives. In 1910, Berry School principal Robert H. Adams wrote to the president of Davidson College seeking suggestions for a new teacher. Based on those recommendations, Adams hired S. Henry Cook, who had received bachelors and masters degrees from Davidson and had directed the gymnasium there for a year. Cook was hired despite the fact that officials at Davidson had indicated that he probably would not stay long at Berry because he was planning to continue his education and to become a minister. Cook began his service at Berry in the fall of 1910 and ten years later wrote a letter of resignation stating, "I can no longer, conscientiously, work in harmony with the authorities in The Berry Schools." Although no further details regarding the situation have been found, someone else had been hired as the school's new principal a few days earlier, and Cook may have hoped to fill that position. Nevertheless, Cook did not leave Berry; rather, he remained until his death in 1975, serving the institution for almost sixty-five years as teacher, coach, dean, acting president, and, for the last eighteen of these years, as adviser to the president.[27] Martha Berry later told this story of Cook's hiring: "I wrote to the president of Davidson to send me a young man to teach math, history, English, athletics, stay in the dormitories to teach good behavior, preside in the dining hall to teach courtesy; a man who didn't have any bad habits—did not smoke, chew, drink or curse. I received this reply: 'Miss Berry, you will have to write to St. Peter for your man. There are no angels in this world, but I am sending you the nearest I have—red-haired Sam Henry Cook.' ”[28]

G. Leland Green, a graduate of the University of Vermont, became principal of the Berry School in August 1920. Green had worked at a Vermont school and had had success in influencing students to return to farm life after receiving their education, and Eagan, the president of the Berry trustees, hoped that Green could do the same in Georgia.[29] After serving as the first principal of the girls' school (responsible for academic work), Alberta Patterson became dean of that school (responsible for conduct), and Elizabeth Brewster assumed the position of principal. Patterson, several other staff members, and some students at the girls' school became very upset that a dance instructor had been brought to the campus to conduct lessons. They, like many people of the rural and religious South, opposed dancing because it involved close contact and touching between boys and girls. These students attempted to stir up the other girls in opposition to dancing, and Martha Berry viewed this response as a personal attack. Berry announced in May 1921 that Patterson was leaving the girls' school and would be replaced as dean by Alice Wingo, head of the English department at the boys' school. Elizabeth Patterson and eleven other girls' school staffers also left because of this controversy.[30]

In 1910, Eagan sent to Berry one of his employees, E. Herman Hoge, to improve the institution's business system, accounting records, and financial reports. Hoge did not expect to remain long at Berry but nevertheless stayed until his retirement in 1953. Berry did not operate with a budget, but Hoge took a firm hand in controlling expenditures. Martha Berry sometimes said he spent both sides of a nickel.

The policy of the Berry Schools was "never [to] go into debt."[31] The schools controlled costs in part by offering faculty and staff members very low salaries and few benefits. The schools provided housing for faculty during the school year but not

Alice Logan Wingo, who became dean of women in 1921, c. 1920.

during the summer unless they were actively working during that time. In some situations, food was also provided, but Berry offered no insurance or retirement benefits, and no tenure system or academic rank existed with the exception of titles for supervisory positions. Under these circumstances, faculty members who stayed for any length of time probably did so because they were dedicated to the schools, often with a missionary spirit of service.

A 1921 accident exemplifies the way the institution sometimes treated its faculty. In a "jubilant spirit" following Berry's basketball victory over the Rome Athletic Club, some Berry students dressed in sheets and, accompanied by the school band, paraded out the front gate onto the highway. No faculty member accompanied them, and they did not have permission to leave the campus. A Berry teacher returning from Rome on his motorcycle did not see the students spread across the highway and knocked down two students, and a third student riding on the back of the motorcycle was thrown into a ditch. A car then ran over two of the students. Three students, one very seriously injured, and the teacher, with a slight skull fracture, were hospitalized. Martha Berry "definitely instructed" the executive committee of the school to call for the "immediate resignation" of the teacher.[32] The reasons for Berry's harsh reaction remain unclear, especially because the students appear to be at least as much at fault as the faculty member, but the faculty member was transporting a student off campus, which would have represented a violation of the rules unless Berry had approved the excursion.

Challenges

At first, Martha Berry maintained contact with the Rome and Floyd County communities and received public as well as private support for her work. After a few years, however, most of her support came from private sources in other parts of the country. Aided by such factors as the creation of a separate post office to serve the campus, the Berry Schools became increasingly isolated from the surrounding community and maintained that isolation in many respects until about 1960. Martha Berry expected teachers and most other workers at the schools to live on the campus. The rather large amount of land bought by the schools (by the mid-1920s, the institution owned more than seven thousand acres of land, with about one thousand acres in cultivation, five hundred in pasture, and the remainder in woodland) and Berry's efforts to close public roads through school property also alienated the community. Some people in the community thought the schools were attempting to remove too much land from the tax books and, in later years, to block local growth and development.[33]

Nevertheless, the schools did maintain contacts with the broader community, offering teachers' institutes, Sunday school conferences, and agricultural institutes. The schools also attempted to serve as a model for agricultural and home products at local and state fairs, perhaps most successfully with a Jersey dairy herd that won 150 prizes at fairs in Georgia, Tennessee, and South Carolina in 1926.[34] The Berry Schools also established a model farm program that demonstrated practical and effective farming methods. The first model farm, occupying 50 acres, was operated in 1915 by Fair Moon, a 1913 graduate of the high school and subsequently the longtime manager of the school store. In the early 1920s, the schools divided a tract of approximately 375 acres into farms of 40 to 50 acres each, equipped the farms, and provided two-thirds of the cost of seeds and fertilizer. Former students of the school became the operators. They received a small cash salary and one-third of the crops produced.[35]

Like the rest of the country, Berry also experienced the effects of World War I. Approximately five hundred Berry students served their country during

Berry students who served in World War I, 1919.

the conflict. Because so many young men were away fighting, Berry's student body shrunk during the war years, and the school experienced a scarcity of teachers. Following the conflict, Berry built Victory Lake and the Road of Remembrance, with trees along both sides and a monument bearing the names of the eleven former students killed in the conflict. The Class of 1920 placed in the foyer of the Mount Berry Chapel a plaque with the names of those who gave their lives, and in 1920 ex-servicemen at Berry founded a campus American Legion post, which was named for two of those who died, Walter H. Levie and John Montgomery.[36]

Nevertheless, Berry's sense of isolation grew, and between 1909 and the early 1920s, Martha Berry and her schools became entangled in three serious con-troversies regarding the location of a rail line, a serious injury to a student, and the matter of the schools' tax status. The first matter involved a railroad right-of-way that would have cut through the heart of the school's property.[37] The R. G. Peters Mining Company owned an iron-ore mine and timber properties near Gore in Chattooga County, approximately seventeen miles from the schools. In 1909, the company proposed a new Rome and Northern Railroad that would extend from existing rail lines west of Rome across Berry property to various mine and timber properties. Peters, a wealthy Michigan businessman, was a major stockholder in the new railroad company.

After the railroad began condemnation proceedings for a right-of-way across the Berry property, the school obtained a temporary restraining order blocking any further efforts on the matter, and a hearing was set to obtain a permanent injunction.[38] Martha Berry began to contact people in Rome and to write other friends for support. Berry claimed "that seclusion and isolation from the general public, from public roads, railroads, and other similar disturbing influences are absolutely necessary to secure the best results from the students in their studies and work in the school, and in order that the school authorities may retain and exercise proper control and discipline over the students." Berry further contended that the proposed location of the rail line would cripple the school's plans for future expansion, which included a great agricultural and industrial school, an agricultural experiment station, a model settlement, and a settlement school: The railroad "would destroy the usefulness of that particular property for the purposes of the school, and would almost necessarily require the removal of the school to another location, in order that the plans and purposes of the school may be fully perfected; and the present buildings would be practically a total loss, so far as using the same for school purposes is concerned."[39] The petition contended both that the railroad would not be a public benefit and "that the school is a public institution"; furthermore, because the property was already dedicated to a "public purpose," the condemnation proceedings were illegal. The hearing for a permanent injunction was deferred, and the railroad began laying tracks for the line in other locations. Berry offered to donate about 1.25 miles of right-of-way in a less damaging area of its property and to pay for the extra grading, laying of track, and surfacing required in the new location.[40]

The Rome Manufacturers and Merchants Association attempted to settle the controversy, and Berry trustee president John Eagan agreed to attend a meeting. On August 14, the railroad and the school agreed on a compromise middle route. The railroad would pay for the right-of-way, with the amount to be determined by arbitration, and the injunction would be withdrawn. The suit was closed at the railroad's cost, and the rail line was completed.[41] On September 30, Martha Berry wrote to George Foster Peabody that after a long and expensive battle, "we have won the victory, and they will run the line only touching the extreme boundary of our property." She was "so thankful that we have overcome such a threatened evil." Ever on the lookout for fund-raising opportunities, she also asked R. G. Peters to donate twenty-five thousand dollars to the school; he sent seven hundred.[42]

The Rome and Northern Railroad began operation in 1910, but it never did very well financially and went into receivership in 1911. The railroad continued to operate both freight and passenger service but "never managed to do more than hold its own," and by 1924 plans were under way to scrap it.[43] Martha Berry proposed to the president of Southern Railway that his company buy the rail line, or at least the part from the Southern line in Rome onto Berry property, so it could be used for shipments to Berry, but the company declined. Berry then considered whether the school should buy about 1.5 miles of the railroad from the junction with the Southern line onto Berry property for use as a sidetrack. She asked the railway president if the idea was practical and whether Southern would use it and received the reply that the railroad would switch shipments arriving in Rome on their rails to the sidetrack without cost to Berry if the institution purchased and maintained the line; however, company officials warned her that the cost of maintaining the rail line might be greater than the cost of hauling the shipments from Rome by other means.

In 1925, Berry purchased the short rail line, including terminal yards, two complete switches, and the crossties. Later that year, she sold the line to the Central of Georgia Railway along with the right-of-way to build an 860-foot sidetrack, terminating in the vicinity of the Emery Barns, which had been constructed in 1915–16 north of the boys' school campus. Berry inserted the provision that the school could repurchase the property for the amount that the Central of Georgia had paid for it—fifteen hundred dollars—should it cease to be used for railroad purposes.[44] Berry also proposed that the Central of Georgia establish a station called Mount Berry and build a branch rail line to the mountain campus, where the foundation school was then located. The company rejected these suggestions because it did not think there would be enough business to justify the expense.[45] After most rail travel to Berry ceased, the school for many years operated the line to a point on the campus just west of Victory Lake. Some of Berry's important supporters, including Henry Ford, used the rail line for their private cars when visiting the campus.

The second major controversy stemmed from the most serious work-related accident involving an on-campus Berry student during the first few decades of the school's existence. The accident occurred in 1916 in the steam laundry, which had operated in Frances Cottage since 1913.[46] Wilma Butler, a sixteen-year-old girl in her first term as a student at Berry, was assigned to work in the laundry. On November 1, supervisor Lula Ray told Butler to take clothes out of the wringer or extractor, a rotating electric-powered tub that removed water from clothes by spinning them. Butler apparently turned off the electricity but opened the lid of the wringer and reached into it without waiting for the spinning to stop. Her fingers became entangled in the clothes, and her right arm suffered extensive damage. As a result of her injuries, her arm was amputated about three inches above the elbow, and she remained in the

hospital for eighteen days. Berry paid her hospital expenses and provided her with an artificial arm.[47]

Wilma Butler and her father wrote to Martha Berry in the summer of 1917. Berry felt "uneasy about the attitude [Wilma Butler] is taking" and considered the letters from Wilma's father "very threatening." The Butlers filed suit against Berry in the City Court on October 29, 1917. The plaintiffs stated that Wilma Butler was in good health before the injury, that the accident was a great shock to her nervous system, that she suffered great physical pain and mental anguish, and that she was in great danger of suffering nervous prostration. They also claimed that her earning capacity had been permanently reduced by at least three-fourths solely because of the school's carelessness and negligence: Butler claimed that no one had instructed her in the use of the equipment or had warned her of the possible danger. Butler requested twenty thousand dollars, while her father asked for three thousand dollars because she was still a minor.[48]

The school's attorneys advised Berry "not to try to compromise" and suggested that she write to the presiding judge that the school had already done a great deal for Butler. Berry continued to worry about the matter, however, writing to Eagan, "It will cause a great deal of trouble and notoriety will be bad for us." Moreover, "If we have to pay the Butlers thirty thousand dollars, it will be the death of the Girls' School."[49] On January 5, 1918, attorneys for Berry filed demurrers and answers to the petitions in the cases, contending that the accident had occurred because of Wilma Butler's negligence.[50] Two and a half years later, on September 25, 1920, a jury found in Berry's favor, noting that the school had already covered Butler's hospital expenses and provided the artificial limb. Not surprisingly, school officials, including Martha Berry, were pleased by the decision.[51]

Martha Berry in her office, 1917.

It did not develop into a significant controversy, but at around the same time as the Butler incident, Berry experienced the death of a student. On August 31, 1917, S. H. Cook and a number of male students went to swim in the Oostanaula River, and Monroe Miles, a twenty-one-year-old from southeast Georgia who had just arrived at the school the night before, drowned. The school chaplain, Rev. J. A. Hubbard, brought the body back to the boy's family and conducted the funeral service.[52]

The third major controversy that created tension between Berry and the surrounding community was whether the school would be required to pay taxes on its land and endowment.[53] In an apparent effort to advance their political ambitions, Floyd County attorney Graham Wright and local lawyers R. A. Denny and Seaborn Wright led an effort that resulted in the requirement that Berry pay taxes on its property for the first time. Martha Berry and some of her supporters feared that as a result of the school's rocky relationship with its neighbors, the Floyd County Board of Commissioners would seek "to levy the heaviest [possible] taxes upon Berry School property."[54] Berry gave permission for her name to be added to a petition favoring a state constitutional amendment to exempt educational endowments from taxation. In response to statewide efforts, the Georgia legislature in 1917 passed a constitutional amendment exempting such endowments from taxation, and a popular vote ratified the amendment in 1918. The next year, the legislature passed a law to implement that amendment, but the amendment and the law specifically excluded from the exemption endowments invested in land.[55]

In 1921 Graham Wright and Denny pointed out that a rich Floyd County corporation was not paying its fair share of county and state taxes. Without naming the corporation, they persuaded Governor Thomas W. Hardwick to hire them to collect the taxes due, with 20 percent of the amount collected earmarked for the attorneys as a fee for their services. The corporation was the Berry Schools.

On September 24, 1921, W. W. Hawkins, tax receiver of Floyd County, notified Berry that it had twenty days to file returns for 1915, 1916, 1917, and 1918 on real estate and on all personal property held as endowment. The notice stated that these taxes were considered delinquent and that the failure to file the returns within the specified time would result in the school's being considered to be in default, and the taxes would be doubled. The notice also indicated that the firm of Denny and Wright was the state's counsel in this matter.

Martha Berry, her staff, alumni, and supporters actively sought to block the collection of back taxes, inviting Governor Hardwick to come to the school. On his October 10 visit, Hardwick encouraged Berry to believe that he would immediately work to put a stop to the state's effort to collect the taxes. People from across the state and in other parts of the country wrote to the governor, the state tax commissioner, Denny and Wright, Berry, and several newspapers opposing the imposition of taxes on the school, and Berry and some others who supported her schools personally visited the governor to request his intercession.

On October 17, 1921, Hardwick wrote to the state tax commissioner that he had not been aware of who the delinquent taxpayer was when he authorized the employment of Denny and Wright to collect the taxes. He implied that although Berry might be legally liable for the levies, the state's policy was to exempt educational institutions from taxation as expressed in the 1918 constitutional amendment. The governor further indicated that he understood that Floyd County was willing to forget its share of these taxes; he believed that the state should do the same.

The Gate of Opportunity, c. 1925.

On October 25, Denny and Wright sent a long letter to the governor defending their effort to collect the back taxes. They believed that Berry was an enormously wealthy institution with an endowment of more than a million dollars. Although the constitutional amendment's implementation legislation had exempted endowments from taxation, they pointed out, those measures specifically stated that endowments invested in land were not exempt. Because Berry owned enormous amounts of land in Floyd County—six thousand acres and counting—exemption of this large acreage from taxation would burden the county's other property owners. Furthermore, Denny and Wright alleged, the state constitution specifically prohibited the legislature from making exemptions to the taxation requirements, and the county commissioners had no more authority

than the legislature; therefore, it would be illegal for the county to forgive Berry's taxes even if it were willing to do so. And the legislature could not act to forgive Berry's past taxes because any such action would have been retroactive and thus unconstitutional. Only a constitutional amendment could authorize any exemption.

But Denny and Wright were not finished. The attorneys implied that the governor may have been misled to believe that the Berry Schools were free and only for the poorer mountain people. In fact, they contended, each student was required to pay $140 in cash or labor each year in addition to sixteen hours of work each week of the school year. Denny and Wright suggested that they and the state tax commissioner be allowed to investigate Berry's books and that money collected could be used to pay public-school teachers' salaries and Confederate veterans' and widows' pensions, both of which were sometimes unpaid. Finally, the lawyers stated that they had received bad publicity as a result of this controversy and that they intended to continue to try to vindicate themselves. They would continue to attempt collection of the taxes unless the governor directly ordered the cancellation of their contract, in which case he should make public his reasons for doing so.

On October 31, the state tax commissioner wrote to Martha Berry that the governor would not arbitrarily end the tax-collection efforts but instead would order a preliminary investigation prior to any action. Berry was angry, having believed that she "had things practically settled" in her favor. She blamed Denny and Wright for the problem and stated that the governor had "gone completely back on his word"; she was "determined that Denny and Wright shall not examine our books."[56] Berry and her supporters redoubled their efforts to pressure the state's political leaders, writing to Georgia's U.S. senators, William Harris and Thomas Watson; the chancellor of the University of Georgia; Berry's trustees; local newspapers; Floyd County teachers; and even former president Woodrow Wilson, among others. In a published letter to alumni, Berry explained the controversy and requested letters of protest to the governor, to Denny and Wright, and to the school. Berry alumni drafted resolutions to the governor and a letter to the editor of the *Rome Tribune-Herald*. And as they had promised the governor, Denny and Wright also took their case to the public, sending a letter to the *Rome News* along with supporting documents that the paper published on November 13.[57]

On November 11, Martha Berry, Berry comptroller E. H. Hoge, and the public auditor for the schools met with the governor. Berry had first been required to pay taxes in 1917, and Hoge certified

that the schools had paid state and county taxes assessed since that time, raising the money through contributions to keep the schools operating. The governor would not say what he would do regarding future taxes.

Five days later, S. L. Graham, clerk of the Superior Court of Floyd County, wrote to Governor Hardwick to request that he withdraw the proceedings to collect back taxes from Berry. Graham observed that a great majority of the area's people did not support the effort and that the "Floyd County Board has dropped the matter so far as this county is concerned." On that same day, a Rome newspaper story stated that Rome and Floyd County were backing Berry in the tax battle.[58]

At the governor's request, the state tax commissioner wrote to Denny and Wright on November 17 informing them that the governor had decided to withdraw his approval of the contract concerning the institution's endowment except for real estate owned by the school. He noted that educational institutions' endowments were normally exempt from taxation in Georgia and that the state could not carry on Berry's work without spending far more than it could recoup in taxes from the institution. The letter stated that Denny and Wright could continue efforts on their own initiative to collect further back taxes on the real estate if they wished. Hardwick was only withdrawing the state's authorization for Denny and Wright to proceed on its behalf. This limited action would still allow any taxpayer the legal right to institute proceedings against Berry for the collection of the taxes in question.

The Berry board of trustees held a special meeting on November 23 and concluded that "in the future tax returns should be made only on those lands from which the school receives a rental." Three days later, Martha Berry wrote to John Eagan that she thought that G. E. Maddox, the school's attorney, "is going to have us pay the taxes on the land. He seems to think that is the best thing to do." Eagan replied that he believed it would be wise to pay taxes on certain lands. On the scheduled date, the schools did so. Denny and Wright did not contest those returns, although Martha Berry continued to hear that Denny and Wright were bad-mouthing her and the schools.[59]

On November 19, the *Rome Tribune-Herald* declared that Berry had won the fight against payment of back taxes. Martha Berry sometimes perceived it as only a "partial victory," but she and Eagan thanked people for their help, and in a published letter to Berry alumni in early 1922 she declared it a "glorious victory."[60]

Prominent Friends

In addition to Theodore Roosevelt and Henry and Clara Ford, several other well-known individuals endorsed Martha Berry's work. Berry became very accomplished at and well known for raising financial support for her schools. She had hoped to obtain contributions from Andrew Carnegie from the time of her early trips to northern cities, but he initially declined to provide direct support because he was already contributing $10,000 a year to the Southern Education Board.[61] Around 1906, Berry met Carnegie at a reception in Atlanta and took the same train as he did to Washington to talk with him. In 1907, Carnegie donated $5,000 for a wood-shop building, and two years later he agreed to contribute $25,000 (approximately $510,000 in 2003) to a $100,000 endowment campaign if the school could raise $75,000 and then persuaded Olivia Sage, another New York philanthropist and the widow of prominent American financier and railroad mogul Russell Sage, to give an additional $25,000. In less than a year, Berry had raised the full sum.[62] Because the 1909 gift was for the boys' school, Carnegie gave an additional $50,000 for the girls' school in 1912

on the condition that other donations match his gift, and Olivia Sage contributed another $25,000 for the girls' school.[63]

The Berry trustees opened a million-dollar endowment campaign in 1915, with plans to approach the General Education Board, supported by John D. Rockefeller, as well as the Carnegie Corporation. When the General Education Board's executive secretary visited the schools, however, Martha Berry was away, and Rockefeller chose not to contribute to her institution.[64] At the request of Andrew Carnegie and his wife, Louise, the Carnegie Corporation agreed in 1917 to provide $100,000 (approximately $1,433,000 in 2003) toward a $250,000 endowment fund for Berry. Two years later, Martha Berry sought support for a library. Louise Carnegie handed the request directly to the corporation's secretary and asked "that it receive most careful consideration," but no funds were approved.[65] Berry followed up with a 1921 request to the Carnegie Corporation for a large gift for a permanent endowment and received $12,500 a year for five years. Nevertheless, it became apparent in early 1922 that the plans for a large national endowment campaign should be abandoned.[66]

Other especially important early donors to the Berry Schools included wealthy mining engineer and businessman G. Lister Carlisle and his wife, Leila Laughlin Carlisle, the daughter of a steel magnate; Kate Macy Ladd, heir to the Macy's department store empire, and her husband, financier and philanthropist Walter G. Ladd; and Emily Vanderbilt Hammond, the great-granddaughter of Cornelius Vanderbilt and wife of corporate lawyer John Henry Hammond. Lister Carlisle served on the Berry board of trustees from 1917 to 1954, and Walter Ladd was a Berry trustee from 1916 to 1924. Leila Carlisle, wealthy in her own right, provided very generous gifts to Berry, including the school's first water system and first electric light system, a steam laundry, dairy barns, books for the school library, the Laughlin Building (now occupied by the communication department) and the Moon Building (now occupied by the art department and the print shop), three faculty/staff cottages, furnishings or heating systems for other cottages, an endowment for the upkeep of the Roosevelt Cabin, and an endowed scholarship. [67]

Kate Macy Ladd made many significant contributions totaling approximately $1,000,000, including Lemley Hall, the original portion of Memorial Library, endowments for these buildings, Victory Lake and the Road of Remembrance, and a box of candy for each student at Christmas during her lifetime. Following the death of Martha Berry's mother, Frances Rhea Berry, at age eighty-eight on December 30, 1926, the Oak Hill mansion was deeded to the schools, and Ladd funded the property's reconstruction and landscaping over the next two years. [68] In 1927, Ladd established a trust fund of $100,000 (approximately $1,058,000 in 2003) to provide income to Martha Berry during her lifetime. The death of Kate Macy Ladd's husband, Walter, in 1933 led to the establishment of a trust with $13,000,000. After fifty years, the remainder of this trust was to be distributed equally to five beneficiaries, including Berry. [69]

Emily Vanderbilt Hammond met Martha Berry at the home of Kate Macy Ladd, thus beginning a long-lasting and very important relationship for the Berry Schools. Each year between 1924 and the 1950s, Hammond would bring to Berry groups of northern friends. These "pilgrimages," as they were known, acquainted many people with the Berry Schools and subsequently resulted in their becoming donors. The pilgrims would unroll a silver scroll with money attached down the main aisle of the Mount Berry Chapel and out the front door onto the walkway. [70]

The support of these donors as well as of the many others who contributed smaller amounts was

Emily Vanderbilt Hammond, Martha Berry, and Corrine Roosevelt Robinson, c. 1930.

Students and the Silver Roll, including funds collected by the Berry Pilgrims in honor of Berry's silver anniversary, in front of Mount Berry Chapel, 1927.

essential to the Berry Schools' survival. A 1907 economic recession caused serious cash-flow problems for the Boys Industrial School, and similar financial problems arose during World War I and again during the early 1920s. In 1916, Martha Berry was having trouble raising funds in New York, as she wrote to John Eagan: "My friends told me they had helped in the past because they were interested in me and that they had no real interest in these boys and girls, that Georgia should take care of her own." Five years later, Berry again lamented about a fund-raising expedition to the Northeast, "I raised nothing except from my actual speaking, and I am very discouraged about finances. It seems that my old-fashioned way of begging is not so effective."[71]

To some extent, Martha Berry as well as Alice Lloyd, the leaders of Berea College, and numerous others used negative stereotypes to persuade people in other parts of the country to contribute to southern educational institutions, depicting the highlanders in particular as ignorant or illiterate and as living in severe poverty and isolation. Although such depictions were effective in generating donations, they sometimes angered the same people the schools proposed to benefit. Conversely, these southern educational leaders also attempted to convince people to donate money by depicting the mountaineers as "contemporary ancestors," noble descendants of the early American pioneers who had been denied opportunities to advance. As "pure" Anglo-Saxons or Scots-Irish, highlanders given education could become leading citizens who could advance their communities.[72] This opinion, while now perceived as overtly racist, was commonly held by white Americans in the first half of the twentieth century.

Fund-raising was also hampered by Martha Berry's various health problems. In 1919, she wrote that her doctors had begged her to take a rest and that it was "almost impossible to raise money sufficient to carry on the work at Berry."[73] In July 1923, Eagan

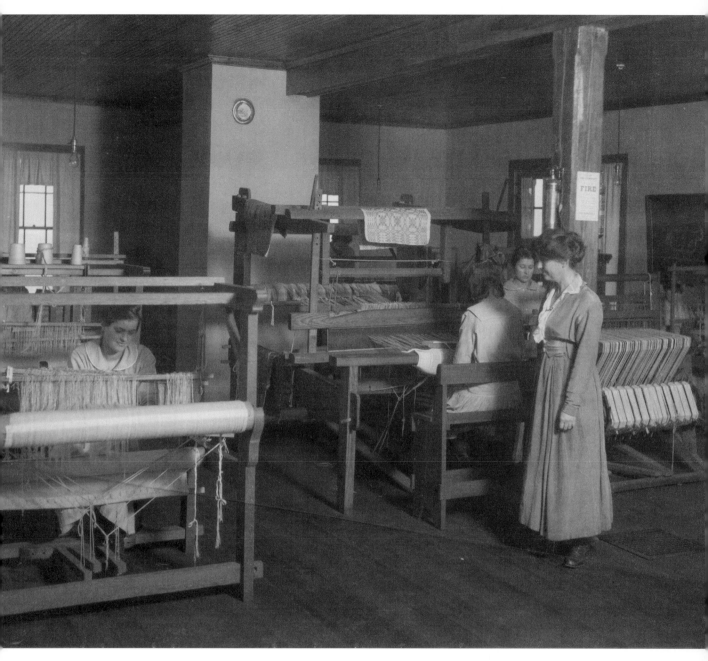

Sarah Nicholoy, weaving room supervisor, with students in Sunshine Cottage, c. 1917.

Students at work in the boys' school laundry, early 1920s.

told the campus executive committee not to trouble Berry and suggested to her that she should not bother herself with school affairs; Berry subsequently took three months off and missed the opening of school in the fall of that year.[74] Because of her inability to raise money, the schools experienced a financial crisis so severe that payroll could not be met on October 1, and all employees were informed that they would receive half their salaries at the beginning of the month and the other half later in the month.[75]

Still, the schools continued to expand. In 1924–25 the Berry Schools had endowments of $1,180,966.72 (approximately $12,400,000 in 2003) and operating expenses of $265,361.79.[76] A total of 695 students from ten different states enrolled that year—297 in the boys' high school, 141 in the girls' high school, 164 in the boys' foundation

school, 71 in the girls' foundation school, and 22 in the log-cabin school for campus children. Since their founding, the schools had educated 5,000 students, and space and resource constraints forced the schools to reject 400 of the 1,000 fall 1924 applicants. From the beginning, Berry's schools were only for people from rural areas, and applicants from cities and towns were still not eligible for admission. Twenty units (courses) were required for a high-school diploma, including agriculture, mechanics, the Bible, and music. The schools offered five programs of study: agricultural, mechanical, normal, literary scientific, and home economics. In addition to the mandatory work requirement for all students, approximately 50 percent of the boys and 20 percent of the girls completely covered their school costs by working on campus. Fewer girls could cover all of their educational costs through work because many jobs such as farm and construction labor were reserved for boys.[77]

Berry also continued to be very active in directing her schools. She discontinued Christmas vacation in 1925 "for the good of the students" because returning students might bring back diseases that would result in loss of time from schoolwork. As she told the executive committee, "I think it best to have only Christmas Day as a holiday. . . . There is always a letdown right after Christmas Day, and the work should go right on after the holiday of one day."[78]

Of the six original trustees, only Martha Berry and her brother, Thomas, remained by 1925. Hoke Smith, the only person to join the original board of trustees of the Boys Industrial School, had also resigned. From January 1908, when the corporation's name was officially changed to the Berry School, to June 1917, when the name was again changed to the Berry Schools, twelve more trustees were named,

with nine others selected for service on the Berry board by 1925. Whereas all seven members of the Boys Industrial School board had been Georgians, by 1908 residents of other parts of the country also served and by 1925 almost half of the board's nineteen members came from outside Georgia, including Massachusetts, New Jersey, New York, Ohio, and Pennsylvania.[79] All of these trustees had been nominated by Martha Berry.[80]

The first head of the board, John J. Eagan, died on March 30, 1924, after having led the board for more than two decades. Another longtime trustee, Moses Wright, Martha Berry's brother-in-law, died on October 5, 1925.[81] The two men had been instrumental in the founding and administration of the schools over their first two decades, and their deaths marked the end of an era. Nonetheless, the institution was ready to embark on a new era, establishing a junior college and subsequently expanding it into a senior college.

Between 1926 and 1942, the Berry Schools faced serious financial problems and received their first significant national negative criticism. Despite these challenges, a junior college and then a senior college were added, and campus facilities, landholdings, the endowment, and enrollment increased significantly before Martha Berry's death.

CHAPTER FOUR

Expanding the Charter

The Beginning of Berry College

In the fall of 1923, Berry planned to begin offering college courses and thereby to enable its graduates to enter other colleges and universities as sophomores or juniors. Berry high-school graduates had performed well at many of the South's leading colleges and universities, but other students who wished to continue their education beyond high school could not do so because of financial limitations. Consequently, Berry's principal, Leland Green, indicated, many Berry graduates who desired further education had no option but to attend second-rate colleges or junior colleges. He recommended that Berry begin to offer two years of post-high-school study, with emphasis on agriculture, premedical, and teacher-preparation courses.[1] Like Berry's high-school students, those in the college program would have the opportunity to work to cover their educational expenses, and graduates of other high schools would

also be able to continue their education at Berry. Despite this expansion, the *Berry Alumni Quarterly* reported, "there was no thought of placing less emphasis upon the grammar- and high-school work. It is expected that these two departments will constitute the chief interest of the Schools as heretofore."[2]

Students graduating from the Berry high schools would be encouraged to remain at Berry for the college courses, and Green suggested that the first two years of the boys' high school could be moved to the mountain campus, while students in their last two years of high school and first two years of college could reside on the lower campus.[3] Berry Junior College initiated its two-year college program in the fall of 1926, with Green serving as the new school's president. The college offered agricultural, commercial, home economics, and literary-scientific programs of study as well as fifteen semester hours of education courses, which a student could combine with any of the four programs of study to receive a professional high-school teaching certificate. To earn a diploma required sixty semester hours of college courses in addition to courses in the Bible and in music. Like the high-schoolers, the college students attended classes four days each week and worked for two days. Unlike the Berry high schools, however, the junior college was co-educational, enrolling ten men and nine women in its first year, four of the women and two of the men from other high schools. The first twelve students received diplomas from the junior college in 1928, and a total of 137 graduated from 1928 through 1931, when the last junior-college diplomas were awarded.[4]

When the junior college opened, along with a new library building, Berry began to increase the size of the faculty and to recruit more teachers with graduate degrees, but no faculty member in 1928–29 had earned a doctorate, although Martha Berry and Leland Green had received honorary doctorates. Only six faculty members held masters degrees.[5] Despite the shortcomings of the fledgling junior college, the early graduates did well at other colleges and universities, and the Southern Association of Colleges and Secondary Schools granted accreditation in December 1929.[6] The two separate high schools, the Mount Berry School for Boys and the Martha Berry School for Girls, continued to receive emphasis as major parts of the total institution, and the boys' and girls' foundation schools continued to prepare students for the high schools. All of the high-school boys had moved to the mountain campus by 1931 to make room for the college men at the former location of the boys' high school.

The cost for attending any of the schools was $215 for the first year—$150 for tuition, $50 for uniforms, and $15 for books. Many students earned their tuition by working on campus during the summers or full-time during a semester. After the first year, the cost of uniforms dropped, and aside from small laboratory, damage, and infirmary fees, there were essentially no other monetary costs.[7]

As of 1931, more than twelve hundred students had graduated from the high schools and junior college and had found employment in a variety of fields: business, 23 percent; teaching, 22 percent; homemaking, 15 percent; farming, 12 percent; nursing, 4 percent; and dairying, 2 percent. In addition, 17 percent of graduates went on to pursue further study, and 1 percent each became doctors, preachers, and school superintendents. Smaller numbers became county agents, dentists, or lawyers or found jobs with the Young Men's Christian Association. Of the more than six thousand students who had left school without graduating, 40 percent were farmers, 17 percent homemakers, 15 percent businesspersons, 15 percent teachers, 2 percent nurses, and 1 percent dairy farmers; 10 percent became students at other institutions.[8] Thus, fewer than 20 percent of those who had enrolled at Berry had graduated. While they may have gained as a result of their experiences, a more effective program might have provided even greater benefits to many more people.

Berry began offering courses for the senior-college program in the fall of 1930, but before the school could award college degrees, it needed a certificate of approval from the Georgia Department of Education, which arrived more than a year later, in November 1931. The Berry trustees then approved a petition requesting extension of the corporate charter for one hundred years as well as authorization to operate a college and grant degrees. The Superior Court of Floyd County amended the charter on April 14, 1932. The first seventeen students to complete senior-college programs of study graduated in the spring of 1932. The senior college at first was called Martha Berry College, but the name was soon shortened to Berry College. G. Leland Green had worked to establish the college, which Martha Berry described as the "crowning achievement of

Interior of the Berry Store (later the Moon Building), where students purchased uniforms, books, and other necessities, c. 1936.

my life."[9] Green became the president, and it was expected that he would hire faculty and run the school; she, as director, would raise the money.

Despite its state certification to award degrees, the senior college was not yet accredited by the Southern Association of Colleges and Secondary Schools. In his 1931 report to the trustees, President Green noted that the junior college had quickly gained accreditation and expressed his confidence that the senior college would do so in three or four years. Per Green's request, the association had already dropped Berry as a junior-college member, and soon after the first students received their senior-college degrees, Berry began to work toward regional accreditation, presenting formal reports to the asso-

ciation in 1933 and 1935 and hosting a visit from the group's executive secretary.[10] Martha Berry spoke at the association's December 1933 annual meeting, describing the development of her schools and college and the education being provided to the students, hoping, as the association's president had suggested, that presenting a paper "might indirectly do your cause some good." The association sent a three-person committee to visit Berry College in May 1936 but did not grant accreditation and would not do so for another twenty years.[11]

Berry College also began efforts to become a member of the Association of American Colleges as early as 1934, when the organization's executive committee carefully considered the college's request

Students constructing the Science Building (later the Cook Building) using bricks made in Berry's brick plant, 1937.

for admission but decided that Berry was not yet ready. Two years later, in January 1936, Berry College was granted full membership despite the fact that the association normally accepted only those institutions recognized by regional accrediting associations. The president of the Association of American Colleges explained, "Martha Berry has created here one of the most significant educational enterprises of the twentieth century, one which when the history of education is written will place her name near the top."[12]

Within a few years of its creation, the senior college was offering five degrees, each requiring 128 semester hours of credit: bachelor of arts, bachelor of science, bachelor of science in agriculture, bachelor of science in home economics, and bachelor of science in industrial arts. The college also was providing, primarily through the required work program, training in thirty lines of work, with more added each year. The occupational-training list included farming, landscaping, forest management,

carpentry, plumbing, brick manufacturing and laying, shoe repair, automobile repair, general merchandising, stenography, typewriting, cooking, sewing, nursing, dental assistant training, teaching, and ministry. The two high schools required twenty units for a diploma and claimed to have standards comparing favorably with those of the country's best secondary schools. A practice school for student teachers operating at Possum Trot enrolled children of that community and children of the Berry teachers and workers.[13]

By 1940 the requirements for those same five college degrees had increased to 130 semester hours. Majors were offered in twenty-one fields of study: agriculture, biology, business administration, chemistry, education, English, fine arts, French, German, home economics, industrial arts, journalism, Latin, mathematics, music, physical education, physics, psychology, Spanish, religious education, and social science. To support the programs of study, the library possessed twelve thousand volumes.[14]

The Depression Years

For the first thirty years of their existence, most publicity regarding the schools was positive. However, Martha Berry's separation of her schools from the larger Rome community resulted in the development of some local animosity, and these feelings were exacerbated by the incidents regarding the rail line across school property, the injury to Wilma Butler, and the school's attempts to avoid paying taxes on its property (see chapter 3).

Prior to late 1933, the negative feelings generated by such matters had been limited almost entirely to the local and state levels. In October of that year, however, the *New Republic* published a letter from Don West, a former student at the Mount Berry School for Boys.[15] West was born in 1906 in the mountains of Gilmer County in northern Georgia, one of nine children of poor farmers. He attended the high school from 1923 until the spring of 1926, when he was expelled, as he indicated, for objecting to the showing of the 1915 film *Birth of a Nation* because he thought it glamorized the Ku Klux Klan. Although he had not graduated from the high school, he was admitted to Lincoln Memorial University in Tennessee, from which he ultimately graduated. He subsequently enrolled in the seminary at Vanderbilt University, graduating in 1932.[16]

Although West had apparently been a disruptive force during his time at Berry and had been expelled, the *Berry Alumni Quarterly* and the *Southern Highlander* recognized his accomplishments as a college and graduate student and as a poet. In April 1932 West visited Berry, where he read from his poetry and lectured on Danish folk schools. Both students and faculty were impressed, and Martha Berry entertained West in her home.[17] Shortly after his visit, West wrote to Berry to express his "sincerest appreciation for the fine spirit in which I was treated. . . . Always I shall be glad and proud to have been a Berry student, and always I shall be happy to tell people of it."[18]

But West's thinking had obviously undergone a major transformation by the time he composed his letter to the *New Republic,* in which he wrote,

> Recently there has been a significant student strike in the Berry Schools at Rome, Georgia. Berry is a school for poor whites which parades itself as a great philanthropic and humanitarian institution. The students pay their tuition by working during the four summer months. Before the depression they were paid from sixteen to eighteen cents an hour, working from ten to twelve hours a day at manual labor of the hardest sort, some of it semi-skilled. This summer, however, the authorities reduced the working students to the disgracefully low wage of ten to twelve cents an hour, while tuition remained the same as before and the prices in the school store, where students must buy their supplies, were raised considerably. Resenting this injustice, the students went out on strike, demanding enough out of four months' work to pay eight months' tuition, and a reduction in the school-store prices. The strike was ended when officials promised to endeavor to meet the demands and not to expel students for striking.
>
> Since they returned to work, students report that the authorities are holding the club of expulsion over their heads. I am an alumnus of Berry and know too well the reality that lies behind their fine story of helping "poor mountain boys and girls." I think the public should be told the nature of this and other missionary institutions with which the South is cursed.[19]

Why had West experienced such a dramatic change of heart? As his letter alleged, student pay had been cut, but faculty pay had also been cut because of financial problems associated with the Great Depression, and the schools claimed that the pay cut would allow more students to enroll and work at Berry.[20] In reaction to the pay cut, Willis Sutton, a Berry student and cousin of West, had helped to organize an August 28, 1933, strike among the students at the boys' high school. According to a leaflet, *Berry Students Demand Justice,* published by the "Committee for Student Rights in Berry High School," the students believed that they were "treated unjustly by the administration" and demanded either lower tuition or higher wages as well as the recognition of an organization representing the student body. The publication also called for more social events involving the boys and the girls and permission for more trips into Rome and to student homes.[21] Furthermore, because of the Great Depression, jobs outside Berry were almost nonexistent, so the on-campus work program represented the only way that many students could obtain an education. Critics accused the school of exploiting people who had no other options.

The details of the strike remain murky. According to *Berry Students Demand Justice,* all the students working at the boys' high school went on strike, while an investigator for the *New Republic* indicated that ninety-six of the school's one hundred students supported the strike and that they pushed the other four into participating. Charles Proctor, a Boston dentist and strong Berry supporter, stated that five or six students quit work, that all but one soon returned to their jobs, and that one "agitator" was removed and one student sent away. Other sources contended that no strike had occurred, that there had been a strike lasting only a few hours, or that it had lasted two days.[22]

On August 28, the executive committee of the schools met to consider a petition in which the students at the boys' high school requested more credit for their summer work and increased cash-withdrawal privileges because of increased supply costs. They also complained that the pay rates for four months of summer work were insufficient to cover eight months of tuition. The executive committee ultimately concluded that it lacked authority to act on the petition. President Green; Gordon Keown, Mount Berry postmaster, resident trustee, and adviser to Martha Berry; and Grady Hamrick, head of the boys' high school, met with the students and urged the boys to honor their summer work contracts, enroll in school in September, and leave consideration of any adjustments to "proper school authorities" in the future.[23]

After the strike ended, some students apparently sought assistance from the Communist-led National Student League, which sent organizer Clyde Johnson from New York to Atlanta, where Don West met him and drove him to the Sutton home. Sutton and Johnson subsequently planned to meet dissident students at the school gate, but when the two men arrived, they were greeted by administrators but no students. Sutton and Johnson were taken to jail but released without charges. Johnson was arrested again the next morning and left the area shortly thereafter.[24] With that, the incident apparently came to an end until the publication of West's letter.

The letter unleashed a fury. Martha Berry wrote to her friend, Emily Vanderbilt Hammond, "I am receiving threatening letters all through the day, saying they are going to ruin my reputation and the reputation of the school."[25] But Berry and her supporters did not take the attack lying down. The *New Republic* reported that it "received about 200 letters from trustees, faculty members, students and friends of the Berry Schools, all of them strongly repudiating Mr. West's general attitude."[26] Dozens of others defended Berry in letters to West, his associates, other publications, educators, trustees, alumni, and friends. The *New Republic*'s correspondents included Atlanta attorney Robert C. Alston, who had become chairman of the Berry board of trustees after John J. Eagan's death in 1924 and who sent a heated telegram to the magazine. In response, the editors agreed to send an investigator to Berry: his report concluded that although the decrease in student wages was an issue in the strike, the students seemed just as concerned about strict rules and limited social activities involving both men and women. In many respects, however, the report criticized the schools' actions, implying, among other points, that students had been threatened and that a detective had been hired to follow the investigator. [27]

Another group of Berry students printed a "Protest of Berry Students against False Propaganda Being Spread about Them by Don West and Others." This four-page resolution was addressed to the Socialist Party of America; to the *New Republic;* to West; to another former Berry student, Walker Martin; and to the National Student League, and the authors rejected the "false statements, propaganda, and literature being circulated by Don West in magazines, newspapers and circulars." [28]

By mid-October, Martha Berry, her top associates, and her major supporters had decided that they should stop fighting and thereby adding to the bad publicity. On October 13, a friend of Hammond, Dr. William J. Schieffelin of New York, wrote to her that he thought it had been unwise to have the students write letters regarding the matter and that little attention should be paid to what the detractors were saying. Hammond forwarded the letter to Martha Berry and added, "I think you made a mistake taking Don West so seriously." Berry apparently agreed, writing to Schieffelin and Proctor that Berry supporters should end their efforts "as the publicity is just what our opponents are after." The furor then died down, with further articles on the subject limited to the *New Republic*'s publication of its investigator's report in April 1934. [29]

Although Martha Berry felt that the controversy was the worst that the schools had yet known, it apparently had little or no lasting effect. [30] Students at the girls' high school and the college did not participate in the strike, and the students generally seem to have emerged from the storm with feelings of even greater loyalty to the institution. Most students of that time and since who participated in the Berry on-campus work program thought they received full educational value for their labor. In fact, many of the students from that period considered the work program one of their fondest memories of Berry, rather than as unjust labor. [31]

West's statement in his letter that the South has been "cursed" by missionary institutions is not particularly unusual. A number of scholars of Appalachia and others have often strongly criticized the efforts of those seeking to change or "improve" the lifestyles and economic circumstances of the people of the southern highlands. David E. Whisnant, for example, has accused teachers, social workers, health-service providers, and others of trying to destroy an entire culture and substitute their own middle-class values, of arbitrarily emphasizing some aspects of the Appalachian culture as original or early-generation American values or skills while attempting to eradicate other, perhaps equally valid, parts of the mountaineer lifestyle. Conversely, P. David Searles has pointed out weaknesses in that argument at least in the case of Alice Lloyd and the college she founded. [32] Martha Berry's work provides another example of benevolent efforts that helped large numbers of rural southerners.

As the reduction in pay that led to the West incident shows, the Berry Schools were hard-hit by the Great Depression. The fund-raising problems the school had experienced in earlier years paled in comparison to those of the 1930s, and whereas students had paid about twenty-seven thousand dollars in cash for tuition in the late 1920s, ten years later that sum had dropped to about seven thousand dollars. [33] Effective January 1, 1933, Martha Berry slashed by 20 percent all faculty members' salaries, which at a maximum of $150 for an eight-month contract had hardly been extravagant even before the cut. Anyone not willing to accept the salary reduction was to be paid for thirty days and then released from employment—during the worst part of the Great Depression. The following March, Berry decreed that all twelve-month employees must take one-month vacations without pay, although married men making $75 or less a month only had to take two-week unpaid vacations. Despite these drastic measures, within two years the amount budgeted for salaries had climbed nearly back to pre-1933 levels. Seeking to increase the schools' income, Berry raised the price of milk ten cents per quart on April 1, 1933, and as of September 1 required families living in campus housing to pay for the electricity they used.[34] Furthermore, as was the practice in many company towns, Berry began to pay its employees in specie and tokens printed and manufactured by the institution instead of in U.S. currency, thereby forcing employees to make their purchases at the campus general store. Such actions increased the financial pressures on the same employees whose salaries had just been sharply reduced.

The Berry Schools' dire financial situation seriously curbed their acquisition of land during the Great Depression, when there was simply no money available for such purchases. In a few cases when the institution did purchase land during those years, Henry Ford provided the funds to do so. The schools also sought to raise cash by increasing the number of students who paid their full tuition rather than working for it, although in recognition of the economic circumstances faced by students' families, the school accepted farm produce at market value as payment.[35] In 1939, Martha Berry directed that the school "must try to have half pay and half work students" and that this goal had to be a factor in the admission of new students.[36]

Despite the Great Depression, some of the school's longtime supporters, including Leila Laughlin Carlisle, Walter G. Ladd, and Kate Macy Ladd, continued their generous donations, and Martha Berry continued to receive widespread approval for her work. George Lister Carlisle Jr., a Berry trustee from 1917 to 1954, sent Tracy Byers to write the institution's story. The result was the first book on Martha Berry and her schools.[37]

In the spring of 1933, Hammond, Proctor, and Martha Berry received the first honorary degrees awarded by Berry College in recognition of their great support of the institution. In 1926, Proctor had donated a dental clinic to the school in honor of his deceased son, and at times he had worked in the clinic or provided other dentists to staff it. Hammond continued to bring "pilgrims" to Berry until the 1950s, including, in April 1933, Sara Delano Roosevelt, the mother of the newly elected U.S. president, and Mina Edison, widow of Thomas A. Edison. The following November 23, Sara and Franklin Roosevelt hosted Martha Berry at the Little White House in Warm Springs, Georgia.[38] As part of Roosevelt's New Deal, a Civilian Conservation Corps camp was established on Berry property. The Berry Schools were also honored by visits from such prominent U.S. educators as Mary Woolley, a former president of Mount Holyoke College who spoke at Berry in 1937, and Mildred McAfee, president of Wellesley College, who came in 1940.[39]

This era also saw the founding of two women's organizations that remain active in the early twenty-first century. The Mount Berry Garden Club was organized on May 26, 1931, with eleven charter members and Gordon Keown's wife, Frances Olmsted Keown, as its first president.[40] Eight years later, Martha Berry initiated the founding of a club for Berry alumnae and the wives of its alumni, the Daughters of Berry, to preserve the ideals and traditions on which Berry had been founded and to work to establish a museum of its history. She invited

Martha Berry and Henry Ford, in front of Mary Hall, 1930.

Iva Lee Hamilton Cannon, whose husband, Geddins, was Martha Berry's driver and groundskeeper at Oak Hill; Frances Olmsted Keown, and Lillian Hulsey Russell, whose husband, Clifton, was head of grounds, to her mountain house in Mentone, Alabama, and they agreed to hold an organizational meeting for the group the following October. Forty-four charter members signed up for the group, which held its first meeting in the Roosevelt Cabin, and Mary Alice Barnes served as the group's first president.[41]

Roany, the horse who had assisted in the early days of the boarding school, died on November 26, 1929, at the reported age of thirty-five. In 1934, a marker was dedicated in his honor on Founder's Day, a ceremonial occasion on which he had pulled a carriage driven by Martha Berry between lines of students.[42]

Faculty and Student Life in the Early 1940s

Even after the worst of the Great Depression had passed, faculty and staff salaries remained low, and the school provided no insurance or retirement plans. The Berry Schools did not permit employees to live in Rome and consequently provided on-campus housing for all workers. These cottages and apartments were provided rent free, furnished with water, and kept in repair, while employees paid for electricity. Faculty still could not remain on the campus during the summer, however, unless they were employed for that time. Martha Berry expected teachers "to go immediately after commencement except those on duty."[43]

At the end of the 1930s, the faculty included thirty-nine persons, five with earned doctoral degrees: chemistry professor Grover Ford had received a doctorate from Iowa State University; English professor Walter Herbert held a Ph.D. from Princeton University; professor Harold Jones had a doctorate in biology from Peabody College; Lawrence McAllister, a physics professor, had a doctorate from the University of Chicago; and George Osborn held a Ph.D. in history from Indiana University.[44] At least two members of Berry's faculty had published books with major scholarly presses in the early 1940s, Herbert's volume on John Wesley released by Princeton University Press and Oxford University Press and Osborn's biography of Senator John Sharp Williams published by Louisiana State University Press.[45]

Of those five men with earned doctorates, Lawrence McAllister—Dr. Mac to his students—remained at Berry for the longest period of time, teaching physics from the early 1930s to the early 1970s and sending dozens of his students on to graduate school and subsequently to contribute to the development of the U.S. space program and other technological advancements. Dr. Mac was actively involved with the seniors who published the first Berry College yearbook, the *Cabin Log*, in 1935 and was responsible for providing sound amplification systems for the campus.[46]

School policies included strict rules for faculty as well as for students. For example, smoking was banned. Martha Berry did not allow faculty members' family to work their way through the Berry Schools: "If they wish their relatives to come to Berry, they must pay." Children of the faculty who were in school at Berry could receive honors but not prize money when competing with other students.[47]

Martha Berry with Roany the Pony, c. 1925.

Faculty residence, 1928.

Dr. Lawrence McAllister, physics professor at Berry from 1932 to 1972, c. 1949.

Of course, not all faculty members left Berry voluntarily. Ralph Hill, a chemistry faculty member, made a statement to the school's executive committee in which he indicated that he thought a number of things at Berry should be corrected: faculty members were treated like grammar-school children and hired for as little salary as possible; excellent teachers were let go in favor of inexperienced teachers who could be paid less; the school's management often acted insincerely and deceitfully, showing visitors only the lovely exterior and not the interior workings of the school while making false statements and giving bad advice to the director; faculty members feared losing their jobs for speaking out and could be dismissed without cause. Members of the executive committee took exception to his statements and tried to explain some misunderstandings and then told him emphatically that if he endeavored to arouse strife on the campus he would be required to leave before his contract expired."[48] Hill was subsequently released from his employment. Martha Berry ruled the schools with a very strong will, making or approving most of the strict rules and expecting her administrators to enforce those regulations firmly. The rules sometimes seemed rather arbitrary, and they might even be administered in an uneven fashion at times.

Dr. John H. Winter, a teacher of sociology since 1930 who also became dean of men at the college, announced in September 1934 that he planned to leave about two months later. He apparently was in good standing with the school at that time, but by the end of October a serious disagreement had clearly developed, and school authorities asked him to leave immediately because "he has made many false and derogatory statements in regard to the School and in regard to Miss Berry, the head of the School, and it has also developed that he has surreptitiously taken advantage of his position to misrepresent the School, and that he has made various and sundry threats as to his future intentions towards the School and

to damage it in the eyes of the public generally."[49] Winter apparently retaliated by hiring an airplane to fly over the campus and drop leaflets presenting his views.[50]

In 1940, the college's enrollment reached 677, outstripping that of the boys' high school (380), the girls' high school (126), and the Possum Trot school (69) combined. However, the college graduated only 101 students that year, while the high schools graduated 105 boys and girls.[51] All candidates for bachelor of arts degrees in 1942 had to complete at least twenty-four semester hours in foreign languages, and all bachelor of science degree candidates had to complete twelve semester hours in one foreign language. All college students were required to take two Bible courses, while all males were required to have one year of agricultural study and all females had to have one year of home economics. Any courses failed had to be repeated.[52] College policies and curriculum were very conservative, and methods of instruction were typically quite traditional.

Very strict rules still governed most aspects of students' campus lives. Regular attendance at classes, Sunday school, church services, and chapel programs was required, while the use of tobacco and alcohol were forbidden. All interactions between men and women were carefully monitored. Students normally could go home during the school year only for a short time at Christmas. Any serious violation of the behavioral rules would result in a student's being sent home (suspended) or permanently expelled, and Martha Berry expected a "publicly expelled" student "to stay away for all time, and not come back as a visitor, even," although she apparently did not stick to her policy in the case of Don West.[53]

In an effort to maintain strict confidentiality regarding school business, Martha Berry directed in 1926 that students not be assigned to work in her office or to handle the *Southern Highlander*, which was intended for donors and might contain inaccurate

Students marching to chapel service at the College Chapel,
c. 1952.

information about students. She was particularly sensitive regarding her relations with contributors and potential donors.

By the early 1940s, campus life for faculty, staff, and students had become much more comfortable than had been the case in the early days but remained rigorous and restrictive compared to college life today. Classes were usually held six days a week and did not end on Saturdays until 6:49 p.m.[54] According to the 1943–44 *Worker's Handbook,* all "workers" (faculty and staff) were expected to teach Sunday school if asked to do so and to build character in their students by precept and example. Workers had to notify the comptroller's office as well as their department heads before leaving campus for a day or longer. Christmas vacation usually lasted seven days. Hospital service was available to employees for one dollar a day in addition to the cost of medicine.[55]

Visitors to the schools could receive lodging at the rate of one dollar a day and could purchase "good meals" at the cafeteria. Faculty and staff could employ students, many of whom looked for extra work, at the same rate as the schools did. Faculty and staff could not, however, employ "colored" help. Berry encouraged its workers to contribute to its Student Aid Fund, which provided loans to students in need, but urged that employees not give financial help to individual students.[56]

Employees received keys to the Gate of Opportunity, the main entrance to the schools, for a deposit of fifty cents and shared responsibility for keeping the gates closed at night and on Sunday. Employees and students abided by the same daily schedule, with an 8:00 a.m. bell signaling the start of the workday and a 5:30 p.m. bell signaling the close of work. Regulations forbade employees with cars from taking students off campus, and faculty members were not allowed to date students.[57]

To meet the requirement that they "keep their mouths and teeth in excellent condition," students paid an annual fee of two dollars for dental services at the schools' clinic. A school physician and two nurses also oversaw the general health of students.[58] Before enrolling, students had to submit evidence of a clean bill of health.

Students rotated their work (two days) and classes (four days) according to their classification—freshman, sophomore, junior, or senior. Sophomores worked Monday and Tuesday and attended classes Wednesday through Saturday; juniors and seniors worked Wednesday and Thursday and attended classes Monday, Tuesday, Friday, and Saturday; freshmen worked Friday and Saturday and attended classes Monday through Thursday. Students could obtain supervised work experience in more than twenty occupations.[59]

Athletics included only intramural or intersociety activity. In the fall the freshman, sophomore, junior, and senior classes played a series of basketball games against each other, and each spring various campus groups played in a basketball tournament. The "varsity" basketball team included eight sophomore, junior, and senior lettermen who were selected at spring tryouts. Similar plans prevailed in baseball, track, and tennis.[60]

Except for Christmas recess, classes continued straight through from the second week in September until the fourth week in May, though the advent of World War II led to changes to accommodate military cadets, who followed a "paced-up" schedule that included summer classes. Students could not go home during the year or leave the campus for more than a few hours at a time without permission, and any departure from campus required a chaperone. Students could not keep automobiles or bicycles on campus.[61]

All students were admitted on a probationary basis, with classification or permanence of enrollment thirty days after entrance. Detailed reports

Students at work in Ford Dining Hall, 1940s.

of students' performance, sent home twice each semester, included room grades. Students' rooms had to be ready for inspection by 8 a.m. each day: clothes and shoes had to be in order in the closet, beds had to be neatly made, and furniture and floors had to be dusted. Electrical appliances were not permitted in dormitory rooms, but students could make coffee on a hot plate in a special room set aside for that purpose.[62]

All students were required to wear uniforms for the sake of "democracy and economy."[63] Female students usually owned three everyday uniforms and one dress uniform each for summer and winter. The everyday uniform of the college women below senior level was pink chambray, while the college seniors wore green chambray and high-school girls wore blue. Sleeves were long, with detachable white cuffs and a matching detachable white collar. In summer, the sleeves could be rolled up before the cuffs were attached. From spring through fall, girls wore plain white dresses with white oxfords on Sundays; the winter Sunday uniform was blue serge with black oxfords. Plain black shoes with low heels were the rule

for the daily winter uniform, with white shoes worn from spring through fall. Students employed in the sewing room made the uniforms, which cost between three and four dollars each. School officials customarily asked clothing manufacturers to donate belt buckles and buttons for the winter Sunday dress.[64] Each girl also had an overcoat, a raincoat, and an umbrella and was required to wear her uniform when leaving the campus to go home and when returning to campus. Men wore jeans or overalls and blue shirts during the week, except for seniors, who wore white shirts. On Sundays, men wore dark suits with white shirts and dark ties.[65]

Each unexcused absence from class, work, Sunday school, or church lowered a student's "citizenship standing" by two points or demerits. Students who made the dean's list were allowed one absence each semester from a course. Being even slightly out of uniform or accessorizing with the exception of a pocket handkerchief elicited a "uniform note," which also affected citizenship standing. Excessive demerits meant disciplinary probation, and extended probations could mean dismissal.[66]

Runner at Berry track and field meet, 1930s.

Students who habitually received unsatisfactory grades were expelled from school. Faculty met periodically to rate students who had applied for summer work and to vote on whether to drop certain students from the roll. Faculty also received reports on the status of students, discussed conduct grades, and reviewed students whose work was not satisfactory.[67] In 1942, President Leland Green requested in writing that the dean, the industrial manager, and the principal refer all serious disciplinary cases to him for a conference and on one occasion wrote to Dean of Women Sophie Payne Alston that too many expulsions had been occurring.[68]

In 1924, the school adopted a set of guidelines for daily life known as the Berry Code in which students pledged to keep their bodies and their minds clean; to cultivate habits that would help them become physically, mentally, and morally strong; and to "walk humbly before God."[69] The girls' school motto, "Not to be ministered unto, but to minister," became the entire institution's motto in the late 1920s, and Martha Berry selected as her personal motto "Prayer Changes Things." In 1935, Professor M. C. Ewing of the music faculty wrote a new alma mater.[70]

The college members of the Athenian and Philomathean literary societies decided in November 1931 to leave those organizations to the high school and form new college literary societies, the Georgians and the Syrrebs, respectively. The literary societies offered competition in scholarly debate, oratory, music, dramatics, and athletics. Students who made half As and half Bs in their courses were eligible for the honor roll, provided their room and conduct grades were As and their work grade was no lower than B. The Honor Club for college men, founded in 1929, and the Excelsior Club for college women, organized in 1932, recognized students with consistently high academic performance. In the spring of 1949, the two organizations merged under the name Excelsior Club. Founded in 1932, the X Club was a secret male organization of campus leaders selected each semester on Tap Day at joint chapel. The club, with its exclusive membership, remained active during the 1930s and 1940s before being disbanded because it was deemed discriminatory.[71]

THE BERRY CODE

❧B☙

I PROMISE at all times to keep my *clothes*, my *body* and my *mind* clean. I will always cultivate those habits which will help me to become *strong physically, mentally* and *morally*, but I will *spurn* those which will harm me.

I *will not* speak vulgar or profane language, get angry when things displease me or allow my mind to harbor foolish or wicked thoughts.

I will *gladly* listen to *advice* of *older* and *wiser* people, but will learn to *think* for myself, *choose* for myself and *act* for myself.

I will always *do* the *right thing* although I may be laughed at and the *crowd* may be against me.

I will be *honest* in *word* and *act.* I will take *nothing* that does not belong to me. I will *never* do wrong in the hope of not being found out. I cannot *hide* the *truth* from *God* and *myself.*

I will never enter a contest or play a game without treating my opponent *politely* and *fairly.* In all group games I will always play for my *team* and my *school* instead of my own glory. I will be a *good loser* or a *generous winner.*

I will *always* do my duty no matter *what difficulty* may appear.

I promise not to be content with slip-shod or merely passable work. I will take an interest in all my work and learn to do the *right thing* in the *right way.*

"Order is Heaven's first law." Therefore I will be *orderly* and *cheerful* in all my work. When working with others, I *promise always* to do *my share* and to help *others* do the same.

I will be kind in *thought, word* and *act.* I will bear no grudge or ill will towards anyone. I will not think myself above any other boy or girl. I will not gossip or speak unkindly of any one.

I will be *polite* under *all circumstances. No Berry boy or girl is ever rude.*

I will be *devotedly faithful* and *loyal* in *every relation* of life.

I will walk *humbly* before *God* and so order my *daily life* that those with whom I come in contact may *know* that I have *learned* of *Him.*

The daily schedule was rigid. Students arose at 5:30, had breakfast at 6:15, had classes in the morning and chapel at 11:30, and had dinner at 12:10 during the week and at 12:30 on Saturday. The women's daily schedule began ten minutes ahead of the men's to allow the women time to walk from classes at the girls' school, where they lived, to the main campus. Supper was at 6:00 p.m. and was followed by a quiet hour for studying. Bedtime was at 11:00 p.m. for the women, while the men had no prescribed bedtime. On Sunday, students arose at 6:30, had breakfast at 6:55, Sunday school at 9:30, church at 11:00, dinner at 12:15, and supper at 5:30 unless they received a sack supper, which was frequent Sunday-evening fare. Couples eagerly anticipated Sunday afternoons, when "Sunday calling" at Ford Quadrangle took place. Men and women met at the main archway at 2:00 and were free to visit with each other on the green or in one of the living rooms until 5:00—properly chaperoned, of course. Students could entertain visitors from off campus on the weekend if such requests were made to and approved by the dean several days beforehand.[72]

E. H. Hoge, Berry's comptroller from 1910 until 1953, c. 1935.

End of an Era

During the 1930s, Martha Berry maintained personal control over her schools when her health and travel schedule would permit, but she found it necessary to give more authority to others as the institution became more complex. As early as 1916, Berry had established an executive committee to assist her in running the schools, and during the 1930s, its members—including President G. Leland Green, comptroller E. H. Hoge, and postmaster and resident trustee M. Gordon Keown—oversaw much of the school's management. O. C. Skinner, a graduate of Alabama Polytechnic Institute (now Auburn University) came to Berry in 1924 as industrial manager, in charge of buildings and grounds, labor

Robert C. Alston, chairman of the board of trustees from 1925 until 1938, c. 1929.

and industries, and firefighting crews that protected Berry's extensive forests, and he joined the executive committee in the late 1920s, as did Grady Hamrick, head of the Mount Berry School for Boys, in 1932. Martha Berry sometimes met with the committee and at other times directed their action through letters. She also relied heavily on S. H. Cook, who had been at Berry since 1910 and had become dean and head of the mathematics department when the college opened, and Sophie Payne Alston, who had come to Berry in 1933 to take over the direction of the home economics department and teach and who had become dean of women four years later.[73] Elizabeth Brewster, who had worked with Martha Berry at the establishment of the boarding school in 1902, died in 1941.[74]

Robert Alston remained chairman of Berry's board of trustees from 1924 until his death in 1938 and was succeeded by J. Bulow Campbell, Martha Berry's brother-in-law, until his death in 1940. John A. Sibley, an Atlanta lawyer and banker, then took over, continuing in that role until 1955.[75]

Now in her midseventies, Martha Berry began to experience serious health problems, partly as a result of cirrhosis of the liver. She had surgery in the latter part of 1940 and was hospitalized in Atlanta by the late summer of 1941.[76] On September 13, the board held a special meeting and authorized Sibley "to appoint such committees as are necessary to carry on the work of the School for the coming year." At Martha Berry's request, the trustees had already begun to seek someone to assume many of her responsibilities.[77]

Martha Berry died in Saint Joseph's Hospital in Atlanta shortly after midnight on the morning of Friday, February 27, 1942. She had experienced periods of ill health for more than two decades, probably caused in part by hard work and worry for her schools. At dawn on Friday, the chapel bell on the college campus tolled once for each year of her life, and at 9:00 the chimes—a gift from the alumni on her birthday the previous October—played "O God Our Help in Ages Past," the school hymn, and some of her other favorite hymns. On Saturday, all work on campus ceased at noon, and students lined both sides of the roadway from the Gate of Opportunity to Barnwell Chapel on the Log Cabin Campus for the founder's final homecoming.

Accompanied by a student guard, Martha Berry's body lay in state in Barnwell Chapel from Saturday afternoon until Sunday afternoon. An Episcopal funeral service was held at 5:00 in the Mount Berry Church, Berry College Chapel, with Dr. John Moore Walker of St. Luke's Episcopal Church in Atlanta, assisted by Berry's chaplain, Dr. Robert Belton, officiating. Berry College's senior men served as pallbearers. There were tremendous numbers of floral arrangements, especially roses. The faculty and students provided a blanket of pink roses, and some alumni had the Original Cabin reproduced in roses. In addition to the faculty, students, and alumni in attendance, many other people came from around the nation to pay their last respects. Martha Berry was buried in a spot she had chosen under a large pecan tree on the chapel's south side. The relatively few other graves near the chapel are all located on the north, so she lies alone. Saturday and Sunday were springlike, sunny days, but by Monday morning a heavy blanket of snow had fallen. [78]

Berry alumni and other supporters sent numerous letters of condolence. Newspapers across the nation carried stories of Martha Berry's life and death. Green and others wrote poems to commemorate the occasion, and Proctor wrote a statement of appreciation. In the spring the alumni laid a marble slab on the grave. [79]

The editors of the *Berry Alumni Quarterly* dedicated the March 1942 edition to Martha Berry's memory, printing her last letter to the alumni as well as the contents of her final letter to the trustees, both of which had been written long before, on July 1, 1925, and designated for opening at her death. She urged the alumni to "be faithful and guard and protect the Berry Schools." [80] In the letter to the trustees, Berry recommended that Keown succeed her as director. She had great faith that he would work with the other administrators, the faculty, and the staff to carry on the school as she had envisioned it. [81] Her recommendation was well received. In his letter supporting the choice, Green wrote that Keown "has been courageous, patient, and wise in assuming the grave responsibility of Miss Berry's position." Green also noted that under Keown's stewardship during Berry's illness, "the year 1941–1942 was one of the best we have known . . . in spite of the loss of our founder, which also made it one of the most difficult years." [82]

For the year ending in May 1942, the Berry Schools had a total enrollment of 1,214–678 in the college, 338 in the boys' high school, 138 in the girls' high school, and 60 in the Possum Trot practice school for campus children. Fifty-two men and fifty-seven women graduated from the college, the largest class in the institution's history. Fifty-eight boys and thirty girls had graduated from the high schools. Residents of 127 of Georgia's counties comprised 60 percent of the student body, with the remainder from twelve other states. [83] The Berry Schools' endowment fund was valued at $3,287,816.16 (more than $37,000,000 in 2003), real estate was valued at $733,196.01, and buildings were valued at $4,355,999.09. [84]

Martha Berry had also left a final letter to the faculty and staff. In it, she expressed her trust that she would "have the help and cooperation of all of the faculty members in carrying out the Berry program, the traditions of orderliness, and combined work and instruction schedules. . . . My earnest wish is that by working together harmoniously and prayerfully,

Martha Berry's funeral, March 1, 1942.

we may measure up to the great responsibilities of helping poor boys and girls for whom the schools were founded."[85] Her death occurred in the midst of World War II, which was transforming Berry as it did the rest of U.S. society. Rather than attending college, potential students were entering the military or other government service, thereby reducing enrollment and creating a shortage of student workers for the industrial departments. Furthermore, the school's leaders had to deal with rationing; government-requested committees, record keeping, and reporting; and adjustments in curriculum and accommodations to train cadets and further the cause of freedom. As the war pulled the economy out

of the Great Depression, Berry's low salaries made it difficult to retain faculty and staff, and increases in the income tax reduced donors' willingness to make monetary gifts. The schools also had less-than-satisfactory equipment and had deferred maintenance and repair of buildings during the economic hard times. In addition, the rules and regulations governing student life had become outdated, and the college remained unaccredited. These difficulties were exacerbated by the loss of a leader who had been the primary decision maker and fund-raiser, and in such situations, it is not at all unusual for a college or other organization to experience a sense of crisis.[86] During most of her lifetime, Martha Berry was constantly making changes, expanding, and attempting to move her schools forward, but at times near the end of her life and in her last letters to the trustees, alumni, and faculty, she seemed to suggest that the schools should not continue to change. She reportedly told Sibley, "My fear isn't death, but that people, perhaps well-meaning ones, may try to make just another school out of Berry. I'd rather see the doors close."[87] Admiration and respect for Martha Berry consequently made many alumni and staffers reluctant to change the institution after her death. New leaders, therefore, often felt bound by the past and pressured not to make modifications necessary to move the institution forward into a new era.

Following Martha Berry's death, Acting Director Gordon Keown and President Leland Green carried on the administration of her schools. Over the twelve years after the two men's tenures ended in 1944, Berry saw a succession of presidents come with high hopes and leave in despair. These men encountered numerous obstacles yet made valuable contributions to the schools' development.

CHAPTER FIVE

Challenges and Changes

The Green and Keown Years

While a committee appointed by the chairman of the board of trustees searched for a replacement for Martha Berry, Acting Director Gordon Keown quietly and efficiently oversaw all the schools' operations. His first responsibilities were to continue contacts with the friends and benefactors developed by Martha Berry and Inez Henry, her assistant, and to cope with problems of staff shortage in wartime. As the coexecutor of Martha Berry's will (along with E. H. Hoge), Keown also had to administer her estate, a task that required him to deal diplomatically with members of the Berry family, some of whom were anxiously asking when they might expect settlement of the estate.[1]

Notwithstanding the loss of the schools' founder and director, Keown and Green entered the new era with optimism. At the end of May 1942, Green told the board that, with Keown's appointment as di-

rector, there had been "no slackening of effort but instead an added determination to push the schools onward and upward." During Green's last talk with Martha Berry, she had told him that she wished that everyone connected with Berry would stand by the schools: "The opportunity is there to make them the greatest Schools in the world. This is my last request." Green indicated that Berry workers had a "unity of purpose" and a "quiet attention to duty that were not evident before." They had "full confidence in Keown's loyalty to Miss Berry's ideals, in his wisdom and in his sense of justice to all."[2]

One of the first issues that arose after Martha Berry's death concerned the significant landholdings (about twenty-seven thousand acres) that the school had accumulated as an investment and with which Martha Berry certainly had been reluctant to part.[3] With the beginning of World War II, the U.S. Army planned to construct a military hospital in Rome. In the fall of 1942, after failing to negotiate

M. Gordon Keown, acting director of the Berry Schools from 1942 to 1944, c. 1943.

G. Leland Green, principal of the Berry Schools from 1920 to 1926 and president of Berry College from 1926 to 1944, c. 1940.

the purchase of the necessary land from Berry, the United States filed suit in the U.S. District Court in Rome to obtain approximately 160 acres from Berry and about .25 acre in two tracts from other owners.[4]

The court authorized the United States to take possession of the property on March 10, 1943, and on June 12 the United States filed its declaration of taking and paid Berry $12,375 as compensation. On August 20, Berry filed a claim with the court, contending the fair market value of the land taken "was greatly in excess" of that amount and exercising its right to have a jury place a valuation on the land. On November 30, 1944, however, the jury found that just compensation for the land totaled only $9,600,

and Berry had to refund the additional money. The land was formally transferred to the United States, and the legal matter was finally concluded by order of the court on January 3, 1945.[5]

The war affected Berry in other ways as well. In April 1942, Green reported to Special Consultant to the U.S. Department of Labor Emory Q. Hawk that as a result of the draft, voluntary enlistments, and defense and other wartime employment opportunities, students were dropping out of school, the college was changing the curriculum to meet wartime needs, and there was "a demand for our graduates far exceeding the number we are able to supply."[6] Registrar John C. Warr wrote to the American Council on Education that as of January 1, 1943, Berry College had lost two-thirds of its male enrollment to the armed forces and that 60 percent of those remaining were in Reserve Corps divisions.[7] Green's May 24, 1943, report to Keown and the board of trustees showed total enrollment of 1,072 (590 females, 482 males) compared with 1,214 in the fall of 1942, with 578 in the college, 260 of them men. Enrollment had dropped in all of the school's divisions, including the Possum Trot school, which closed later in 1943 because there was no gasoline to run the bus, no teachers were available, and some of the men from the mountain community went to towns in search of work in defense plants.[8] On March 15, as one of 110 colleges around the country participating in the Army Air Corps college training program, Berry had taken on 170 Air Crew students, raising enrollment to 1,242 for the year.[9]

The possibility of having cadets on campus in 1943 had caused much concern among Dean of Women Sophie Payne Alston and some of her staff, who wrote lengthy recommendations concerning impending problems with arrival of the military units and the need to chaperone the female students. The girls, they suggested, should "not be given free run of the campus as now."[10] These concerns were largely unfounded, however. Two female students of the time remembered no fraternizing between the students and the cadets, as the dean of women had directed, and heard no rumors of misbehavior during that period, although they did recall that the cadets looked for opportunities to communicate with the female students even though they were forbidden to socialize. The women observed the cadets marching down Berry's main thoroughfare, now Opportunity Drive, and drilling in the open field near Thomas Berry Hall. Women did not attend classes with the cadets or sit with them in the dining hall.[11]

Berry had not chosen to accept the cadets but had been selected, inspected, and approved for the program by the Army Air Force.[12] On April 9, 1942, Colonel William Dick of the Army Air Forces War Department had authorized Green to procure aviation cadets for training and to appoint a faculty adviser for them. Green chose S. H. Cook.[13] "The cadets received instruction with the other students from Berry instructors, except for military training, which officers in residence conducted."[14] Dr. Harold Jones of the biology faculty taught first-aid classes, and several faculty members became Red Cross instructors. At the request of the military, school officials set up an efficient dispensary and saw that milk was pasteurized and that drinking water was checked carefully for cleanliness and safety.[15]

Berry had contracted to train air crewmen from the second semester of 1943 for the duration of the war, but the work actually began earlier, in the middle of March, and ended in June 1944. In May of that year, Green acknowledged that both the U.S. government and the schools had benefited from the arrangement, which provided twelve-month employment for practically all of the college teachers and some of the high-school teachers while helping all to feel that they were contributing directly to the war effort.[16]

Records compiled by the registrar in the spring of 1943 showed that 527 Berry men and women were in active service; of these, 124 were commissioned officers and 111 were noncommissioned officers.[17] Four Berry men had lost their lives and five were missing in action. By the following summer, more than 700 Berry men and women were serving in the armed forces, and by the end of the conflict, more than 1,200 men and women from Berry had served in World War II; fifty-eight lost their lives and are remembered with a bronze plaque in the foyer of the Berry College Chapel.[18]

Members of Berry's faculty also answered the call to serve their country. Several staffers were reserve officers, and others took on additional committee

*Some of the 170 Air Corps Cadets
stationed at Berry, in the dining hall,
1943.*

and clerical work, including registration for the draft and ration duties. Berry employees participated in Navy relief, Red Cross, and bond drives, and the Defense Committee cooperated with other such area bodies in promoting fire prevention, air-raid protection, waste prevention, economy in transportation, and dissemination of important information.[19] The *Berry Alumni Quarterly* listed Berry alumni known to be serving in the armed forces and called on its readers to give savings stamps and bonds to Berry, thus promoting both national defense and the schools.[20]

In a message to the staff on "The Task Ahead," Green asked, "How can we make our greatest contribution toward victory?" His answers included buying war bonds, observing all regulations, and maintaining a confident, cheerful spirit, all part of what had to be done "to keep the home front solid." He believed that the college had a particular role in maintaining President Franklin Delano Roosevelt's four

freedoms: freedom from want, freedom of speech, freedom of the press, and freedom of worship. Green's observation on freedom of worship defined the Berry Schools' approach to religion in life: "Our concern is not with denominations, creeds, nor brands of religion. Each individual must accept and interpret his relationship to the Eternal in his own way. . . . We have never identified ourselves with any particular cult, creed, nor theological belief, but we have welcomed all whose souls earnestly long to know and to obey God."[21]

The college's lack of accreditation had become a problem for its graduates, especially those seeking admission to graduate schools or teacher certification. In the fall of 1942, Green learned from W. Morrison McCall, director of Alabama's Division of Instruction, that it could not certify graduates of Berry College to teach in that state "since we would be granting your students a concession not granted to other unaccredited colleges."[22] Green had already begun to work toward gaining accreditation for Berry College from the Southern Association of Colleges and Secondary Schools (SACS). The response to his initial efforts was not encouraging. In June 1942, M. C. Huntley, executive secretary of the SACS Commission on Higher Education, wrote to Green that "unless the college has altered its program considerably, I do not know that it would be wise to bring the matter of membership up at this time."[23] Green later recalled that the SACS "refused Berry admission for three reasons: (1) inadequate salaries, tenure, and retirement systems; (2) lack of a provision for sabbaticals to further graduate study [by faculty]; and (3) the sixteen hours of required work each week, which was too much out of line with Southern Association requirements."[24] Berry clearly needed to remedy these problems as well as inadequacies in the curriculum, in academic rigorousness and grading standards, and in faculty credentials.

Dr. Victor Butterfield, acting president of Wesleyan University in Connecticut, evaluated Berry in 1942 and cited certain strengths: spiritual vitality, stronger among students than faculty, accompanied by a nice sense of service; beauty and utility of the physical plant; and the work program, appreciated by the students but in need of better coordination with classroom work. He noted that the academic program seemed in greatest need of help, especially in building up a strong, more permanent faculty and in improving faculty morale, which implied sense of security, better pay, and systems of tenure, retirement, and insurance. Butterfield also stressed the importance of dealing with the faculty openly and allowing them a voice in determining educational policy and procedure. Butterfield further recommended employing a skilled businessman to supervise forestry, animal breeding, and diversified crops and seeking a strong new leader who would guide the schools within the framework of Martha Berry's

threefold purpose while continuing to progress and adjust.[25]

On May 24, 1943, Green recommended to the board of trustees that Berry's program not be changed but that both its liberal and its technical education be perfected with balanced emphasis on the education of the head, the heart, and the hands. He further stressed the importance of gaining SACS membership, establishing a retirement system, making all work educational, and operating the schools year-round. To accommodate children of alumni and other special cases, he recommended allowing 5 percent of students to come from urban areas. None of these changes were implemented at this time, as further study was deemed necessary.

After Green made his recommendations, Berry's leaders engaged in serious discussions about what direction the schools should take. Dr. Philip Weltner, an attorney from Atlanta, joined the board of trustees in 1943 and became chairman of a study committee that focused on keeping Berry's aims and ideals alive while proposing changes that might keep the schools relevant to new times. Others serving on the committee included Green, Cook, Alston, and O. C. Skinner.[26]

Weltner initially ignored such factors as finances, faculties, and campus arrangements yet also suggested several serious reforms for the board's consideration. He assumed that Berry would offer professional training in certain vocations and suggested that it "reconstitute" its college and secondary schools into an "upper school" covering the last two years of high school and the first two years of college and a "preparatory school to include the first two years of high school." He proposed tackling the upper-school problem first to establish a general education "to be dovetailed into the work of the professional schools." The faculty in this upper school would be grouped into four departments—science, humanities, social sciences, and mathematics—"flanked by the industrial and domestic arts and work on the campus and on the farms." He also submitted a list of the knowledge, skills, and experiences necessary to fit a person for general farming.[27]

After some months of studying all aspects of Berry's operations, Weltner told the board of trustees that the institution's survival would depend on its educational program, not its beauty and physical plant. He recommended that the position of director be dropped since it was peculiar to Martha Berry, that the title of president be given to the head of the schools, and that the schools have four general officers: president, comptroller, dean of instruction, and director of operations. He also recommended developing a budget; including two or three divisions (agriculture, home economics, and rural education); building more creativity into the work program; and making many changes in the faculty and staff. Weltner also proposed amendments to the bylaws that created committees of the board of trustees, including an executive committee and committees on investment, education, budget, and buildings and grounds. The board accepted the recommendation regarding the creation of the board committees as well as the suggestion to eliminate the directorship and on January 28, 1944, unanimously appointed William Jesse Baird, a native of Knox County, Kentucky, as president of the Berry Schools.[28] Keown became the school's postmaster and resident trustee.

By this time, Green had served Berry for twenty-four years, and the board granted him a year's leave of absence with pay. His letter to the "Men and Women of Berry" acknowledged Baird as the "wisest possible choice" as head of the Berry Schools and support for the new president's program. Green planned to use the year to travel, study, and rest and then to return to Berry to develop "a Department of Teacher Training second to none in the country."[29]

The Baird Years

William Jesse Baird came to Berry with impressive credentials. He held a bachelors degree from Berea College and a masters from Cornell University and had completed further graduate work at the Universities of Wisconsin and Kentucky as well as at Columbia University. He had taught at Berea before becoming head of the school's Department of Agriculture, dean of Berea's foundation school, and subsequently director of teacher training at the college. In 1942–43, he had worked with the Danforth Foundation, which sponsored faculty fellows to promote good relationships between college faculty and students. Emphasis was on religious and philosophical readings, discussions, and fellowship in faculty homes. While not claiming to be a religious leader, Baird focused his visits to college campuses on strengthening the colleges' religious organizations, and the colleges commended Baird's efforts.[30] He was highly recommended as an educator and an able administrator, and his public relations work with Berea had been outstanding. He was active in state and national educational and administrative associations and in civic organizations. In recommending him to Berry, former Berea president Charles T. Morgan described Baird as "one of the greatest educators in America today." Morgan also said that Baird would "bring a fine attitude toward the race question. He will exercise the utmost tact and understanding in regard to it, and insofar as it is humanly possible, will lead you into no embarrassment over it."[31] The race question had not become an issue at Berry, however, and would not do so for two decades. It was simply not discussed.

Baird arrived at Berry quietly and without ceremony in the summer of 1944 and used the *Berry Alumni Quarterly* to introduce himself to the school community, writing of his belief in the foundation stones of Berry—"learning, labor, simplicity, and

William Jesse Baird, Berry's president from 1944 to 1946, c. 1945.

character."[32] His official titles were president and chief executive officer, with responsibility for financial management, fund-raising, promotion, program development, and other matters previously directed by Martha Berry, Green, and Keown.[33] He worked to develop good relationships with alumni, taking what he termed his "Gallup Poll" to acquire information on Berry principles in practice. The poll acquainted him, he wrote, with Berry alumni who were "practicing the principles they had learned and seen put into operation at The Berry Schools to create stronger, better communities."[34]

Although he had studied Berry extensively, had visited on several occasions, had attended the spring meeting of the board of trustees, and felt at home with the institution's focus, Baird inadvertently stepped on some toes shortly after his arrival. Because Green was still occupying the president's office, Baird began his work in the office that Martha Berry had used, thereby ruffling the feathers of some of those who had been close to Berry. Furthermore, Baird had brought along his secretary and other employees from Berea, increasing the hurt feelings. And although Keown had for many years signed the school's important legal documents and expected to continue that role, the new president insisted on assuming that duty. Even without these missteps, however, the circumstances of the job were such that Baird faced an uphill climb. He was an outsider coming to an institution that for forty years had operated completely at the direction of the founder. The decline in male enrollment continued in 1944 and 1945: the spring 1944 college roster included only fifty men, and only one man graduated from the college the following year. This lack of laborers threatened the continuing operation of the farm projects and maintenance of the extensive plant, which depended considerably on male students' work. As was the case across the country, women stepped in to fill such traditional male roles as plowing fields and baling hay. The problem

Students baking bread in Girls' School kitchen, late 1940s.

remained acute, however: in October 1945, Baird wrote, "we have had such terrific problems in securing required personnel for The Berry Schools that I am trying to beg, borrow, buy, or steal just about any qualified person."[35] Fortunately for the school, the picture would change when men began returning from their wartime service in 1946.

Baird had a wide variety of goals for the schools as well as plans for accomplishing those goals, which included strengthening the work program's educational and spiritual value; giving greater emphasis to the religion program; maintaining schools of liberal arts, agriculture, home economics, and industrial arts with appropriate teacher-education courses; and offering extension courses to the rural community from which Berry students came.[36]

The newly created executive committee of the board of trustees readily accepted Baird's plans, which were unlikely to cause dissension because they essentially kept Berry on the path it had previously pursued and merely sought to improve and strengthen the existing program; only the extension department would be novel. A newly approved assistant would work closely with the president to develop and maintain donors' interest, to create closer relations with various constituencies, and to edit certain institutional publications. Inez Henry became the first person to fill that position. The trustees also agreed that the president of the alumni association should sit in on board meetings.[37]

During his presidency, Baird adjusted the college's program and procedures in accordance with the proposals the board had approved; instituted the election of department heads by faculty members; established a new curriculum for the college, eliminating the Latin requirement and mandating eight semester hours of laboratory science and six semester hours of social science as part of students' general-education requirements during their first two years of school; and improved library facilities and faculty qualifications. Baird also authorized necessary repairs to the physical plant and installed gas heat in the Ford Buildings. To help improve the educational program, he required the faculty to provide students with course syllabi. To improve planning and accountability, he required

Students sewing women's uniforms, c. 1951.

departments to prepare and submit budgets. Baird maintained good relations with the faculty and staff, hosting informal dinners (deemed the most interesting campus social events of the time) that allowed small groups to get to know one another. Baird also quickly won the affection of the students, in part by having the men's uniform modified from overalls to blue denim pants and the color of the women's stockings changed from black to neutral; the senior class of 1946 dedicated the *Cabin Log,* the yearbook, to him.[38]

During these years O. C. Skinner assumed a new role as Berry's director of natural resources, establishing permanent pastures, overseeing the water system and agricultural production, and managing the forests.[39] Baird authorized a winter 1944 survey, conducted by a representative of the Tennessee Valley Authority, of the schools' farm and timber properties to determine to what degree they were suitable for intensive farming. This study concluded that only a small fraction of the lands were suitable for field crops and recommended that the lands be converted to permanent pastures or reverted to natu-

ral forest under scientific management, a suggestion that would have long-range impact.[40]

Trustee G. Lister Carlisle began to study the possibility of a pension system for Berry's employees. Baird contacted Louise Whitfield Carnegie, widow of Andrew Carnegie; in response, her secretary, Archibald Barrow, suggested that Berry join the Teachers Insurance and Annuity Association to provide retirement benefits for the faculty and staff. Baird replied that Berry would like to do just that, but it would require a pension endowment of $200,000, "the income from which would make it possible for the schools to match the amount our teachers would put into the annuity."[41] These efforts did not meet with immediate success.

Baird's tenure coincided with the illness and death of several persons who had long been important to the institution. On April 24, 1945, Gordon Keown's wife, Frances Cone Olmsted Keown, who had been instrumental in the founding of two of Berry's women's organizations, died suddenly at her home on the campus, and Alice Wingo, a Shakespeare scholar and former dean of women who had previously been admitted to the Madison Rural Sanitarium (an arm of Madison College in Tennessee) near Reeves, Georgia, because of her failing health, died on August 4.[42] The Berry community was also saddened in 1945 by the death of Kate Macy Ladd, "one of the first and most loyal friends Martha Berry made for the work."[43]

In the spring semester of 1946, Berry welcomed back eighteen men who had served in the military, with twelve of them enrolling in the college and six in the high school.[44] Their return did not change the makeup of the college's senior class, which had thirty-nine women and no men, but it did have implications for Berry's income from the Servicemen's Readjustment Act of 1944, which provided benefits such as college tuition that would help veterans readjust to civilian life.[45] Further, the more mature returning students with world experience added a broader dimension to the campus environment and a deeper seriousness of purpose than existed among the typical eighteen- to twenty-year-old students.

The role of athletics at Berry expanded during this period. Registrar John C. Warr formed an intercollegiate basketball team in the fall of 1945, marking the end of the board of trustees' longtime ban on intercollegiate sports. The Berry team played high-school teams, independent teams, and junior-college and college teams from Georgia, Tennessee, and Alabama, achieving little success but nevertheless remaining hopeful.[46]

The education of the heart continued as an important facet of Berry's mission under Baird. In the spring of 1946, the *Southern Highlander* reminded its readers that the schools promoted religious education through many channels, including classes in the Bible at both the high school and the college and Sunday school programs. Programs at the beginning of the year focused on the meaning of the schools' coat of arms and the four segments of its seal—the Bible for religious ideals, the plow for work, the lamp

for learning, and the cabin for simplicity of living— as well as the school promise: "I the Lord do keep it; I will water it every moment lest any hurt it, and I will keep it night and day." Other aspects of religious focus included the high school and college Young Men's and Young Women's Christian Associations and their Thursday evening programs, Sunday evening vespers, and biblical inscriptions on the walls of various buildings.[47]

During this era, the minimum age for admission to the Berry Schools was fourteen. The college awarded general bachelors of arts and sciences degrees as well as bachelors of science degrees in agriculture, home economics, and industrial arts.[48] The college had six divisions: agriculture, education, general studies (encompassing business as well as fine art and music), home economics, mechanics and industrial arts, and science. According to the December 1946 school catalog, ten of Berry College's thirty-five faculty members had earned doctorates.[49] Despite the progress in this area, the number of faculty with terminal degrees remained too small for the school to win accreditation.

For the first time since the outbreak of the war, Berry held a homecoming Alumni Weekend in conjunction with the spring 1946 commencement. The events included a "splendid speech" by Baird to the Alumni Council and a memorial service honoring fifty-two men who had lost their lives in the war.[50] Despite Baird's very public presence throughout the weekend, he resigned as Berry's president just over a week later, at the annual meeting of the board of trustees on June 10, and took the presidency of Morehead State College in Kentucky, where he remained until his death in 1951.[51] He gave no reason for his seemingly sudden decision, and it seemed an incongruous action for a man whose recommendations indicated that he would persevere in any circumstance. Nearly twenty years later, journalist Tracy Byers, who had worked at Berry with Inez

Students at the Mount Berry School for Boys, c. 1943.

Henry before Martha Berry's death, returned to the school and lunched with Henry and Bertha Hackett Ewing, a longtime Berry secretary. Discussing the "passing scene of Berry presidents," the women concluded, "We really made a mistake in getting rid of Dr. Baird. He just came too soon. We'd of run off the Lord Himself in those early days. . . . He really was the right man. They said we . . . broke his heart and shortened his life when we ran him off from Berry." Baird was the victim of a concerted effort to rid the school of a president who envisioned worthwhile—and largely nonthreatening—changes but was blocked from making them, a fate that awaited others as well.[52] Late in July 1946, Baird "left the Berry campus as quietly and unnoticed as he had entered two years earlier." The longtime head of Berry's chemistry department, Willis Pirkle, later lamented, "It is a sad circumstance in Berry history that no formal goodbyes were said."[53]

Miffed at what he perceived as the usurping of his position, Keown had become Baird's chief op-

ponent. Alston, a strong personality who believed in strict discipline of the students, refused to cooperate in the new president's attempts to ease restrictions on student social life. When Baird removed her as head of the home economics department, which enforced uniform rules, she retaliated by lodging unfair complaints with the trustees. Baird and Academic Dean Sam Henry Cook also had differences that hampered their working relationship, and this chasm widened when Cook learned that Baird had allegedly commented that he could not do a thing until he got a dean.

Pirkle claimed that Baird never received a briefing on the institution and had to find his own way into the presidency. Moreover, Green's return as head of the education department may have caused Baird some anxiety. In Pirkle's view, Baird had the outlook of the executive and the will to make changes, but to question local leadership on policies relating to traditional values was as hazardous as to "question the Norman Conquest." Pirkle concluded that "people with unbiased judgment would give approval to most of Baird's suggestions for improvement, but his quick-action strategy confused some of the leaders." The board of trustees apparently was not ready to support fully a president with "vested authority, original in his thinking, and capable of changing social customs and traditional school policy." In his own analysis of his time at Berry, Baird reputedly said, "I missed Miss Berry's spirit, but I encountered her ghost wherever I went."[54]

The Lindsay Years

At the same June 10, 1946, meeting at which Baird submitted his resignation, the board of trustees elected William McChesney Martin Jr. to its membership, reelected John A. Sibley as chairman, and chose James Armour Lindsay, principal of the Mount Berry School for Boys, to succeed Baird as president of the Berry Schools and College. Lindsay and his wife, Tulley Borden Lindsay, had joined the faculty of the education department in 1944, and James had served as interim chair during Green's leave. When Grady Hamrick retired in 1945, James Lindsay had become principal of the boys' school. He had also consulted on the curriculum for the girls' school, and both Lindsays had been active in the community and in campus religious life.[55]

Lindsay came to Berry from Mississippi State College, where he was an associate professor of education. He had also served as superintendent of public schools in Bloomington, Illinois; North Arlington, New Jersey; and Johnstown, Colorado, and as an associate professor of education at the University of Alabama. A native of Colorado, he held bachelors and masters degrees from the University of Colorado as well as a Ph.D. in educational administration from Columbia University and had done postdoctoral work at the University of Chicago. Tulley Lindsay, a native of Alabama, had studied at

James Armour Lindsay, Berry's president from 1946 to 1951, c. 1947.

Peabody College and at Columbia University before earning a doctorate from Yale.[56]

As head of the Mount Berry School for Boys, Lindsay had been enthusiastic and attentive to all aspects of the program, from work to academics. His tendency to show up at work sites unannounced threw some workers off guard and seemed to cause some confusion. Still, his promptness and forthrightness, his inspection tours, and his encouragement helped to reverse the lax supervision that had existed in some areas. This change in approach and attitude made him unpopular among some staff. One former faculty member and department chair described him as a "man of great charm, approachable and friendly . . . an indefatigable worker" but also as impulsive and impatient. "He often made snap judgments . . . that confused rather than aided the question." By the end of Baird's first year, Lindsay had needed support to maintain his position, so he placed himself "in league with the Old Guard at Berry and utter[ed] pronouncements which he thought would be in line with their thinking." He supposedly denounced Baird's proposals for educational reform and sent "personal letters of question" to the trustees. He argued that everything at Berry should be left "much the same as Miss Berry had decreed in her writings and testament." This logic won favor with Berry's conservative leaders but offered little hope for those who thought differently.[57] In one of the first public announcements of his strategy, at the summer convocation on July 9, 1946, Lindsay addressed the staff on "Enduring Essentials at Berry," stressing tradition's role in Berry's strength, the need for Berry's employees to join together to work toward a common cause, and the regenerating power of progress.[58]

The Lindsays were quick to respond to the campus community's needs. For example, the school gardens had an exceedingly productive year in 1946, and the surplus of fruits and vegetables triggered a call for help from the cannery, which, as was the custom, was preserving surplus produce. In the fall of 1946, the Lindsays, S. H. Cook, and other faculty, staff, and student volunteers turned out for "Operation Bean-Snapping," storing more than twelve thousand gallons of food, including eleven hundred gallons of beans.[59] The surplus proved fortuitous when the "worst flood since 1872" covered the old highway and marooned the Berry Schools the following spring. Rains flooded the gardens, damaged the winter crops, and flooded campus basements. Students rowed boats through the underpass on U.S. Highway 27 to deliver mail to the Rome post office and collect mail for Mount Berry.[60]

Also at the same time that Lindsay assumed the presidency, the Berry Alumni Association acquired its first full-time secretary and coordinator of alumni affairs, Walter Johnson, an alumnus who had just returned from military service. Johnson took over many of the tasks that had previously been performed by Berry employees in jobs not dedicated exclusively to the alumni association. For about twenty-five years prior to the war, Johnson had filled this role while working as a bookkeeper at the schools. His new job provided no salary, but he was provided with a home, Boxwood Cottage.

Berry continued to need money for maintenance, programming, equipment and supplies, and growth. The *Southern Highlander* continued its long-standing role of publicizing the schools' urgent needs, which in the summer of 1946 included such items as farm equipment, a station wagon, working scholarships, endowed scholarships, endowed days, and operating expenses. Endowing a permanent scholarship took five thousand dollars. A donor could endow a day of special significance for twenty-five hundred dollars or, if that was too much, could endow a portion of a day.[61] Later the same year, the *Southern Highlander* solicited donations for a newly created "Fund for Our Faithful Workers," the

Inez Henry (center left) *and James Armour Lindsay* (center right) *during "Operation Bean-Snapping," 1946.*

first retirement fund in Berry's history. Subsequent issues presented profiles of such older workers as Sam Henry Cook and E. H. Hoge.[62]

Under the guidance of Berry graduates Garland Dickey and Edward Dickey, the intercollegiate athletic program expanded in 1946–47, initially with a basketball team, known as the Blue Jackets, and with baseball and track by 1949.[63] Six basketball lettermen returned to the 1947–48 squad, playing Georgia schools Oglethorpe, Young Harris, West Georgia, North Georgia, Abraham Baldwin Agricultural College, and Piedmont College as well as two institutions located in Alabama, Snead and Jacksonville State Teachers College.[64]

Christmas was a special time at Berry. The 1947 celebration included the chapel choir's presentation of the *Messiah* on the Sunday before Christmas as well as the carol service, which had first been presented by Alice B. Warden twenty-five years earlier and in which the wise men wore robes that Warden had brought from the Holy Land. There was also

a Christmas tree, and on Christmas afternoon, all those who remained on campus received gifts provided by a generous donor.[65]

At this time the Mount Berry Garden Club decided to convert an old railway station on the southwest side of Victory Lake into a picnic spot for faculty and students. On March 21, 1948, the Frances Olmsted Keown Picnic Center was dedicated in honor of the club's first president.[66]

Lindsay, interested in gathering information from various sources to guide his administration, initiated several conferences and studies of the condition of the schools. The objectives committee of the board of trustees recommended in July 1948 that students spend two years of high school (the upper two) studying some definite vocational field, such as beef production, dairying, or weaving, with possible continuation of that study through junior college or through senior college for specialized training in agriculture, education, home economics, industrial arts, or mechanics. The number of students who

Walter Johnson, a 1912 graduate of the Mount Berry School for Boys and Berry's first paid alumni secretary, c. 1953.

entered Berry and remained through graduation (believed to have been only 30–40 percent of all those who enrolled, although no statistics were kept) was a concern, and the school worked to instill the desire to graduate in first- and second-year students.[67]

W. B. Stubbs, executive director of the John Bulow Campbell Foundation, an Atlanta organization established by Campbell, founder of the Campbell Coal Company, Martha Berry's brother-in-law, and a Berry trustee, submitted to the Berry board in November 1948 a report, "Facts Suggested for Consideration of the Trustees with Reference to the Report of the Objectives Committee of the Board of Trustees." He observed that the South remained predominantly rural and that population increases would put heavier demands on facilities for public education. While states in the Southeast had assumed responsibility for educating all students through age sixteen, they had not come up to the national average in meeting this responsibility. He further observed that educational opportunities had

increased for boys and girls in the area served by Berry. Total enrollment at the schools had peaked at 1,252 in 1940 and after dropping during the war had rebounded by 1947, when it reached 922, which was considered full capacity. Stubbs cautioned that if the first two years of the high school were discontinued, too few acceptable students might apply for the higher grades to fill the schools to capacity.[68]

Accompanying such concerns as maintaining enrollment and proper focus in programs was recognition of the need for internal adjustments directed at upholding quality. Realizing the effects of inflation in the grading system, Dean S. H. Cook announced that effective January 18, 1949, a grade of seventy rather than sixty-five would be necessary to pass each course, a change that produced no noticeable negative student reaction.[69] Cook also announced the addition of several courses that had not been taught before the war: astronomy, materials and methods of teaching (in various disciplines), reading and comprehension, church history, and forestry. The

Georgia Department of Education, which had recently approved Berry's teacher-education program, required the methods and materials course for those planning to teach in the state system. Berry's education division formed a group, the Future Teachers of America, for its teacher trainees.[70]

In 1950, a trustees' committee of George Winship, Harmon Caldwell, E. W. Moise, and Philip Weltner restated Berry's aims and presented a survey of Berry's property and programs. The reports pointed out the handicap that lack of accreditation presented to Berry graduates and noted that some students had transferred so that they would graduate from recognized institutions. The committee's report recommended that each student should follow a general program as well as a specialized program in agriculture, forestry, home economics, industrial arts, or elementary education. The school should seek SACS accreditation as a way to raise the quality of the academic work but should not jeopardize the benefits gained through the two-day work requirement. Educational expenditures, the committee said, should focus on the college level to achieve outstanding programs in the areas recommended.[71]

Fred Loveday, who became principal of the Mount Berry School for Boys when Lindsay became president, conducted a survey that showed that the high school supplemented the college, often serving a different kind of student. He objected to the proposed merger of the Martha Berry School for Girls and the Mount Berry School for Boys, and he pointed out extra expenses that would be entailed in providing extra dormitory and dining space on the mountain campus as well as other accommodations. A merger would discontinue the separate boys' and girls' schools and would create a new coeducational school with a new name. Loveday's survey and arguments came after the committee's recommendations seemed to detract from the lower levels (below the top two grades) of the schools and seemed to indicate

that more emphasis was being placed on the college. About 70 percent of Berry's alumni were graduates of the high schools, and they would probably not wish to have the schools discontinued. A visiting committee in 1951 recommended closer coordination of the two high schools, more teaching aids, a guidance director, and more aptitude tests.[72]

Lindsay paid attention to the surveys and suggestions and created opportunities for the faculty to express their views, establishing the Faculty Council and allowing its members to take part in policy formulation, in accordance with SACS recommendations. The Faculty Council's actions led to a statement of philosophy of education and life through which all of Berry's activities could be related as well as a brief statement of objectives for the Berry Schools: "To help youth (a) to understand himself, his capacities and possibilities, (b) to understand others and to develop acceptable ways of getting along with people, (c) to explore the physical world and find the relationship to it and its Creator, (d) to find his life's work and prepare for it, and (e) to build character and grow in spiritual insight."[73] The council also planned and carried out studies on ways to improve the Berry program, providing information to faculty members on methods of teaching, preparing materials that showed how academic offerings and vocational activities could be correlated, and demonstrating the need for additional improvement in the areas of guidance, health, and reading.

The new practice of having student teachers intern under a supervisor working jointly with Berry and the State Department of Education improved the student-teaching experience. Through the efforts of the Faculty Council, the college approved vocational home economics and the addition of a nursery school as a laboratory that made possible a course in child care and implemented a reading-improvement program sponsored by the Campbell Foundation.

Improvements to the library further enhanced the learning environment.

Under Lindsay's stewardship, the school established the Inter-Society Council, which included the presidents of all organized student groups and sought to improve student-faculty relations, strengthen students' leadership skills, and develop in students "a deeper sense of responsibility to the Schools." In a sense, this organization was paving the way for student government. Summer sessions, begun in 1947, enabled students to graduate more quickly than would otherwise have been possible and provided additional income to faculty.

The schools devoted greater attention to the selection of faculty and staff, improved employee housing, raised salaries, and made Social Security benefits available to the staff. A campus newsletter increased employees' awareness of campus happenings. Faculty turnover decreased following these improvements.[74]

Because Lindsay had little experience in the areas of business and finance, the trustees amended the statutes and bylaws of the Berry Schools to provide for a business manager and director of finance with responsibility for business, industrial, and financial affairs. Clarence Walker, a Berry alumnus with broad business experience, was hired for this position, with responsibility for the budget, real estate, maintenance of the physical plant, oversight of industrial departments, and cooperation with fund-raising efforts.[75] When Skinner resigned as director of natural resources and chairman of the division of mechanics and industrial arts in July 1948, Walker assumed many of Skinner's duties and made numerous improvements.[76] Under Walker's supervision, a five-year permanent pasture plan financed by the Campbell Foundation was put into place, the forestry program was expanded, and managed timber cutting became an important source of income. In April 1948 the Wildlife Service of the U.S. Fish and Game Commission designated Berry property a game sanctuary.[77]

Lindsay decided to revive the Possum Trot School and community and to reinstitute a model training school for future teachers.[78] The ringing of the old bell at the historic Possum Trot Church on January 13, 1949, the forty-seventh anniversary of the opening of the first boarding school, marked the accomplishment of this goal. Mary Carden was the principal; she and Mrs. Clarence Arthur Wood, assisted by college students majoring in education, taught the grade-school children.[79]

In 1950, however, the United States became involved in the Korean conflict, forcing Berry again to confront declining enrollment and shortages of industrial workers as well as rising costs that necessitated an increase in tuition. To accommodate students, the school raised wages proportionately. As was always the case, buildings needed repairs, equipment needed updating, and salaries needed enhancing, and the administration struggled but ultimately succeeded in maintaining a balance between income and expenditures.[80]

As had been the case for most of their existence, the Berry Schools remained isolated from the outside community, even the area of Rome, with only those on official business normally permitted to enter the guarded gates, virtually all workers living on campus, and students infrequently permitted off campus. However, occasional visitors from around the country brought entertainment and enlightenment beyond the routine experiences of its students. During this period, the school hosted such notables as Georgia Governor M. E. Thompson, African American tenor Roland Hayes, and acclaimed writer Dr. Archibald Rutledge.

As was inevitable for an institution that had existed for more than forty years with the assistance of many long-standing supporters and staffers, Berry continued to mourn the passing of some of those who had been integral to its history. On April 8, 1947, little more than a week after a visit to Berry, staunch supporter Henry Ford died in Dearborn, Michigan, at age eighty-three.[81] Albert Shaw, publisher of the *Review of Reviews* and a board member for nearly forty years, died about two and a half months later, on June 27.[82] In the summer of 1949, John Henry Hammond, husband of Emily Vanderbilt Hammond, died. The Hammonds had celebrated their golden wedding anniversary at Berry the preceding April, and Emily Hammond had presented Berry with the Pilgrims' "Golden Roll" of almost seven thousand dollars in gifts from her and her friends.[83] On March 20, 1950, music teacher Alice B. Warden, who had taught at Berry since 1922, died after several months' illness.[84] Henry Ford's wife, Clara, died on September 19, 1950, and was memorialized at a service at Berry on September 30.[85]

Near the close of the Lindsay era, the institution began planning for its fiftieth anniversary celebration, and Lindsay announced the building of Morton Hall, a new dormitory for men.[86] Toward the end of the 1950–51 academic year, the board of trustees accepted Lindsay's request for a year's leave of absence from the faculty for further study, and there was some speculation that Lindsay was ill.[87] The Lindsays returned to Alabama and later moved to California; they never returned to Berry. While serving as a special consultant to the California State Department of Education, he died of a heart attack on September 16, 1954.[88]

As Pirkle observed, "the Lindsay years were quieter and freer from controversy and other disturbing influences than any other administration that has followed it." Furthermore, in Pirkle's view, Lindsay did more "useful and successful ground work for the accreditation that Berry College eventually received than any other person, perhaps." His time at Berry was a rather happy one of routine work in all departments that avoided debt and deficits, and he

"carried The Berry Schools through a very critical period of its history . . . with greater credit to himself than biographies and histories and documents of the institution have indicated."[89]

The Cook Interregnum

With Lindsay's departure, Sam Henry Cook was a logical choice to serve as acting president while a permanent president was sought. Cook had spent forty-one years at the Berry Schools and had been involved in all facets of the institution—monitoring the men's dormitories and the dining hall, making work and class-schedule assignments, teaching courses in a number of disciplines, and serving as treasurer and deacon of the Mount Berry Church. When the board of trustees appointed Cook, Chairman John A. Sibley referred to him as the Mr. Chips of the Berry Schools.[90] Pirkle described Cook as "a man of few words, reserved, and devoid of foolishness." If students "went too far in their familiarities toward him, he took them down a notch or two; but they loved him anyway."[91] Cook was not interested in becoming the school's permanent president, but he was willing to serve until an appropriate person could be found. He was not a promoter or fund-raiser; he was a man of his word, conservative in his views, and critical of deficit spending.

Because of the Korean conflict and consequent government demands for manpower, Berry's enrollment again declined in the early 1950s, with fewer than fifty men enrolled at the school in 1950–51. Furthermore, the Georgia school system had added a twelfth grade in 1950–51, with the result that fewer freshmen were entering college than in previous years. The need for the girls' school was declining, and in February 1953, the board decided not to accept any more freshman girls for the high school. The school would use dormitory space in Clara Hall for college women. Evelyn Pendley, who

Samuel Henry Cook, longtime Berry faculty member, dean, and acting president from 1951 to 1953, c. 1951.

grew up on the campus and graduated from Berry, felt that prospective female students had become reluctant to apply to Berry because of the schools' strict, old-fashioned discipline and restricted social life. As a result, Cook recommended to the board in February 1953 that the girls' school be closed. The last class would graduate in 1956.[92]

Sophie Payne Alston, "a complex personality . . . demanding of students in regard to deportment and conforming to the rules" who had served as dean of women at the girls' school since 1937 and who had clashed sharply with Baird, was relieved of her duties in July 1951 as a result of problems stemming from her "personal idiosyncrasies." Her successor, Betty Barbour, and Dean of Men Hudon Vann organized the student-welfare life program, which included nonacademic regulations, activities, and student concerns, and put it "on a basis of sound educational control hitherto not realized."[93]

In 1951–52, the school's jubilee year, a total of roughly a thousand students enrolled in the Possum Trot School, the Mount Berry School for Boys, the Martha Berry School for Girls, and Berry College.[94]

The institution observed its Golden Anniversary on the weekend of January 12–14, 1952, coinciding with the winter commencement. Dr. James G. K. McClure, president of the Asheville, North Carolina, Farmer's Federation and later a member of Berry's board of trustees, spoke at the opening chapel service, and Dr. Wallace Alston, president of Agnes Scott College in Atlanta, preached the baccalaureate and Founder's Day sermon.[95] Emily Vanderbilt Hammond received an honorary membership in the Daughters of Berry, an award previously bestowed only on Martha Berry, Clara Ford, and Leila Laughlin Carlisle, on Sunday afternoon and delivered the commencement address the following day.[96]

J. M. Goddard, executive secretary of the SACS Commission on Higher Education, evaluated the college during 1951–52 and declared that Berry must meet accreditation standards if it intended to continue offering baccalaureate degrees. He made meaningful observations that indicated the magnitude of the work to be done: Too many degrees were being offered in relation to the size of the student body, the faculty, and the degree of faculty training. Grades were too high. Faculty training and salaries remained below standard, and faculty members needed to be encouraged to participate in learned societies. The institution's financial stability was in question, and too much money was being spent on administration relative to instruction. The library lacked college-level resources. Too

The Grand March, a Mountain Day tradition originated during the 1920s, 1950s.

many people reported to the trustees. Measures of performance of Berry graduates in relation to that of graduates of other institutions were needed. The faculty responded to Goddard's criticisms by conducting an intensive study and implementing improvements to the testing and grading system, including the adoption of testing in general education for seniors, as Goddard had suggested.[97] A student editorial in the *Mount Berry News* supported these changes, noting, "We should realize we will be expected to pass tests all through life . . . tests with only two grades, passing or failing."[98]

Cook served two years as acting president before resigning in anticipation of the appointment of a new permanent officeholder, for whom a search had begun in September 1952. Cook returned to his position as dean of Berry College. The 1953 spring commencement, which marked the end of Cook's tenure and at which 107 students received diplomas, featured former Georgia governor Ellis Arnall as graduation speaker; Dr. Robert S. Lambert of Cincinnati preached the baccalaureate sermon.[99]

The Lambert Years

The search committee for a new president for the Berry Schools included Chairman James McClure, G. Lister Carlisle, Virginia Campbell Courts, Harmon Caldwell, and Philip Weltner. At the July 1953 meeting of the executive committee of the board of trustees, McClure recommended for the position the same Dr. Robert Stanley Lambert who had preached the baccalaureate sermon at the school's recent commencement exercises. The executive committee unanimously approved the nomination.[100]

A native of Syracuse, New York, who had served as rector of Cincinnati's Calvary Episcopal Church since 1931, Lambert and his wife, Sylvia, had long been connected with Berry. He had delivered the 1937 and 1949 baccalaureate addresses, and both Lamberts had visited Berry in the 1930s and the 1940s. Like Emily Vanderbilt Hammond, Sylvia Lambert had brought with her a group of interested "pilgrims" from Cincinnati.[101] Lambert had worked his way through Lehigh University, done graduate work at Columbia University and Union Theological Seminary, and received a doctor of divinity degree from Elon College in North Carolina. He had served as a captain in the field artillery in World War I and as a U.S. Navy chaplain in both the Pacific and European theaters during World War II.[102]

Lambert did not arrive on campus until a few weeks after the opening of the 1953–54 school year because of an earlier commitment to fill a pulpit in Massachusetts. Although his late appearance may have displeased some members of the Berry community, he nonetheless received a cordial welcome. The Berry staff held a reception in the Lamberts' honor on September 23, two days after their arrival, and the alumni hosted a similar reception on October 10 as part of homecoming.[103] In an October 27 letter to alumni, Lambert expressed his appreciation for the reception and assured them that he had a "program" and that he would periodically acquaint them with "goings-on" around the campus and with "any new developments we are contemplating." He welcomed alumni comments and assistance.[104] In January 1954 President Lambert thanked alumni for their response to the questionnaires and assured them that he would continue to emphasize "the wonderful record of our graduates and the program."[105] A warm relationship developed between the Lamberts and the alumni.

At his first meeting with the board of trustees, Lambert made suggestions, some of which echoed those of previous administrations, including substantially raising faculty salaries, establishing a retirement system, and making staff living quarters more attractive. In response, the board designated twenty-five thousand dollars to improve salaries and authorized the renovations of Lemley Hall and the Pine Lodge apartments. The board agreed to study Lambert's other suggestions and authorized trustee Philip Weltner to oversee a committee that would complete an evaluation of Berry. Weltner was the president of Oglethorpe University, and his Educational Study Committee included several recognized professionals from other institutions.[106]

The trustees authorized an official inauguration ceremony for President Lambert on April 9, 1954. Representatives of 130 universities and colleges marched in a procession into the Mount Berry Chapel in the order of their founding, with Harvard University first. Faculty, trustees, and program participants followed. Dr. Raymond Walters, president of the University of Cincinnati, made the principal address. Berry's conservative old guard thought the event was too costly and ostentatious and was not in keeping with Berry tradition, although some perceived that the publicity in the academic world was advantageous for the school.[107] Nevertheless, the tradition of presidential inaugurations at Berry had been initiated.

Lambert exhibited great enthusiasm for the presidency and the college, and his energy was contagious. He frequently drove around campus at dawn to see what needed attention. A popular speaker, Lambert received "more invitations than he could possibly fill," and during his first year at Berry, he spoke before many civic, religious, and social clubs in Rome and the surrounding area.[108]

The Lamberts often entertained friends and student groups in their home. Sylvia Lambert was an experienced hostess who endeared herself to many people. Enthusiastic and energetic, she also became involved in improving student life. For example, early on, she noticed that students had no activity center, so she guided the development of a recreation center in the basement of the east wing of Mary Hall, which had previously been cluttered with empty

Robert Stanley Lambert, Berry's president from 1953 to 1955, c. 1954.

trunks and miscellaneous items. The result was a thoroughly cleaned and attractively decorated facility equipped with a variety of games that college men and women could at times enjoy together, another revision of Berry's traditions. President Lambert told the college women's assembly that he felt engaged couples deserved some time together without benefit of chaperone and subsequently approved a new policy that allowed men to escort college women around Victory Lake on Sunday afternoons. However, the failure to relax other rules at the time resulted in the Victory Lake Paradox: "One could escort a date to the woods with a blanket under arm and around the lake without chaperone, but could be sent to his or her room by a dance chaperone for dancing too close." Although students were happy with these changes, they sensed that some old-line faculty were not pleased. [109]

In his February 1954 report to the board, Lambert expressed the opinion that students' ability to pay should have no bearing on the expectation of an educational opportunity equal to or even better than that at any other school. Improvements had occurred in the area of health and hygiene with the remodeling of Cherokee Lodge into an infirmary and quarters for convalescence. A main switchboard had been established at the Ford Buildings for better communication, student government was under way, and prospects for corporate gifts were good. He expressed the feeling that the schools should provide offices for faculty, complete improvements to faculty houses, and provide recreational areas such as bowling alleys and an outdoor swimming pool for students and faculty. He also called for an assessment of the landscaping and planting of the campus and for the development of an arboretum as an industrial department. [110]

A 1954 report submitted by a committee of external educators Berry had invited to review its programs found that Berry's student qualifications were too low and that the policy of accepting only students from rural areas should be examined; that the catalog was misleading, as many courses listed were not frequently offered; and that an assessment of the curriculum, including adequate testing, was needed. In numerous instances, faculty lacked qualifications for the subjects they were teaching. The faculty needed to be strengthened and given responsibility in educational matters, teachers remained underpaid, academic rank needed to be established, and educational expenditures per student needed to be increased. The library fell short in management, holdings, and use. Berry's greatest need, however, was a "dean of instruction whose principal duty was to be concerned with leadership and formulation of instructional procedures and the development and procurement of adequate personnel." Numerous other recommendations dealt with the plant, the students, the alumni association, and the academic standing of the college. Furthermore, the report recommended the disestablishment of the Possum Trot Community School. In May 1954, Dr. Lambert announced that the Possum Trot teachers' contracts were not being renewed. Little community need probably existed for the school, and its reestablishment after World War II had probably represented a forced effort. [111]

Apparently in response to the committee's findings, Lambert attempted to implement some changes. He engaged Dr. Robert E. Lee as professor, assistant dean, and head of the mathematics department, a position previously held by S. H. Cook. [112] This appointment intensified insecurities that some long-term employees had felt with regard to Lambert, and confusion occurred when faculty and students were unsure about which dean to consult on particular matters. Cook, long the dean of Berry College, was not yet ready for retirement and seemed to have been surprised by Lee's appointment. It appeared that he was being stripped of the adminis-

Students socializing in the Tea Room, late 1940s or early 1950s.

trative responsibilities he had held since 1926. Cook and some of his allies, including Hudon Vann, assistant to the president Harvey Roberts, and Inez Henry, ceased to support Lambert. Furthermore, longtime Berry employees bristled at rumors that Lambert planned to discontinue the practice of having students march into chapel with the men on one side and the women on the other, although such a change never occurred during Lambert's tenure.[113]

Lambert also hired additional faculty with doctorates, including in 1954 Thomas D. Cobb, acting registrar and head of the English department; Garland M. Dickey, returning after a year's leave of absence, as dean of men, replacing Vann, who left in the spring of 1954; Harold C. Jones, returning after a seven-year absence from campus, head of the biology department; John Lounsbury, chairman of the division of education; and David Randall, chemistry. With these additions eleven of the college's forty-three faculty members held terminal degrees.[114]

In May 1954 the board made retirement provisions for longtime employees E. H. Hoge, who had retired in 1953, G. Leland Green, who was retiring that year, and S. H. Cook and Inez Henry, both of whom were scheduled to retire in the near future. Each person could receive $150 a month or could live in a home provided by the schools and receive $100 a month, and the board would vote each year on whether to extend these retirement benefits for another year. The following October, administrators' long effort to establish a retirement fund finally came to fruition when "the Board of Trustees by unanimous vote adopted a plan whereby the increments [contributions] of Berry Staff members would be" matched by the school.[115]

Both Berry's visibility and its facilities had improved markedly by the fall of 1954. A new avenue for promoting the schools had opened with the state's creation of a "College Day" program in which the registrar and several faculty members met and talked with prospective students. The college had built two new staff cottages and a new feed mill and had renovated several buildings.[116] A new dormitory to accommodate one hundred men, Morton Hall, named for major contributor Mary Morton, was dedicated on November 22, 1954.[117]

Lee, chairman of the Faculty Committee on Accreditation appointed in the fall of 1954, announced the following spring that a March 1954 SACS visit had determined that the college was making strides in its bid to attain accreditation.[118] The faculty continued to make changes to achieve that goal. In the spring of 1955, the faculty agreed to reduce the number of degrees offered to just two, the bachelor of arts (for English and social-science majors) and the bachelor of science (for agriculture, industrial-education, and elementary-education majors). Biology, chemistry, physics, mathematics, and general-science majors could receive either degree, with the major difference the requirement of two years of foreign language for the B.A. All students had to take 57 hours of general education and complete 126 semester hours to earn a degree.[119]

In June 1955, Lambert summarized Berry's progress toward accreditation, noting the expansion of the general-education program, the revised grading system, the reduction in number of degrees offered, a plan for ranking the faculty, and a program to evaluate student progress. Other accomplishments included increases in the value of the

forests, the modernization of the bookkeeping system, and the closing of a public county road that ran through the campus near the school store (now Moon Building) and beyond the Log Cabin Campus and Ford Buildings. Student employees in the new bookbinding department had already bound twelve hundred volumes. In Lambert's assessment, things had gone smoothly at the college during the year.[120]

During the spring 1955 semester, however, Lambert had "made a re-appraisal of the Boys' School and observed that it was a rather 'loosely run' institution." Although the practice had been to notify staff members by March 15 whether their contracts would be renewed, late in the semester Lambert requested the resignation of the boys' school principal, Fred Loveday, who had held that position for approximately nine years and enjoyed the support of the long-term administrators. Loveday appealed to the board of trustees, who sided with the principal. Unwilling to accept the board's decision, Lambert turned in his resignation, which was immediately accepted. At the urging of the president of the alumni association, Lambert offered to withdraw his resignation and accept reappointment, but Martin, who had become the board's chairman in 1955, upheld its decision. With Lambert's departure, Berry had lost another good leader.[121] During his tenure as Berry's president, Lambert had reportedly refused payment for his services and had paid the utilities on his campus residence out of his own funds. At the time of his departure, however, he accepted twenty-five hundred dollars in severance pay and an automobile.[122]

Lambert's resignation appeared on the front page of the *Rome News-Tribune* on June 10, 1955. In it, he cited "the lack of support and cooperation on the part of the trustees and my assistants on campus."[123] Like Baird, Lambert had been victimized by the dogged resistance to change that was characteristic of Berry's entrenched bureaucrats. Lambert's departure was not mentioned at the first staff convocation or the first joint chapel of the 1955–56 academic year. William McChesney Martin Jr. became acting president while continuing to serve as chairman of the board of trustees. [124]

The Martin Interregnum

Martin had majored in English and Latin at Yale University and had become president of the New York Stock Exchange at age thirty-one, the "boy wonder of Wall Street." His father had helped design the Federal Reserve System, and while serving as Berry's acting president, Martin was also chairman of the board of governors of the Federal Reserve Board. Martin's other responsibilities prevented him from frequently coming to campus; nevertheless, he had been a longtime friend of Martha Berry and took his duties seriously, visiting Berry as often as he could. He would arrive quietly and take his usual room in Emily Cottage for a two- or three-day stay, refusing the use of a campus vehicle and preferring to walk from the Log Cabin Campus to the administration building and to Blackstone Dining Hall, where he took most of his meals with the male students, the unmarried faculty members who lived on the lower campus, the dean of the college, and frequently the dean of men. Sometimes he sought a game of tennis in lieu of lunch and would ask Garland Dickey, dean of men, to find a partner. Faculty and staff were honored that such a man was willing to give his time to such a small institution. [125]

One of Martin's first deeds after assuming office was to send letters to long-term faculty announcing their classification in rank, as suggested by the SACS. [126] On September 5, 1955, at the first staff convocation of the fall term, Martin delivered a typically engaging and enthusiastic address: "I want to talk to you simply, directly and informally about my hopes and aspirations for Berry. These Schools have a heritage that is unshakeable. They are built on the

William McChesney Martin, longtime chairman of Berry's board of trustees and acting president from 1955 to 1956, late 1950s.

Rock of Ages. . . . The spirit of cooperation given me from the staff and students has been remarkable, encouraging and inspiring. . . . At this time I truthfully say that I feel a real sense of commitment. . . . I want to leave this thought with you. The torch has been given to us. Let us carry it forward, remembering that the Scripture teaches us that 'all good things work together for good to them that love the Lord.' " Martin added that he would rather be a trustee of Berry than of any other school he knew.[127] However, he was not willing to rest on the achievements of bygone days: "Our job is to improve and enrich our intellectual pursuits, deepen our spiritual insight and understanding, and make more fruitful our work experiences."[128]

Martin's year as acting president coincided with the last year of operation of the Martha Berry School for Girls. The 1955–56 *Berry Schools Bulletin* carried a brief announcement that the school was offering only the twelfth grade that year. This final graduating class had thirty-one young women.[129]

On November 27, 1955, fire destroyed most of the recitation hall at the boys' high school. Work crews converted space in the shop-gymnasium building and furnished it with blackboards, desks, and chairs, and no classes were missed. Students, faculty, and staff made gifts toward a new building, as did some of the school's longtime contributors and the Kresge Foundation.[130]

In February 1956, Martin asked Sam Cook to assume the on-campus leadership role. Later that spring, Martin nominated and the board elected Dr. John Bertrand as Berry's new president.[131] Martin continued as chairman of Berry's board of trustees until 1973 and remained an active trustee until 1977, when he became trustee emeritus. On July 28, 1998, at the age of ninety-one, he died at his home in Washington, D.C.[132]

John Bertrand's 1956 arrival as Berry's fifth president signaled changes to come, but not without struggle. While some longtime Berry loyalists decried his plans, others saw him as the Moses who would lead Berry out of its wilderness of uncertainty. Bertrand proved to be the man of the hour, guiding Berry through difficult transitions and significant accomplishments until 1980.

CHAPTER SIX

Foundation for the Future

Accepting the Challenge

William McChesney Martin Jr., chairman of Berry's board of trustees and the schools' acting president, had met John R. Bertrand through Charles N. Shepardson, a member of the Federal Reserve Board. Shepardson had been dean of agriculture at Texas A & M University, and Bertrand had served as Shepardson's assistant dean. On a business trip to Washington in the fall of 1955, Bertrand called Shepardson and was invited to have lunch in the Federal Reserve Board chairman's dining room, where he met Martin. Two years earlier, Shepardson had introduced Bertrand to Philip Weltner as a possible candidate for Berry's presidency, but Robert Stanley Lambert had been hired.[1]

Bertrand, a native of Texas, held bachelors and masters degrees from Texas Technological College and a Ph.D. from Cornell University. Before completing his formal education he had been a farmer. He later served as associate professor of sociology and acting dean of men at Sam Houston State Teachers' College in Texas, as a research fellow in the University of Missouri, and as dean of the Basic Division at Texas A & M University. He also served several years as a consultant to a handful of Texas junior colleges. For three years prior to coming to Berry, he had been dean and director of the Fleischmann College of Agriculture and Home Economics at the University of Nevada. Bertrand had served as a submarine officer in the Pacific during World War II and had received numerous decorations, including the Silver Star and the Gold Star. He was very active in a variety of civic and professional organizations, and his wife, Annabel, an Alabama native, was an artist.[2]

Bertrand's decision to come to Berry was not an easy one. After some years of serious work toward achieving accreditation, its proponents were meeting with opposition from some longtime members of the administrative staff. Some younger staff members

John R. Bertrand, Berry's president from 1956 to 1979, c. 1958.

who had contributed to the progress had not been invited to return to Berry, and others were considering leaving.

Martin visited Bertrand in Reno and subsequently wrote to him on March 15, 1956, that Berry offered a great opportunity for someone who had the patience to build on the solid foundation that was there. He added there were "two areas of disagreement which cause trouble: (1) the work program, and (2) the nature and purpose of accreditation." Martin explained that the tendency to look at the work program as a way to give an education to those who could not otherwise afford one had caused donors to think of their gifts as charity. He, however, felt that the work program was designed to use the schools' resources as a part of the educational process. Some longtime Berry staffers saw in accreditation the risk of reorienting the schools' emphasis toward the liberal arts and destroying its traditional areas of emphasis. In Martin's view, it was important for the school to become accredited as soon as possible to show that the liberal-arts work met accepted standards and that accreditation should not minimize other aspects of Berry's program. He wanted to have all-around first-class programs—in the liberal arts, in home economics, in industrial arts, in education, and the school's other activities. Martin indicated his willingness to launch a ten-year program for progress, to include accreditation, if Bertrand was still interested and advised Bertrand to visit Berry.[3]

Bertrand did so on April 5–6. In his customary careful and orderly manner, he analyzed the factors in favor of and against coming to Berry and compared them to the advantages and disadvantages of remaining in Nevada. A major problem he foresaw was the tendency of many people at Berry to idolize Martha Berry personally rather than her ideals. Another obstacle was the administration's instability in the fourteen years since her death. The only point of stability, it seemed, was Martin. If Bertrand came to Berry, he would be putting his faith in a single person and in his belief in what they could do together rather than in the stability of an institution. He was uncertain about whether this would be a wise course of action. [4]

In the spring of 1956, students had begun to show concern about the situation on campus. Three graduating seniors wrote to Martin,

> Under present circumstances and without making changes, the potentialities of the Schools cannot be reached. . . . Although considerable progress has been made in the past few years, it appears we are in for a setback. We students have been conscious of the great efforts of the faculty in working for accreditation and are concerned lest they go for nothing. . . . All we ask for is a decent change for progress in the midst of tradition. Yet every time someone mentions a change at Berry, he is labeled a heretic. . . . We fear that if something is not done in the very near future . . . the status of our staff will lower itself considerably. We students are very much aware of the uneasiness among the faculty. [5]

Alumni and faculty members shared these concerns.

After weighing the pros and cons, Bertrand decided to accept the challenge. In so doing, he moved on a "plank of faith" such as that often referred to by Martha Berry, accepting a salary somewhat lower than Nevada had offered. John and Annabel Bertrand believed in Berry's mission. On May 25, 1956, following a motion by Dr. Harmon Caldwell, chancellor of the University System of Georgia, the board of trustees unanimously elected Bertrand as the schools' new president. When Martin informed alumni at their annual banquet that evening, they responded enthusiastically. [6]

Although the introductory years of President Bertrand's long connection with Berry proved laborious, his constancy and persistence brought accom-

plishments long desired but not earlier achieved. Bertrand conquered numerous obstacles, thereby helping to provide a foundation on which the schools' could build their future success.

Achieving Accreditation

In 1957, Berry finally achieved accreditation by the Southern Association of Colleges and Secondary Schools, for which the college had worked for more than twenty years. In the twentieth century, recognition by regional accrediting agencies became a mark of distinction for an educational institution, indicating that institution offered timely educational programs of high quality befitting its mission and purpose, provided adequate facilities, and provided for the well-being of its faculty, staff, and students.

While the Berry high schools had been accredited since 1922 and the junior college was accredited during its brief existence, the four-year college had never reached that goal. Many longtime employees and alumni felt that Berry, a private institution offering a unique threefold education of "the head, the heart, and the hands," was serving the needs of its students well, training men and women from the rural South primarily to return to the agricultural environment from which they came. Adherents to this view saw no need for Berry to become accredited and feared that the changes such status required would rob Berry of its distinctiveness. Industrialization was rapidly overtaking the agricultural environment, however, and students were feeling the need for educational and social experiences that would prepare them to move into a world beyond their rural southern upbringing. Lack of accreditation and opposition to the changes necessary to achieve it made retaining a president, as well as faculty and students, difficult after Martha Berry's death.

Accreditation had also been delayed by the financial challenges of the Great Depression and the personnel shortages of the World War II years. While Berry's leaders had at various times over the preceding twenty years requested Southern Association membership, no formal report was filed until 1951, at the end of James Armour Lindsay's five-year term. This report indicated that Berry enrolled 703 full-time students in 1950–51, with a teaching staff equivalent to forty-eight full-time faculty. No formalized system of rank and tenure or retirement existed, though records appeared to show that funding was adequate. At the time, 70 percent of the schools' income was earmarked for the college, while the remainder went to the high schools. The library held 10,227 books but could seat only 78 students. The college offered three intercollegiate sports for men—basketball, baseball, and track—but provided no athletic scholarships or grants and did not belong to an athletic conference.[7]

An important factor in accreditation of an institution is the extent of its alumni support. In 1951 approximately 25 percent of alumni whose addresses were known contributed to the college. The school lacked job-placement services for graduates but contended that little need for such services existed because the demand for Berry graduates outstripped the supply. The college required no comparative measurements of the performance of its graduates, such as the Graduate Record Examination.

For the next two years, during S. H. Cook's tenure as acting president, little progress toward accreditation occurred, and faculty qualifications, library facilities and resources, and other factors such as salaries still did not meet the Southern Association's standards. During the two years of Lambert's presidency and in the year following his departure, the college devoted much effort to achieving accreditation, with faculty and staff committees conducting studies and recommending improvements. The college expanded its general-education program, raised grading standards, reduced the number of degrees offered, implemented student evaluations, hired new faculty, devised a formula for ranking the faculty, expanded the library, and devised a retirement system. Robert E. Lee, dean of instruction from 1955 to 1956, observed that the college was very near achieving accreditation following this period of intense efforts.[8] By this time, the college planned for a visit by the Southern Association of Colleges and Secondary Schools Committee on Accreditation in the spring of 1956. However, in light of the fact that Berry was about to hire a new president, Dr. Donald C. Agnew, executive secretary of the Southern Association of Colleges and Secondary Schools, wrote to Martin, the acting president, that it would be best to postpone the visit until the fall, when, Agnew hoped, the "question of stability of the administration might possibly be closer to solution."[9]

The Southern Association's visit was eventually postponed for another year, during which the college continued its work toward meeting accreditation requirements. In the fall of 1956, eleven holders of doctorates were teaching in chemistry, education, English and speech, industrial education, mathematics, physical education, physics, religious education, and social sciences, in keeping with the requirement that at least one holder of an earned doctorate teach in each major field.[10] On December 1, 1956, President Bertrand submitted to the Southern Association of Colleges and Secondary Schools a report covering the 1955–56 academic year and the fiscal year ending December 31, 1955. The report detailed the school's many advancements over the preceding five years. Bertrand had requested funds to improve salaries and had received approval of his tenure policy. The school had employed still more qualified faculty, and other efforts were under way to bring all aspects of the college to accrediting standards.[11]

On October 1, 1957, Berry submitted a new

report to the Southern Association's Commission on Colleges and Universities.[12] The association sent a team of three college leaders from outside Georgia to the Berry campus on October 9–11: the committee members attended classes; visited administrators, faculty, work supervisors, and others; and talked to numerous members of the campus community. Just over two months later, on December 16, Berry received official notification that it had received accreditation.[13]

Establishing Credibility

Although S. H. Cook had planned to retire effective September 1, 1956, Bertrand persuaded the long-time dean to remain at Berry for another year until a successor could be found.[14] Cook also agreed to serve as an adviser to the president after retiring, thereby providing the new president with an important element of stability as well as credibility with Berry's old guard.

Bertrand also smoothed the way for his acceptance by the Berry community by writing letters to longtime Berry staffers prior to his arrival in which he carefully broached the subject of change, laying the groundwork that would enable the school to move forward. He wrote to Inez Henry that he had closely read Tracy Byers's 1932 book, *Martha Berry, the Sunday Lady of Possum Trot,* and seen in it evidence of Martha Berry's adaptability to ever-changing conditions. He added, "I am confident that as all of us move ahead together with the intention of accomplishing most fully Miss Berry's original purpose . . . , we will look to the future and be ready to make adjustments as we find them to be sound. . . . I expect to move very slowly in the beginning and am deeply grateful that both you and Dr. Cook are going to be near me to guide and counsel me."[15]

At the opening convocation on September 3, 1956, Bertrand spoke of how changes in the need for educational opportunity required the same intelligent reappraisal they had continuously received under Martha Berry's leadership. He mentioned societal changes wrought by World War II and the resulting new perspectives and opportunities for youth that demanded that Berry compete with other institutions in a distinctive way. He stressed Berry employees' collective responsibility to continue to grow in effectiveness; otherwise, the schools would fail Martha Berry. So that there would be no mystery or confusion about his intentions, he cited among "Things I Believe" democratic procedures and the responsibility of individual faculty members for making recommendations, suggestions, and criticisms. He also emphasized his belief in the soundness of standing committees, in shared planning, in the need for all the people to take part in the democracy, and in respect for authority. He then expressed his willingness to accept responsibility for final decisions.[16]

Bertrand also outlined his early objectives: to study the institution's organizational structure and define the responsibilities for each position; to develop a teamwork approach and a strong esprit de corps; to clear up internal problems and increase endowments to improve salaries; and to focus all efforts on achieving accreditation. Bertrand pledged to devote "efforts toward bringing to an early fruition the fine work toward this goal which has been done during the last several years and which began well before the last administration."[17] That statement exemplified his usual graciousness in giving credit where it was due and forthrightly established his expectations. He indicated the likelihood that a committee would be charged with studying the existing staff rules and suggesting needed changes.[18]

Bertrand reiterated much the same message to alumni later that fall and added that the aims for Berry's future would be based on the spiritual values on which the schools were founded but that the methods of implementing these aims would have to be realistic and consistent with the times. He invited members of the institutional community to help him by sharing ideas and suggestions.[19]

Speaking to the board of trustees on November 24, Bertrand cited matters that needed clarifying and requested consideration of several recommendations, including changing the fiscal year from the calendar year to July 1 through June 30 to coincide with the academic year and employing a dean of the college, since Cook had asked to be relieved of administrative duties. The new president also suggested creating the position of dean of students, to whom the dean of men, the dean of women, the registrar, the director of admissions, and the director of medical services would report. The new dean would also coordinate the student work program in all units of the institution. Bertrand also recommended creating the position of director of development, who would initiate and direct an extensive fund-raising campaign, working primarily with foundations and businesses, and would be responsible for school publications. The board approved these proposals and reaffirmed its March 5, 1955, actions concerning retirement: all staff members would retire at sixty-five; any exceptions would have to be approved by special vote of the board. Retirement could not be postponed beyond the age of seventy. They also established a policy allowing staff members with twenty-five or more years of service and retired staff with ten or more years of service to build homes on land owned or acquired by the Berry Schools. The homes would be the property of Berry but could be used by the former staff members and/or their spouses during their lifetimes.[20]

In the fall Bertrand issued confidential opinion surveys to faculty and staff, seeking information—ranging from a description of official responsibilities to needed organizational changes—to assist him in planning.[21] Such surveys were repeated periodically during the Bertrand era. In the spring Bertrand initiated student evaluation of the faculty, noting on the form that it was one of several means for arriving at an objective appraisal of faculty members.

Because having the Berry president involved in the larger Georgia educational scene seemed important, the college decided to affiliate with the Georgia Foundation for Independent Colleges, and Bertrand later served as the group's president.[22] He also served as the founding president of the Association of Private Colleges and Universities in Georgia.[23]

As with any change in leadership, constituents needed to be reminded of expectations. The president told staff and faculty at the April 1957 convocation that they were expected to participate on committee assignments and to help with some of the student events, such as the required chaperoning of activities; previously, only a few of the staff had carried out this role. He could not condone grumbling about these assignments. He also indicated the likelihood that the board would take action on the tenure policy at its next meeting: As he had expected, the board established tenure for members of the college faculty on May 25 to go into effect July 1.[24] The institution thus committed itself to academic freedom as well as the support of all citizenship rights of faculty and staff as well as students.[25]

The establishment of Academic Council in 1957 provided an avenue for cooperative planning and broader opportunities for faculty participation in college governance. Represented on this council were departments, librarians, admissions and registrar personnel, and deans. The council dealt with matters relating to students' academic experience, including not only such items as curriculum, academic calendar, and course schedules but also often seemingly minor items that could improve life for both students and faculty. Prior to the fall of 1957, students had only a three-minute break between classes, forcing students to race from class to class.

In September 1957, the council extended this break time to five minutes, hardly generous but certainly an improvement. [26]

Other changes implemented in the fall of 1957 included the assignment of students to the heads of work areas and then the students' assignment to specific jobs by those department heads as well as a new organizational structure that featured the positions of academic dean, dean of students, business manager, assistant to the president, principal of the Mount Berry School for Boys, director of information, director of the physical plant, director of agriculture and forestry resources, dean emeritus, and chaplain. The board also approved the admission of a limited number of foreign students, thereby promoting the development among the members of the Berry student body of a broader world perspective that included a range of cultures rather than simply that of the southern United States. [27] Also in 1957, in keeping with Bertrand's recommendation, the fiscal year was changed to coincide with the academic year.

Some members of the Berry community did not buy into Bertrand's program for progress. For example, at around this time Bertrand became concerned about the dean of women, Betty Barbour, who was apparently reluctant to support the administrative reorganization, had failed to adjust to change, had failed to maintain discipline in areas of student conduct, and had criticized Rome Day, when the campus was open to visitors from the surrounding area. Bertrand spoke to the dean, stressing the importance of lending support, to the extent of one's ability and intelligence, for the program outlined and agreed upon by the administrators. [28] Thereafter, Barbour appeared to cooperate.

When Bertrand arrived at Berry, he had found the institution operating with a budget deficit, paying quite low salaries, and greatly in need of building maintenance and repair. Getting the institution on a fiscally sound basis was not to be a quickly ac-complished task. In May 1957, the board approved the use of unrestricted reserve funds up to $400,000 to make up the deficit over a two-year period, an accepted practice among colleges at the time. The board approved the use of $238,000 of these funds for 1957–58 and in February 1958 approved selective salary adjustments for 1958–59. Because of additional expenses incurred in other areas and despite the fact that $37,000 of the amount budgeted for salaries would be unexpended at the end of the fiscal year, well over $238,000 of the reserve funds would be used. Furthermore, cutting from the forest had declined because of wet weather, reducing income from that source, and income from donations for operating expenses would fall far short of the $152,000 anticipated in the budget. Needs commanding attention were great, and the institution could not postpone some items, including a new boiler for pasteurization in the dairy and repairing the organ in the Mount Berry Chapel. Also, the insurance company's engineers had given high priority to extensive repairs along with an increase in the capacity of the water-filtration plant. An immediate austerity program appeared mandatory, but delays in maintenance usually proved more costly in the long run. Much more money was necessary for instructional purposes, according to Bertrand, including more nearly adequate salaries for the faculty if Berry were to provide a first-rate academic program. [29]

In a May 1958 report to the board of trustees, "Problems Provide Opportunities for Berry," Bertrand pointed to Martha Berry's 1931 change in the charter—the last such change—stating that the institution would "continue to conduct and maintain a school for mountain boys and girls . . . and to likewise maintain such a school for boys and girls and young men and young women from other locations" in addition to offering college work. He emphasized that limited funds made it necessary immediately to "examine objectively all parts of Berry's program with a determination to make such adjustments by both elimination and addition as necessary to serve these needs."[30]

To make his point, the president sought to clarify certain principles of operation. He reminded the board that Berry's purpose was education: the industrial programs should exist to serve the educational programs. The dairy, the farm, the poultry farm, the swine operations, and other such programs needed to provide sound work experience for students and to produce income for the schools. Each enterprise should show a profit either by adding income or by adding to the educational program value that outweighed the financial deficit incurred. Internally, all employees and projects should be subject to the president's direction. A sound budgetary system was necessary with controls to ensure that each department operated within its budget, and maintaining such a system fell under the purview of the business manager, who was also to act as the sole purchasing agent and to obtain the best values possible.[31]

To ease the severity of the financial crisis and provide better benefits for the schools and their faculty, Bertrand looked for every opportunity to achieve economies. Consequently, he observed, Berry could no longer continue to provide rent-free housing to most of its staff as a fringe benefit because of the high costs of maintaining such housing. Free housing had been a part of the Berry culture from the beginning, since Martha Berry had always insisted that all workers live on campus. As a trade-off, however, salaries had been abysmally low. For example, a study conducted a few years later showed that Berry's top three salary ranks trailed those at LaGrange College, West Georgia College, North Georgia College, and the University of Georgia (a Berry professor earned $7,133, while someone of the same rank at the University of Georgia made $9,631). At the instructor level, Berry's salaries fell in the middle of the range among those schools, with North Georgia at the bottom and the University of Georgia at the top.[32] Salaries at the Mount Berry School for Boys were above the approximate midpoint between salary scales of Westminster School in Atlanta and Rome City Schools; however, the Mount Berry School for Boys lacked any teachers with more than four years of college, whereas Westminster and Rome had teachers with more advanced education.[33]

Bertrand suggested that a business study might result in Berry's adopting a competitive cash salary structure and rental rates comparable to those in the community. An alternative would be to allow faculty to find housing off campus. Offering salaries at less than the going rate often meant that only those with lesser qualifications would take positions at Berry. Bertrand argued that the president, with the help of the faculty, should make decisions about the educational program, subject to the policy of the board of trustees, and he believed that it was erroneous to assume that students who enrolled at Berry could not have gone elsewhere, since opportunities for the economically disadvantaged now abounded. Berry's niche for the future seemed to lie in continuing to provide for deserving young people an educational program combining the academic, work, and religious aspects for which Berry had been noted. He believed, however, that Berry needed to adopt a plan whereby parents and students would pay, in keeping with their means, a larger share of the cost of their distinctive opportunity at the school.[34]

In 1958 John A. Sibley, previous board chairman, had recommended that a committee of faculty and staff conduct an educational study. Because of circumstances within the institution and staffers' limited experience and time, it seemed wise to have educators from other institutions assist in this study, and Berry had requested outside financial assistance. Through part of a bequest allowing trustees to use the securities "in such a manner as they shall think to be most useful," funds became

Students in the weaving room, 1950s.

available. The school also needed a comprehensive analysis of business operations and the student labor program, but because it had become imperative to have funds, Bertrand suggested that preliminary steps toward a fund-raising campaign for operation of the school be taken without waiting for the results of these studies.[35]

The board of trustees authorized the use of twenty-five thousand dollars in Berry funds if outside funding could not be obtained, and Bertrand engaged educators, business management personnel, a successful institutional fund-raiser, and others to study the schools' various programs and operations, with reports to be presented to the board in the fall of 1958. Ernest V. Hollis, director of college and university administration of the U.S. Office of Education, chaired the study's advisory committee; Laurence Campbell, a professor of journalism and dean of Florida State University, served as the study's executive officer. Other participants included George Kavanaugh of the University of Kentucky; Charles N. Shepardson; Julian F. McGowin, a consultant to Berry on forest operations since 1939; B. F. Grant of the University of Georgia School of Forestry; Walter Mann, trustee and consultant; Dixon Bush of the cooperative program at Antioch College; and G. E. Mattison, Berry's fund-raising counsel.[36]

Bertrand studied these reports before making recommendations to the board of trustees on December 6, 1958. He again reminded the members of Martha Berry's habit of constantly adopting new ideas and making adjustments in procedures to realize the institution's basic purposes and objectives, of how Berry had founded Berry College in anticipation of the need for education beyond high school, and of how Berry devoted the lion's share of the schools' resources to the college program. Bertrand stressed that the adoption of his recommendations would assist in moving confidently toward the creation of a prestigious institution that would conform to Martha Berry's fundamental principles.[37] The board had received the reports from the studies as supporting evidence for Bertrand's recommendations, which would change several important aspects of the college's operations while remaining loyal to the founder's ideals.

Bertrand advised placing auxiliary enterprises on a self-supporting basis while eliminating industrial enterprises that did not cover their costs unless the educational value of the enterprise outweighed the financial losses. In any case, the college should avoid using endowment income to cover any enterprise's losses. Tuition charges should be increased and scholarships should be established and awarded to students on the basis of proven need and academic achievement, though all students would be expected to pay for their education in accordance with their financial means.[38]

Bertrand also encouraged the admission only of capable students, based on their academic achievement and College Board scores with full documentation of their financial status. Day students should be admitted and required to pay their tuition in cash. Qualified students from other states and countries should be accepted, though preference should be given to applicants from the South. Work assignments should be made only on the basis of actual labor needs and the minimum work requirement should be reduced to no fewer than six hours per week. Students should be paid in cash and at varying levels based on experience, job requirements, and productivity. Also, students should be able to meet this requirement in either on- or off-campus jobs, and the college should establish cooperative work programs with business and industry. By September 1, 1959, the college should move away from its traditional schedule of four classroom days and two work days, substituting classes spread over five and a half days a week; a year later, the college should replace semesters with a four-quarter academic year.[39]

Students repairing flagstones around the reflection pool, 1950s.

Bertrand also recommended several modifications directed toward encouraging excellence in the academic program. Those responsible for admission and hiring should select students and teachers carefully according to high standards. The institution should strengthen educational requirements for and salaries of faculty members and should no longer require most employees to live on campus, though housing and services should remain available for some. Despite the focus on the college, Bertrand encouraged continuation of the Mount Berry School for Boys with a high-quality curriculum. To sustain this curriculum, the school should increase tuition substantially, awarding scholarships on the basis of proven need and academic achievement.[40]

After lengthy debate at the December 1958 meeting, the trustees agreed to vote on many of the recommendations, but Bertrand asked them to pass on only

one—that regarding use of unrestricted legacies to balance board-approved budgets until deficits could be eliminated in operations. All the other recommendations, he thought, should be studied more fully to avoid misunderstanding or misinterpretation. He wanted everyone to have adequate time to study and understand the proposals and completely support them.[41]

As word of the president's recommendations spread among Berry's faculty, students, alumni, and donors, Bertrand found himself explaining and defending his proposals, which engendered concern particularly because of objections expressed by Inez Henry, assistant to the president and trustee, and Betty Barbour, dean of women.[42] On February 7, 1959, former business manager Clarence Walker, a friend of former board chairman John A. Sibley, introduced a motion to the alumni association opposing many of the president's recommendations, particularly reducing the number of hours worked, permitting students to work off campus, and eliminating enterprises that did not cover their operating costs, which included most of the mechanical, industrial, and agricultural program. He commented, "Such changes could result in substantial and radical departures from the well-established and recognized purposes, policies, plans and operations of the Schools." He urged the trustees to "oppose any action, authority or approval that would permit any substantial changes or modifications in the fundamental purposes, plans, and policies of the Schools."[43] Some donors threatened to remove Berry from their wills if the schools made these changes.[44]

Rather than present his original recommendations for approval at the February meeting, Bertrand made a special report to clarify his position. It was important for each person involved in the decision to know that Bertrand did not intend to close the gate of opportunity to capable and worthy students who had no financial resources or to take arbitrary action in closing industrial projects as the result of poor past performance. Rather, he intended to establish sound educational and economic principles to be followed while giving academic personnel and project supervisors the time and backing necessary to put their areas of responsibility on sound bases.[45]

Following careful study of Berry's program, Bertrand had concluded that it would be unsound "to conduct auxiliary enterprises on other than a self-sustaining basis . . . to guarantee every student two days of work on the campus without consideration of Berry's need for the labor or the student's need . . . for his work; to make labor commitments beyond the actual labor needs of . . . enterprises . . . to carry on a work program without use of the incentive system generally accepted by those who believe in our democratic way of life . . . to 'buy' students through summer work without consideration of their aca-

demic potential and attraction to Berry's total educational program." The president also thought it unsound to attempt to maintain an institution with a limited endowment exclusively for students who could not afford to attend other institutions, since other institutions were making it possible for capable students without resources to obtain education. It was also unsound to gear the academic program or the work program to outmoded practices, to attempt to build a quality academic program around a rigid two-day work program, and to build a quality program on a staff salary scale shockingly low even among sister institutions in the South. He stressed that adoption of his December 6 recommendations would put the institution on the road to further achievement.[46] At the February 1959 meeting, the board accepted recommendations that allowed the college to use standardized tests for admission purposes, to issue separate catalogs for the college and the boys' school, and to accept its first international student, Ariadne Papadopoulou from Thessaloníki, Greece, but Bertrand did not present the December 6 recommendations because he sensed widespread misunderstanding of their meaning.

Bertrand attempted to clarify the recommendations and his intentions to alumni, faculty, and others through a speech, "Making History at Berry," delivered to the Berry faculty and to alumni groups in Atlanta, Macon, and Rome in the spring of 1959 and printed in the April 1959 *Berry Alumni Quarterly.* The speech "inspired many . . . to greater confidence in the president."[47] Although Sibley had objected to many of the president's recommendations, Martin wrote to Bertrand that the former chairman of the board of trustees "wants to do everything in his power to be helpful." Despite suffering from an illness, Martin kept in close contact with Bertrand and assured him that he was "doing a fine job." Trustee Lamar Westcott was also especially supportive of the president's efforts.[48]

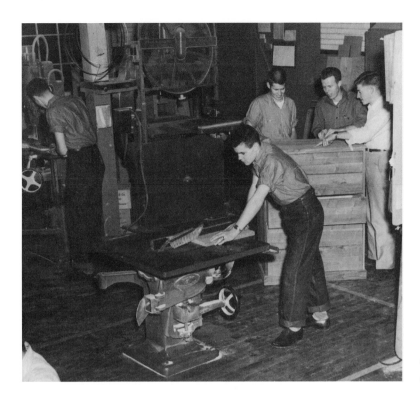

Students in the woodworking shop, building campus furniture, 1950s.

Antagonized by negative communication from some Berry staff, such longtime Berry friends as Emily Vanderbilt Hammond and Leila Laughlin Carlisle withdrew their support from the schools as a result of this conflict. Martha Berry's sister, Laura Berry Campbell, was quite concerned about Berry's accepting students from Rome and pondered her inclusion of Berry in her will. Another of Berry's sisters, Frances Berry Bonnyman, also expressed her negative views on the president's recommendations.[49] While visiting in Inez Henry's home, Tracy Byers heard "bitter attacks" on Bertrand and the schools from Henry, Bonnyman, and Campbell, describing the encounter as "like some fantastic nightmare portrayed in a play, with each [woman] well-schooled and practiced in her part. . . . To hear [them] tearing the school and its administration apart was [a] bitter shock." Responding to a request from Campbell and her daughter, Virginia Campbell Courts, for his observations of the schools, Byers

wrote in praise of the great progress being made, of the flowering of Berry. Neither woman replied to the report.[50]

Bertrand felt the situation appeared quite serious and suggested that his resignation might reassure Henry, Courts, Campbell, Carlisle, Hammond, Geraldine Gebbie Bellinger (another New York benefactor), and several others influenced by these women. The president wrote to Martin, "I certainly will understand fully if it seems best for me to step down. I am quite willing to compromise if it does not involve principle."[51] Martin rejected the offer.

A solution to the problem of the seeming lack of foresight of the board, many of whom were perceived not to be free agents but to be influenced by the past chairman, whose attitude toward Bertrand remained uncertain, was to enlarge the membership and place them on a rotational system. Bertrand and others proposed a large number of names for board membership, and the chairman agreed on this move.[52] Letters came from prominent alumni supporting the president's efforts.

J. Battle Hall, a 1930s graduate of the college, later a faculty member, and now the newly elected president of the alumni association, appointed a special committee of Alumni Council members to study President Bertrand's recommendations and report back to the council through Hall. The special committee unanimously supported Bertrand's recommendations, and in October 1959, the *Berry Alumni Quarterly* published the report and encouraged all alumni to support fully the schools' administration.[53] Although a small core of alumni resident on the campus opposed these views, a large majority of the alumni wholeheartedly backed the program.[54]

Residents of Rome commended the president for the progress made during his administration and for his contributions toward improving the schools' relations with the broader community. In response to a request from the board of directors of the Merchants Association, the group's president wrote, "the folk in our community are feeling that Berry Schools are a part of Rome—not just an isolated institution out on the Summerville Highway."[55] For the first time in nearly sixty years, Berry was no longer completely separated from its surroundings.

Bertrand regretted that during his first three years at Berry he was not able to give Martin more protection from the schools' problems. The two men corresponded frequently and met occasionally in Washington. Bertrand understood the demands of Martin's job as chairman of the Federal Reserve Board and reiterated that Martin's continuing as chairman of the board of trustees was vital to the school's future and to Bertrand's remaining at Berry. In a July 1959 note to Martin, Bertrand wrote, "When accepting the presidency of Berry, I did so intending a lifetime commitment because of my belief in you and the basic principles held by you for

Berry. You were the only hope for stability that I saw in Berry at that time and this remains my evaluation at this time." Bertrand again offered to step aside if Martin saw fit, but if the board decided that Bertrand should continue at Berry, he would commit himself to doing so under certain conditions: Martin would continue as chairman of the board; several active members would be added to the board; and a new vice chairman, who would also serve as chairman of the board's executive committee, would be selected. Bertrand suggested Westcott for this position. An executive committee of about five board members, headed by the new vice chairman, would be appointed to advise the president and the chairman between board meetings. All board members, new and old, would have to agree that they lacked individual authority to direct either the president or other staff members: their authority could be exercised only through board action. The president, employed by the board, was to direct the institution's affairs. A systematic plan would be developed, applicable to all persons not at the time on the board, for selecting future board members. Any future board member would have to retire at the end of the fiscal year during which he or she turned seventy, after which the board would grant honorary board membership, without vote. Also, in a jab at Inez Henry, any paid employee of the institution would be ineligible for future board membership.[56]

Meeting in Washington, D.C., on October 6, Martin reassured Bertrand with continuing support of his policies. Martin had talked with Sibley again two weeks previously but had made no apparent progress in getting him to accept "our viewpoint." Sibley's earlier pledge to cooperate had apparently been insincere, and he did not seem to understand what the authority of a college president should be. Sibley had said that he had confidence in Bertrand as a college president but did not believe Bertrand was the right person to carry on the heritage of the Berry

Schools. Bertrand interpreted Sibley's concept of a college president to be that more commonly applied to an academic dean.[57]

Sibley apparently wanted to turn the school over to the direction of Inez Henry but also wanted Martin to remain on the board, which Martin was unwilling to do under such conditions. Because of Sibley's long connection with Berry, Martin was willing to defer to Sibley's judgment, provided he would again assume the chairmanship or would arrange for a substitute chairman. If Sibley was unwilling to assume the responsibility for the board and for rebuilding it to his own liking, or if he was unwilling to support Martin's policies, Martin believed that Sibley should resign from the board. But Sibley had not indicated a willingness either to resign or to become chairman again, nor had he decided on a suitable substitute chairman. Martin faced a dilemma: he wanted to resign because of his obligations on the Federal Reserve Board even if Sibley did not assume the chairmanship, but he also believed that unless board leaders were "committed to our viewpoint," to resign would be to abdicate his moral commitments to Berry.[58]

Martin and Sibley met again in Washington, D.C., on November 16 and 17, at which time Martin felt that they had to reach a conclusion about what do with regard to remaining in their positions on the board. If they agreed that both should step aside, they would need to decide on the most appropriate way to transfer their authority. If both committed to remaining at Berry for an extended period of time, they would embark on a plan to rebuild the board of trustees and Bertrand would receive a commitment from the board for several years in office. They adjourned without resolving the matter, but Martin authorized Bertrand to tell Walter Mann, a consultant to Bertrand and a trustee of the Dana Foundation, and Charles Dana, a friend of Bertrand and a Berry benefactor, during their planned October 11–13 visit to Berry that Bertrand and Martin had agreed on policy but had as yet been unable to obtain board support on certain essential points.[59]

Bertrand and his wife preferred to remain at Berry but felt that they could not be fair to Berry or to themselves if they compromised on principle.[60] Bertrand was preparing for a change if the circumstances indicated that it would be necessary, but he hoped that by December there would be adequate support for moving ahead at Berry.[61]

Bertrand wrote to Martin on December 11 that he should come to Berry to see the situation for himself before the two of them made any decision on a commitment to the institution. Bertrand assumed that Martin had not heard from Sibley and expressed his view of the situation: "If John remains on the board in his previous role which has permitted him to prevent items from coming up for the action of the board as a whole, then nothing will be gained by adding to the membership of the board. If he can remain on the board as a single board member with the right and responsibility of every other board member to speak to the board as a whole about whatever he believes to be right, I would be more than pleased to cast my future with Berry knowing that whatever is right would come out of the board. Up to the present, nothing has come to me which would indicate that he is willing to assume a single-member role. Am I wrong in my evaluation?"[62] Sibley's actions perceivably influenced those of other board members whom Bertrand saw as making it difficult for him to act.

Yet unbeknownst to Bertrand, Sibley was already backing off his strong opposition. On December 10, Sibley wrote that he disagreed with the recommendation to offer variable rates of pay for student work and argued that the existing system was fair because students rotated among jobs. All learned that the important thing was not the nature of the work but how well the work was done, regardless of its nature. On other points Sibley offered "practical suggestions." He agreed with the suggestion to enlarge and strengthen the board of trustees as rapidly as circumstances would permit, and he offered to help in whatever way he could. He suggested that management depth was far too thin and needed to be strengthened "at the top" so that there might be continuous succession: "This is essential to great accomplishments. Miss Berry did not need or have this necessary depth of management; and upon her passing, a great void was left. I failed in remedying this situation." He added that a capable, well-educated person should be brought in with primary responsibility for finances, operation of various enterprises, and coordinating student labor with the academic program. Apparently having rethought his stance on giving every student full-time work, Sibley offered the opinion that this "well-educated" person should establish budgets for labor requirements for each enterprise so that "we would know how many students we can give full-time work with definiteness and certainty and can arrange our program accordingly." Sibley indicated that he was writing under the assumption that Martin wanted the trustees to express themselves freely, that there was no contest between him and Martin or between him and Bertrand, and that differences of opinion were invited with a view to maintaining the Berry program, stabilizing the management, and launching the schools on the way to greater usefulness. Sibley added, "I hope you will take Bertrand's suggestions, consider them in the light of all discussions, and then make your own recommendations as to changes you now wish. I want to repeat what I said orally: I will not oppose your program, whether or not I agree in all respects. We are working for the same ends; the great responsibility is upon you."[63] The board at the time had nine members, and the number would decline to eight by 1960 because of retirements and deaths and inattention to its development by the chairman. With Martin and Bertrand's efforts, several new members were added by 1961, and the board seemed able to function better. Today the board has eighteen members and is searching for additional candidates to boost its total to a maximum of twenty-three.[64]

In the winter of 1968, Martin announced that nineteen prominent U.S. executives had accepted charter appointments to the Berry College Board of Visitors, which would meet annually and would work actively in furthering Berry's progress.[65] Throughout the remainder of Berry's first century, the board of visitors would bring valuable ideas for strengthening the school's various programs and would bring support to the institution, and with its assistance and that of the enlarged board of trustees, Bertrand accomplished much during his long tenure.

Coping with Student-Life Policies

Rather lax enforcement of the rules guiding student life, particularly uniforms and campus privileges, prompted Bertrand to issue a series of announcements and memoranda beginning in the summer of 1957. Uniforms for the men during the week, breakfast through evening meal, included dark-blue denim trousers, blue chambray shirts (white for seniors), and belts. For night meetings and special programs attended by guests, the uniform of the day was the rule. The schools provided work uniforms or white overalls and black overshoes for the dairy crew. Work assignments generally required the uniform of the day, but supervisors and individual students could determine whether old clothes were more practical in particular situations. Students had to wear clean uniforms to meals, and late afternoon special activities ended in time to allow students to change for dinner. Sunday uniforms for men included suits or dress trousers, white shirts, conservative ties in good taste, and belts. For trips to town or parties, specifications were more general—clean clothes, neat and in good taste. For the time being, male students could wear sport shirts to town, to movies, or to parties while the rules would be subject to further study.[66]

Lengthy guidelines for women's uniforms appeared in the *Handbook for Women Students* and in an October 21, 1957, statement. As in the past, seniors were directed to wear uniforms of green chambray, while juniors, sophomores, and freshmen wore pink chambray. All had white collars, but white cuffs were no longer required. These uniforms were for daily wear and for times when women were working in the dining halls on Sundays. Some students apparently were becoming bold, so the regulations mandated that the necks of dresses not be turned down below the first button. A handkerchief might be worn in one pocket of the uniform; the skirt had to have a three-inch hem. On Sundays and formal occasions, women were to wear navy cotton regulation skirts with white blouses in summer and navy sacony suits with white blouses in winter. Hose had to be of a neutral shade and have seams; socks had to be white, medium weight, and narrow ribbed. Each woman could wear a moderate amount of lipstick in a conservative shade and natural nail polish, but hair could not be tinted or jewelry worn, with the exception of class and club pins.[67]

Bertrand expected faculty and staff to help monitor adherence to the revised regulations. As long as such rules were in effect, they should be followed. It was clear, however, that further consideration of the rules would soon be under way. Bertrand told the faculty, staff, and students that he would give a hearing to a special committee representing the male student body before he made another announcement.[68] The required uniform and other restrictive regulations were becoming obsolete, and Bertrand eliminated the uniform requirement in 1962.[69]

Students managing beef cattle, 1950s.

*Student demonstrating weaving at an exhibition highlighting Berry's work program
and its preservation of traditional highland crafts, c. 1960.*

These changes concerned more than just uniforms, however. Bertrand clearly defined the campus areas that were out-of-bounds for men and women students and extended women's freedom to areas of the campus not previously enjoyed. In his October 2, 1957, document, Bertrand granted women the right to use the path from the administration building to Redmond Road commonly known as the Crack of Opportunity and long used by male students going into Rome during the week, thereby giving women direct access to the bus route on Redmond Road. All women still had to sign out when going into Rome and sign back in with the dean of women by 7 p.m. on weekdays; however, female freshmen and sophomores no longer needed passes to go into Rome during the week. [70]

With written permission from a parent or guardian, a woman could have one four-hour pass per month to leave campus on Sunday afternoon with a friend or family. Women granted such passes were to wear Sunday uniforms and to return to campus and sign in at the office of the dean of women no later than 9:30 p.m. After 5:00 p.m., all women had to return to the archway at the Ford Quadrangle by bus, by taxi, or by automobile. Negotiations were under way with the Rome city bus company regarding a regular schedule of routes between Mount Berry and Rome, operating seven days a week. Berry had ordered a sixty-passenger bus for use between Ford and the lower campus and for travel between Mount Berry and Rome. [71]

Men could call for their dates between 7:45 and 8:00 p.m. in the living room at Clara Hall or the television living room of Mary Hall. After 8:00 p.m., men had to wait for their dates at the entrance to the gymnasium or the auditorium. After the event was over, dating couples left promptly for the archway of Mary Hall or the doorway to the Clara Hall living room, where they were to part. [72]

Each senior man and woman of the college could invite an off-campus guest to attend the traditional senior breakfasts and senior callings but not the senior party. The Student Life Council, which was established in 1957 with faculty, staff, and student members, gave students the opportunity to share in decisions affecting their lives at Berry. The council passed policies on student life and defined student privileges. A caution for exercise of modesty, dignity, and refinement to mark all actions came with these privileges, the continuation of which would depend on students' maturity in using them. [73]

Building on Student Strengths and Programs

In 1959, Berry for the first time accepted students from towns and cities with populations greater than twenty-five hundred, made scholarships and loans available to students, and eliminated the restriction that no more than 10 percent of the students could come from outside the South. The same year, the institution first admitted international students, with day students and married students following in 1961. These changes increased the college's enrollment from 614 in 1956 to 1,692 in 1976, although it remained committed to continuing as a small institution. Although some members of the Berry community may have objected, the implementation of title IX of federal regulations, which required equal treatment of men and women, necessitated the removal of curfew restrictions from the women's residence halls, but locked halls provided security. By 1974, students could reside off campus if they obtained parental permission and college approval. [74]

The Charles A. Dana Scholarships, a large number of which became available in 1963, recognized academic achievement at various levels, and the creation of a chapter of a national honor society, Alpha Chi, in the 1970s gave added emphasis to scholarship.[75] To accommodate the academic program, the school changed its calendar to academic quarters in 1962 and eliminated the two-day-a-week work plan. Students then scheduled their required six hours of work per week (minimum) around their classes, although students were later required to work in blocks of at least two hours.[76] Most students continued to work from fifteen to twenty hours a week. The employment of a full-time director of student work in 1975 gave the program better focus.[77]

Bertrand formalized in 1963 a statement of support of the citizenship rights of all students, faculty, and staff. His guaranteed tuition plan, instituted in 1964 and continuing into the 1980s, assured students that their tuition would not increase during their normal progress through school. Overall, student financial aid increased almost 400 percent over those two decades, reaching more than $1.5 million annually.[78]

Between the mid-1950s and the mid-1970s, tuition rose steadily, from $300 for two semesters in 1956 to $380 for two semesters in 1960 to $600 for three quarters in 1964 and $1,500 for three quarters in 1975. However, these increases did not reflect commensurate growth in the students' share of the cost of their education: Berry's supplement to the cost of its students' education also increased.[79]

Georgia's university system dramatically expanded during the 1960s. While the University of Georgia, West Georgia College, and North Georgia College had been Berry's prime competitors among the public institutions, three new institutions entered Berry's immediate market area in northwest Georgia: Kennesaw Junior College in Cobb County, Dalton Junior College in Whitfield County, and Floyd Junior College in Floyd County.[80] Kennesaw's primary market was older students who held jobs in the area and who needed nearby educational opportunities, and it provided some transfer students and later graduate students to Berry. A partnership between Berry and Floyd preferred by local planning committee members did not transpire, and the idea of Floyd's and Dalton's drawing prospective students away from Berry remained a concern.[81]

Thus, Berry needed to generate the increases in revenues that would enable the schools to offer a program that would be a vital force in education and to determine how best to channel those resources. As president of the Association of Private Colleges and Universities of Georgia, Bertrand worked with the Georgia legislature for a proposed constitutional amendment to authorize a program of state-supported grants for Georgia students attending accredited private colleges, as was the case in twenty-eight other states. Bertrand stressed that the considerable resources of the state's private colleges and universities could be used more fully than was currently the case. He argued that grants of less than the state subsidy per student at tax-supported institutions ($1,123 per student in 1968–69) would aid taxpayers while providing students an opportunity to attend private colleges.[82] These Georgia Tuition Equalization Grants were approved and remain available today.

Berry continued to supplement tuition costs not covered by its students, usually at a rate close to 50 percent. The institution limited its total awards of student financial aid, including tuition-equalization grants and scholarships (but not including student work) to the total the student was paying to Berry for tuition, fees, room, board, and books.[83] By 1973, Sidney Tickton, an educational consultant and cofounder of the Academy for Educational Development, found that Bucknell University and Berry were the only two private liberal-arts colleges with growing enrollments during what he called the "new depression in higher education," a depression not only in money but also in students.[84]

Of much concern to Berry, its students, and other constituencies in the mid-1960s was the planned expansion of the Eisenhower Interstate Highway System. I-75 would pass through north Georgia, and debate focused on whether the road should run west or east of Cartersville, about twenty-five miles east of Rome and Berry. Berry and other communities west of Cartersville advocated the western route, which would provide easier access for students, visitors, and commerce, but by June 1965 U.S. Department of Transportation engineers had decided on the eastern route. While having a major interstate within thirty miles has been an asset to Berry, its location on the "other side" of Cartersville has remained a point of concern, and plans are now under way for a connector to be built from Rome to I-75 just north of Cartersville. [85]

The schools established a student judiciary system in 1968 and included students as voting members of faculty/staff councils and committees in 1969. Also in 1969, the board of trustees added student and faculty representatives to its meetings as liaisons between the trustees and those groups. When the previously required attendance at the campus interdenominational church service became optional in 1969, the campus chaplain made available an expanded religion-in-life program throughout the week. The college then encouraged students to participate in local and hometown churches. [86]

Intercollegiate athletics came into their own during the Bertrand years. An important dimension, conference competition, arrived with the 1958 formation of the Georgia Intercollegiate Athletics Association under the leadership of athletic directors Garland Dickey of Berry and Garland Pinholster of Oglethorpe University. New sports, including tennis, cross-country, golf, soccer, and volleyball, supplemented the established basketball, baseball, and track programs. Berry also became affiliated with

Garland Dickey, athletic director and professor of physical education from 1946 to 1981, c. 1956.

The 1976 Berry's women's basketball team, which won the 1976 NAIA national championship: (left to right) Sharon Adamson, Paula Dean, Coach Kay James, Berry President John Bertrand, Debra Rice, and Nancy Paris.

the National Association of Intercollegiate Athletics. In 1962, a special committee of students and other officials met to suggest nicknames for Berry College's intercollegiate teams. After a vote was held, the name "Vikings" was selected to describe "the skillful, fearless, and daring athlete warriors at Berry College."[87] A program of intercollegiate sports for women beginning with volleyball and basketball evolved under the guidance of Joanne Rowe, who was instrumental in forming the Southern Women's Athletic Conference and who coached the Berry women's basketball team to the conference title in 1967. In 1976, the women's basketball team won the National Association of Intercollegiate Athletics national championship. Two years later, women's track became a part of the athletic program: Berry teams won numerous district titles during this period, and several advanced to national competition.[88]

Expanding Berry Academy

What had formerly been the Mount Berry School for Boys became Berry Academy in 1964. The name change signaled a shift toward establishing the school as a college-preparatory academy. The academy began accepting female day students in 1971 and made residence accommodations available for high-school girls in Friendship Hall in 1973. The academy added a middle school for grades six through eight in 1972, with classes held in the renovated athletic and shops complex that came to be known as WinShape Center in the 1980s. Faculty and staff members and local residents wished to have available to their children private educational opportunities because of perceived inadequacies in the area's public-school systems. Enrollment increases, salary improvements, and reconstruction of the interior of the Hamrick Hall classroom building following a fire in 1972 added to the academy's viability.[89]

Like much of the nation, Berry experienced periods of unrest during the 1960s and 1970s. Students and faculty were swept up in such social issues as desegregation and opposition to the war in Vietnam, as were most colleges and universities across the country. Yet at Berry, these issues that escalated into acts of violence at other institutions were resolved in a relatively quiet fashion. The school's leadership steered a course through student and faculty unrest with great success, and the institution emerged at the end of the Bertrand era stronger and more robust than ever.

CHAPTER SEVEN

Triumphs and Tribulations

The 1960s: Integration and the Vietnam War

Prior to the twentieth century, private and church-related institutions of higher learning were among the major initiators of change, with public institutions in time following suit. Such was the case with desegregation. Oberlin Collegiate Institute, begun in 1834 by missionaries, established in 1835 a policy of admitting students without regard to color, and the institute became the "first college to declare its instruction open to all races."[1]

Berea College in Kentucky, often considered a sister school to Berry because of its work program and other similarities, was founded in 1855 as a one-room district school that "would be to Kentucky what Oberlin was to Ohio, anti-slavery, anti-caste, anti-rum, and anti-sin."[2] Because of sentiment against the antislavery ideas purportedly developing at the school, Berea was "coerced" into discontinuance in 1859 but reopened in 1866 with a precollegiate curriculum. In 1869 the school admitted its first integrated college freshman class, with ninety-six blacks and ninety-one whites. When the Kentucky legislature prohibited interracial education in 1904, Berea became all-white, remaining so until the law was changed in 1950, when it admitted two blacks.[3]

Martha Berry advertised her school as being for white boys at its opening in 1902.[4] Although the *Berry Schools Bulletin,* the schools' catalog, made no mention of race in its statement of purpose, it did list the *Southern Highlander* as a quarterly magazine published by the school "to promote the cause of adequate education for white boys and girls of the rural districts of the South."[5] The school remained segregated until the 1960s, however, possibly because of custom and the social penalty that might have ensued if it did not conform. No black students requested admission to Berry until 1963, and that applicant was denied admission because, according to President John R. Bertrand, the academy and the college were not "in position to accept Negro students."[6] The school served only students from rural areas, and particularly Georgia: northwest Georgia's mountains had few blacks. Furthermore, whatever blacks wanted education may not have bothered to apply to Berry, knowing that it took only white students. In 1950, no blacks applied for admission to the state universities in Georgia, Alabama, Mississippi, or Tennessee.[7] In 1956, when Bertrand came to Berry, the issue of desegregation had come to the forefront in the South. Although some three hundred thousand black students in the region attended integrated schools, most of these were in border states rather than in the Deep South, and bloodshed and violence accompanied attempts at desegregation. The National Guard had to be called into action to preserve law and order.[8]

When the U.S. Supreme Court outlawed segregation in public education with its 1954 *Brown v. Board of Education* decision, Georgia's legislature responded by enacting laws that provided for the abolition of public education if the federal courts ordered integration.[9] Abolition of public education was not a popular alternative, so in January 1961 the legislature created a special committee headed by John A. Sibley, an Atlanta banker and a member and former chairman of Berry's board of trustees, to study the situation. Following hearings around the state, the Sibley Committee recommended that Georgia repeal its resistance laws and substitute a local-option plan that would allow communities to determine how to approach school integration. The federal district court ordered that two black students be admitted to the University of Georgia in 1961; to avoid closing the university, the legislature relented and allowed the students' enrollment. In the fall of 1961, the Atlanta schools began integrating, and the process spread throughout the state over the next several years.[10]

Questions concerning integration first came to Berry's attention in 1959, when President Bertrand received a letter from the faculty of Oglethorpe University requesting that Berry's faculty support publicly a statement advocating continuance of public schools despite integration. Because Berry was not yet integrated, Bertrand saw little to be accomplished by a private institution's recommending to others a policy that it did not follow, but he allowed individuals associated with the schools to take public stands as long as it was understood they were not speaking for Berry, its board, or its president. Although the faculty as a group did not take a public stand, several members openly expressed their support for integration.[11]

In December 1960, Bertrand approved an exchange of tape recordings between a small group of students at Berry and a small group of students from Atlanta University Center, and this communication led to an invitation to the African American group to visit the Berry campus on April 29, 1961. Bertrand approved a visit at the home of William Gordon, an associate professor of speech who had guided the tape-exchange experience. Bertrand also offered to escort the students around campus and to receive them in his home, but he did not plan for the group to visit the dining halls or snack bar. While in New York on school matters on April 26, Bertrand received word of student unrest caused by the forthcoming visit. Later that day, he telephoned Berry students a message in which he stressed the school's long practice of graciousness to blacks as well as to whites and gave as examples the many years of stock-judging contests for African American high-school students and campus performances by such artists as singer Roland Hayes. Bertrand called a chapel meeting for April 28, 1961, but, fearing an embarrassing protest by the students, he postponed the visit of the African American group. On the evening of April 26, approximately twenty-five male students gathered in protest and marched to the Log Cabin Campus, seemingly intending to go to Gordon's home. Learning of the plan, the dean of students met the marchers at the entrance to that area (according to one observer with camera in hand), and they dispersed. At the chapel meeting two days later, Bertrand discussed the circumstances of the invitation and took full responsibility. He invited students to discuss their views with him in an orderly and dignified manner and expressed his desire to meet issues on a Christian-like basis. [12]

This incident at the Log Cabin Campus elicited a number of letters in the next issue of the student newspaper, the *Campus Carrier*. David Stubbs, one of the participants in the march, wrote, "Our march was not directed against the principle of integration alone; it was directed as well against those who would dictate how we must think." Stubbs noted that the protesters had "accomplished our purpose of letting it be known that we will not acquiesce like bleating sheep to an administrative decision that contradicts all which we have been taught since infancy." He invoked imagery of the Ku Klux Klan as he explained that the marchers "did not intend violence; we had no clubs, no ropes, no flaming crosses, no bedsheet robes." In contrast, student Lynda King expressed dismay at the male students' actions, reminding the marchers that such demonstrations were unlikely to solve anything. King encouraged her fellow students to "have our own good common sense rather than allow ourselves to be led by the claims of our emotional feelings and our Southern pride!" [13]

While Bertrand wrestled with the racial issue at the administrative level, no more incidents of student unrest were reported. A survey conducted three years later by the *Campus Carrier* found that 60 percent of Berry students were willing to attend classes with a "qualified Negro student" and that 51 percent were willing to eat in the dining hall with such a student; however, a resounding 74 percent declared their unwillingness to share a dorm room with an African American student. Although one student commented, "The races are not equal and never will be equal," the majority of the students indicated their support for equal opportunities for all races. One student wrote, "I think that if a Negro is qualified, Berry College or any other college should accept him," while another stated, "No man should be held back from an education simply because he is of another race, Negro or other." [14]

As in Greensboro, Birmingham, and other southern cities, high-school and college students staged a series of sit-ins at lunch counters in Rome beginning in 1963. On March 29 of that year, two Berry boys participated in one of the demonstrations, sitting between two African American youths for about forty-five minutes at a counter but leaving before those youths were arrested. The Berry students were orderly, courteous, and respectful to officers and complied when asked for their names. Local authorities reported the incident to Bertrand, but no action was taken against the students, and there is no evidence of a reaction from the student body. [15]

Just over six months later, near midnight on October 14, Bertrand received a telephone call expressing concern that two Berry employees had attended that evening's meeting of the interracial Rome Council on Human Relations and threatening tar and feathers. The caller thought that Bertrand had sent the employees to represent him and warned him about the contents of a speech Bertrand was to give to a group to which the caller belonged. Although the caller had given Bertrand a false name, the president determined that the caller was a member of the Coosa School Parent-Teacher Association, to which Bertrand was scheduled to speak on November 7, and he chose to give two speeches to the group, "College Is Helpful but Not Essential to Success in Life" and "Freedom within the Law." [16]

In the second talk, Bertrand explained that for many years he had defended the right to express one's personal views, whatever they might be, but that he was hard pressed to defend views expressed in the name of someone else at midnight. Further, the idea of tar and feathers was outside his experience. No one represented Bertrand but himself, but he defended the right of Berry students and faculty to have freedom of action and expression within the law. He reviewed comments he had made to the press in 1960 concerning the travesty that would occur if the public schools were closed. He saw quality education for all as an absolute necessity for retaining freedom, and it was unrealistic to think that private schools could meet Georgia's entire educational need.[17] He also reviewed the message he had given to Berry students at the opening of school the preceding September, in which he cited Berry as an American, Christ-centered, democratic institution interested in fostering academic and religious principles in which the teachings of Jesus were the standards for human relations. He had reminded the students and faculty, as he told the Coosa group, that interest in interracial matters went back to the founding of the institution. In addition to Sibley's work to keep Georgia's schools operating even in the event of court-ordered integration, John J. Eagan, Berry's first board chairman, had headed the Commission on Interracial Cooperation, which had been formed in 1919 in response to increasing racial discrimination in the South. Initially led by six white southern men who sought to discuss ways to avoid misunderstandings between the races, the commission grew to include men and women, blacks and whites before merging with the newly formed Southern Regional Council in 1944. Upon his death, Eagan had left his company, the American Cast Iron Pipe Company of Birmingham, to his employees without regard to color or creed. Martha Berry had sought the counsel of recognized African American leaders such as Booker T. Washington and George Washington Carver. Bertrand added, "Ours is a rapidly changing time, and I would be foolish to predict that Berry's enrollment for the next sixty-one years would be limited to white students."[18]

In a report to his faculty, staff, and students at the beginning of the fall quarter in September 1964, Bertrand outlined the moral issues related to segregation and took a position favoring nondiscrimination. Although since the school's beginning, the institution's published admission policy had not referred to race, no African Americans had applied for admission to the college, presumably on the assumption that they would be rejected if they applied.[19] Bertrand also spoke about the financial aspects of accepting African Americans. Because state institutions were beginning to seek funds from the same sources—private individuals, business, and industry—as private institutions did, it was crucial for Berry to seek additional sources of income. Under title VI of the Civil Rights Act, the federal government was beginning to limit assistance only to institutions that accepted students without regard to race, creed, or national origin, and some private individuals and foundations were following suit.[20] Berry was in danger of losing National Science Foundation and National Defense Education Loan funds, and Bertrand had already been forced to return to donors personal gift checks whose use depended on Berry's becoming integrated. He was committed to helping meet the educational needs of a cross-section of young people. After weighing the situation's moral and financial considerations, he had begun in the summer of 1964 to seek African Americans to apply for admission to Berry College. Three African American students from Rome had responded and had been accepted for enrollment. These students—two women, Evelyn Hamilton and Marisue Harrison, and one man, Frank Twyman Jr.—would begin classes the next day.[21]

Patricia Robinson, one of Berry's first African American students, in Memorial Library, c. 1967.

Bertrand expected Berry students to show these new enrollees the same courtesy that the school extended to all students. He reminded the Berry community that the schools' long-standing policy was not to condone involvement in demonstrations or disturbances likely to become riotous and that persons doing so would be subject to prompt disciplinary measures, including dismissal from the college. He offered to refund all money to students not willing to attend Berry under the new circumstances, provided they withdrew the next day and were not involved in disruptive activity prior to withdrawal. The *Berry Alumni Quarterly* noted that the three students arrived the following day without incident and, contrary to the rumor that 50 percent of the student body would withdraw from school in protest of Bertrand's decision, only three male students left. The transition occurred relatively smoothly.[22] Bertrand later revealed that he had been burned in effigy in front of Blackstone Dining Hall on the day the African American students enrolled, but no other incidents occurred, and he perceived that most students accepted the African American students. By the time of the publication of this news, the Berry College Alumni Council had unanimously endorsed Bertrand's action, and

several alumni groups had also declared their full support of the decision.[23]

The following fall, Bertrand's message to accepted students included the statement that "Berry College accepts qualified students without regard to race, creed, or national origin."[24] In January 1966 Bertrand provided information for a study on race relations and integration to Dr. Sam Wiggins, director of Southern Study in Higher Education, George Peabody College for Teachers. Bertrand said, "The first year, we recruited our Negro students (we had [received] no applications) from the community and they attended as day students. Since then we have accepted applicants solely on the basis of qualifications and since June 1965 have had Negro students living in our residence halls as well as attending as day students. . . . We have been proud of the fine attitude of acceptance and cooperation by everyone."[25] As Berry's president, Bertrand set the tone of Berry's internal climate and worked diligently with the board of trustees to achieve agreement on controversial issues. Furthermore, Berry's faculty and students appeared to have had a commitment to the idea of equal opportunity.[26] With all these forces working together, positive change could occur in an atmosphere of congeniality.[27]

Another example of Berry's relatively calm atmosphere can be seen in the campus's reaction to the Vietnam War. Berry's students did not typify those of the 1960s as described by Kenneth Heineman in his study of student revolt in that period, but they nevertheless cared about broader national and global events.[28] The campus did not experience public demonstrations either for or against the war, as occurred at many other colleges across the country, but the conflict was discussed rationally in classes, according to retired history professor Herman Higgins.[29] Burl Horton, who returned to Berry from Vietnam in 1967 and graduated in 1972, recalled that he was treated as a "hero," that the historical event of the war was talked about in classes, that he was asked to write papers about his experiences, and that the campus seemed peaceful and not angry.[30]

An example of the type of student activity on campus at this time was an October 1969 forum at which students were invited to express their views about the Vietnam War. Approximately 150 students attended the two-hour meeting. The dean of students expressed pride, noting that "of 1,174 students, the vast majority are interested in their educational program and are making progress as well as contributing in a positive way to activities on campus. . . . In comparison to some other campuses, Berry has been fortunate. . . . Students calling on the faculty and staff are received favorably." The president of the Student Government Association (SGA) cited this practice as one of the reasons Berry did not experience some of the problems found on other campuses.[31]

Strengthening Faculty and Related Programs

A Faculty Council had been in place under James Lindsay's and Robert Lambert's administrations but had languished during S. H. Cook's tenure at Berry's helm. Bertrand reestablished it in 1967 to provide

a forum in which all faculty could discuss matters affecting Berry's program and their work in it as well as make recommendations to the administration. Revision, expansion, and strengthening of the curriculum, along with addition of the bachelor of music and associate of science (agriculture) degrees in 1967 and 1973, respectively, provided added benefits and opportunities to students and faculty, as did the addition of the master of education degree in 1972 and the master of business administration in 1973.[32] An academic administrative realignment in fall 1973, in which newly appointed Associate Academic Dean Ouida Dickey shared with Dean William Moran the coordination of departments, increased responsiveness to departmental needs through weekly information and planning sessions.[33]

After the arrival of Doyle Mathis as dean of the college in the fall of 1975, an intensive study of the general-education program resulted in the reduction of required semester hours in this area from seventy-seven to seventy-four, including fifty-five hours in the areas of behavioral sciences, humanities, mathematics and natural sciences, and electives plus nineteen hours of basic courses in English, speech, and physical education. These changes allowed students more flexibility in choosing classes.[34] A committee of faculty studied promotion and tenure guidelines and made recommendations that resulted in their updating. The grouping of departments under the coordination of two new associate deans, Barbara Abels and James Scott, in 1976 made possible the sharing of common interests among disciplines and improved organization and planning. The new organization also facilitated the conduct of several studies over the next two years. Departments would engage in thorough self-studies prior to the next institutional self-study for reaffirmation of accreditation.[35]

Until the 1960s, the college offered little support for faculty efforts to remain up to date in their disciplines by attending professional and scholarly meetings, presenting papers, pursuing courses, and engaging in research. Small annual allocations of approximately one hundred dollars for each faculty member allowed some to attend professional meetings, but no other funds were available. Prior to that time, faculty regularly paid the full cost of their own advanced schooling, participation in scholarly meetings, or research. The regional accrediting association had stressed the importance of the institution's providing for such development as a means of retaining qualified professors. A ninety-thousand-dollar gift from Agnes Dana Cowperthwaite, daughter of Charles A. Dana, established an expendable fund whose purpose was to enlarge the faculty-improvement program. She specified that the funds were to be used at the discretion of the president to improve and recruit faculty; specifically, she directed her funds to aid "carefully selected able young men toward the completion of their graduate study, to aid present faculty members in obtaining advanced degrees, and to aid present faculty members in courses of summer study approved by the president."[36] Cowperthwaite wanted to "improve the general caliber of the faculty by grants-in-aid rather than salary increases." Faculty members received grants for graduate study, research, and educational travel for a little more than a decade until the funds were depleted. According to Bertrand, ten faculty received small Cowperthwaite grants in 1965–66. In 1968–69 faculty and a few staff members received $25,846, and for 1970–71, the college awarded $13,800 from this fund.[37] This assistance enabled many faculty to complete their doctorates.

Also important for retaining good faculty was the availability of endowed professorships, whose primary purpose was to enhance salaries of the holders. Better salaries could provide funds for additional resources such as secretarial assistance, scholarly materials, and travel funds or could enable teachers to participate more regularly in development and enrichment efforts. The Charles A. Dana Foundation, which supports innovative ideas for strengthening American education, endowed Berry's first four professorships in 1965, providing $250,000 and requiring a matching $250,000.[38] Berry raised the funds and established the professorships in 1969. The school subsequently created additional professorships.

In 1973 the Lilly Endowment, a private philanthropic foundation that supports the causes of religion, education, and community development, granted Berry $133,000 for faculty-development efforts under the college's plan to have twenty-six faculty members take a quarter to study and work either in the United States or abroad in 1974–77.[39] While all the faculty-development projects had value to the recipients and their departmental colleagues, that conducted by Jorge González, a professor of religion, held special significance, for it set the framework for Berry's enhanced foreign-student recruitment and advising program. González and his wife, Ondina, the college librarian, explored new territories for possible recruitment, learned the needs of foreign students, and established connections with organizations both within and outside the United States to recruit foreign students. On the basis of the González study, Berry appointed a foreign-student adviser who benefited from training grants provided by the National Association of International Educators.[40] In 1976–77 Berry enrolled foreign students from nine countries.[41]

Berry College continued to expect that new faculty, insofar as possible, should hold the highest degrees available in their fields. Dr. Mathis, the dean of the college, announced that by the fall of 1976, 58 percent of the college faculty should hold doctorates.[42] During the implementation of the Lilly Endowment faculty-development program, the board approved a faculty-development plan proposed by

Koji Yoda, Berry's first fully enrolled international student, with his father and Annabel and John Bertrand, 1961.

Mathis and funded by the Gulf Life Insurance Company that would allow faculty a short period away from their teaching to pursue development efforts. The 1979 appointment of a director of research gave the faculty part-time support in developing proposals for funding their research and publications, and the office grew into a faculty-research support unit with two full-time employees plus student assistants.

Berry College's Department of Education spent several years during the 1970s preparing for a team visit from the National Council for Accreditation of Teacher Education (NCATE). Certification by NCATE would have great value for Berry graduates in education, particularly because such certification provides reciprocity among the states on the issue of teacher qualification. In October 1977, NCATE representatives came to Berry and evaluated its teacher-preparation programs in much the same way that the school had been evaluated for accreditation twenty years earlier. Berry received NCATE approval, placing the school among the

first private teacher-education institutions in Georgia to do so, and periodic reviews have maintained this certification.[43] Since 1974, Berry's music program has been recognized by the National Association of Schools of Music.[44] In 2003, the Department of Chemistry received certification from the American Chemical Society, and as of 2005, the Campbell School of Business's accreditation by the Association to Advance Collegiate Schools of Business, International was pending.

Campus Unrest during the 1970s

During the mid-1970s, Berry faculty first began to lodge formal complaints against some of the administration's practices, primarily with regard to compensation, promotion, and tenure. In some of these cases, faculty members had attorneys write letters; in others, complaints were filed in the local superior court, in federal court, or with the Equal Employment Opportunity Commission. The two most significant such matters arose in 1975, with both plaintiffs alleging that the college engaged in unfair labor practices.

In the spring of 1974, well-known educational consultant Sidney Tickton noted Berry's low salaries relative to other colleges nationwide and recommended a minimum 10 percent raise for faculty in 1974–75. In four of the five previous years, Berry faculty had received average cost-of-living increases of 4–5 percent, with no increase at all during the fifth year. In a time of severe recession, however, Berry's trustees felt that the school lacked the funds for such substantial raises. The basis for salary increases was standard cost of living, adjusted for changing responsibilities and/or existing inequities, with other increases merited by outstanding performance. During this period, the institution had tightened its belt, funding only essential positions and requiring the approval of the executive committee for administration before a vacancy could be filled. No department could create new positions. Meeting on March 30, the trustees stated that they would consider merit increases "in the event sufficient undesignated, unanticipated funds become available for use in 1974–1975, and providing continuing funds are in sight to sustain those increases in future years."[45]

Dr. Joyce Jackson, an associate professor of education and chair of the Faculty Relations Committee of the Faculty Council, discussed with her committee and the council the problems Berry's faculty members were facing as a result of the combined effects of inflation, then at 10.8 percent, and Berry's low salaries, and the council voted unanimously to send Jackson's May 28, 1974, report on these matters to the school's president. The report stated the Faculty Council's hope that the development office was seeking funds to allow pay raises as early as the fall of 1974.[46]

In June, the Faculty Council asked the president to release a report on the range of salaries at Berry College. Reportedly angered by the request,

Bertrand refused to do so. The president invited Jackson to report on the salary situation to the board of trustees at its July meeting. As was the practice, he asked her to submit a copy of her report to him in advance of the meeting, but she declined, fearing that she would be censored, and was not allowed to speak to the board. By the time of that meeting, however, the school had received an unexpected distribution of income from the Henry Gund estate fund totaling $18,500. Bertrand announced to the board that in accordance with its provisional authorization on March 30, he would use approximately $12,000 of that amount for "small, highly selective merit salary increases for the college faculty." The balance of the unanticipated distribution would be applied to 1974–75 faculty salary increases already offered but not specifically funded.[47]

In the fall of 1974, Jackson applied with the Faculty Committee on Promotion, Tenure, and Leaves of Absence for promotion from associate to full professor the following spring. The head of the education department, Dr. Milton McDonald, and other administrative personnel who worked with Jackson met to discuss her application and voiced concerns about her readiness for promotion to full professor.[48] Nevertheless, the committee recommended Jackson for promotion to full professor. The academic dean, Dr. William Moran, vacillated but finally agreed with the committee to recommend Jackson; however, McDonald and Bertrand concluded that they could not support Jackson's promotion on grounds of lack of professional maturity and demonstrated academic achievements in teaching, and Bertrand refused to recommend the promotion to the board.[49]

In the spring of 1975, President Bertrand announced that he would recommend to the board of trustees a modest, uniformly applied salary increase for the following year. Jackson called a meeting of "concerned faculty" members. She appointed an ad hoc committee, chaired by Dr. Gordon Carper, to

A student protest regarding the dismissal of a faculty member, 1975.

investigate the advantages to the faculty of collective bargaining and subsequently notified Bertrand of this meeting and of the group's "unanimous mandate to consider the merits of the Berry College faculty's constituting itself as a self-organized collective-bargaining agent through election processes prescribed by the National Labor Relations Board."[50]

On March 25, 1975, Bertrand held a meeting of the entire faculty at which he explained why he believed collective bargaining to be out of place at a small private institution with limited endowment and tuition income. He referred to "a small power block . . . maneuvering . . . to seek control [over] the larger number" of the faculty. These comments clearly indicated that the president and the board were unwilling to recognize the faculty's right to organize. The president was to meet that afternoon with the executive committee of the board of trustees and planned to discuss salaries, tenure, and promo-

tion recommendations and changes in administrative assignments. He delivered the same speech to college staff the following day. Jackson responded to each of these speeches on behalf of the faculty. She and more than fifty other Berry employees, including Carper and Carper's wife, Joyce, a secretary in the Social Science Department, attended an April 4 meeting of the board's Personnel Relations Committee at which faculty salaries and "viable alternatives to collective bargaining" were discussed.[51]

The full board of trustees met on April 5 and approved a general salary increase of 8 percent with the knowledge that additional amounts might be necessary due to promotion, inequities, and increases in responsibilities. The salary increases were to come from the Gund fund.[52] Ten days later, Bertrand called a meeting of all faculty and staff to announce the salary increases (an unusual step) as well as various administrative changes. Carper would no longer serve as chair of the Social Science Department but instead would teach full time. When Bertrand announced promotions, Jackson's was not among them.[53]

Students subsequently rallied to express their lack of confidence in the school's administration. Of 1,422 students enrolled, 671 voted, with 410 expressing "no confidence" in the trustees and the president. The board's chair, William Bowdoin, reported to the board of trustees on July 12 that a minority of Berry students expressed a lack of confidence. The board's Personnel Relations Committee unanimously recommended a vote of full confidence in the chair and the president, with approval of all action taken by the president, the chair, and the executive committee; the board as a whole gave Bertrand a full vote of confidence.[54]

In a claim filed with a National Labor Relations Board (NLRB) administrative law judge, Gordon Carper alleged that his removal as department chair was the result of his engaging in "protected concerted activity" and that the action put rank-and-file employees in fear of losing their jobs. In addition, Joyce Carper filed charges of discrimination against the college. The judge found that as chair, Gordon Carper had exercised supervisory power and consequently was not protected by the National Labor Relations Act. Carper appealed to the NLRB itself, in Washington, and it ruled that an unfair labor practice had not occurred because he had indeed exercised supervisory powers. The NLRB also dismissed Joyce Carper's claims, finding that they were derivative to her husband's and that the faculty gathering she had attended did not apply to her as an employee. The U.S. Court of Appeals for the Fifth Circuit in its review upheld the NLRB's decisions with regard to both Carpers' claims.[55]

Jackson also took legal action against Berry College, claiming that her failure to attain promotion was an unfair labor practice, the result of her engaging

in protected activity. The administrative law judge concluded that the president's failure to recommend Jackson had been illegally motivated, and the NLRB also ruled for Jackson, stating that the failure to promote her constituted an unfair labor practice. Berry appealed the ruling, and the Fifth Circuit Court concluded that Berry had overwhelming reasons not to promote Jackson at that time and declined to support the NLRB's finding. The court concluded that both the NLRB and the court "must give some deference to the discretion of the administration in determining who among the ranks of associate professors will achieve the distinct honor of full professorship."[56] Pleased with the outcome of these cases, the board of trustees on December 6, 1975, passed a resolution commending Bertrand for his handling of the NLRB matter and thanked the local trustees for attending the hearings.[57]

While the decision in his first case was pending, Gordon Carper brought another action, claiming that he had failed to get a larger salary increase as a result of his protected activity. Testimony showed that after his removal as department chair, he had continued to speak against certain administrative practices and to create student unrest on various fronts. He was displeased with his assigned class schedule; he clashed with his department head over several matters and was rated "below average" on his year's performance. He recommended to the Faculty Council a 10 percent salary increase and the renewal of an earlier short-lived sabbatical program. The council endorsed these recommendations and sent them to the president. President Bertrand felt these requests to be excessive, given the institution's economic position, and rejected them. The administrative law judge concluded that there was insufficient evidence to show that Carper had been discriminated against because of his protected activity. The NLRB did not dispute the administrative law judge's finding that Carper was not discriminated against in comparison

Berry's award-winning 1974 College Bowl team: (left to right) *Coach Gordon Carper, Karen Holly, Scott Hooker, Keith Parsons, John McBride, and Coach Brian Hampton.*

with other professors who received below-average evaluations; however, the NLRB decided that the timing of the poor evaluation discredited Berry's reasons for rating Carper below average and thus that the low rating was illegally motivated.[58]

Berry appealed this decision as well, and the U.S. Court of Appeals for the Fifth Circuit again found in the college's favor. The court reasoned that Carper's substandard salary increase could properly have resulted from his poor evaluation but could not find sufficient evidence to permit the NLRB to conclude that the evaluations were illegally motivated. Further, the court stated, "Management can [take unfavorable action] for good cause, or bad cause, or no cause at all."[59]

Both Gordon Carper and Joyce Jackson continued to teach at Berry, and she was eventually promoted to full professor; both were designated professors emeriti when they retired. In 2000 Carper received Berry College's Teaching Excellence Award for making "a distinct difference in the teaching climate of the college." Despite his disagreements with the administration, Carper remained popular

with students. He was instrumental in the revival of Berry's College Bowl team in 1969–70 and served as the team's sponsor until 2002. Under Carper's leadership, the team won trips to three national competitions, and in 2000, the Georgia Legislature honored Carper for his work with Berry teams, including five Southeastern Conference championships and three regional championships.[60]

At around the same time, Berry found itself embroiled in another legal fight when an assistant professor of English, Richard Munn, filed a lawsuit in Floyd Superior Court charging Berry with breach of contract.[61] Berry had received from the Lilly Endowment a grant that would allow faculty to engage in development projects with the understanding that a recipient would return to Berry and work for five years. In 1974, Munn had received a development grant that would allow him to study motion pictures at the University of California, Los Angeles, in the summer of 1975. On March 14, 1975, Dr. Dean Cantrell, the chair of the English department, recommended placing Munn on notice that he must improve his performance in 1975–76 if he wished to be considered for a contract offer for the following academic year. The letter conveying this message also contained the information that the previously approved Lilly grant would be delayed one year until Munn had demonstrated improvement in his performance. On April 29, 1975, Munn filed a $65,000 suit.[62] The college then contended that the filing of the civil suit voided Munn's 1975–76 employment contract. Munn appealed that decision and requested a hearing before a committee of Berry tenured faculty members, who concluded that Munn had shown "incompetence in terms of his ability to function as a working member of the institution."[63]

On October 8, 1975, Munn amended his suit: he was now seeking more than one million dollars for damage to his professional reputation, invasion of privacy, humiliation, mental anguish, and breach of contract. On December 17, the case was further amended to include invasion of privacy and libel. On the same day, the court directed a verdict to the jury to rule only on Munn's salary at Berry for the upcoming year. Berry had claimed that the contract was terminated for cause. A week later, the jury awarded Munn one dollar. The college subsequently paid him an undisclosed amount to avoid potential appeals and to end the matter.[64]

Campus reactions ran the gamut from commendations of President Bertrand's leadership to a protest in the form of a cross burning. On November 13, 1975, the Faculty Council, under the leadership of Dr. Lee Clendenning, sent Bertrand a resolution of appreciation, citing his development and encouragement of faculty participation in college governance as exemplified by his creating or encouraging such organizations as the Academic Council, the Faculty Council, the Graduate Council, the Berry Forum, and a chapter of the American Association of University Professors; his encouragement and defense of the right of academic freedom; his defense of the

The effects of integration, the elimination of Berry's dress code, and changing cultural standards can be seen at this meeting held during the early 1970s, when Berry hosted outside speakers on freedom and held colloquia on the "black cultural experience" and when members of the campus community created organizations such as Students for Peace and Justice.

rights of all faculty members to seek redress; his openness and fairness in dealing with all individuals; and his consistent encouragement of faculty development through assistance grants.[65] Conversely, students burned a cross in front of Hermann Hall on July 8, 1978, at 2:00 a.m., presumably in protest of the administration's treatment of the faculty.[66]

Another incident occurred during the spring of 1978 as a committee of the Southern Association of Colleges and Schools (SACS) was visiting the campus. A small group of faculty members wrote and distributed a "Minority Report" that disputed some of the items included in the self-study committee's report to the SACS. The visiting committee read and disregarded the claims. The study committee learned of this report only after the visiting committee had left campus and reconvened to study the minority report and provide facts that cleared up its errors and distortions.[67]

Improving Facilities and Managing the Land

Beginning in the mid-1950s, Berry's facilities improved dramatically as a result of numerous generous gifts and the college's continued strategy of professional management and planned land development.[68] The college library received additions in 1957 and in 1976–77, enabling its collections to grow from 25,000 volumes to more than 295,000 items. A gift from the Max C. Fleischmann Foundation made possible the first and larger of these expansions, which is named in honor of Fleischmann's wife, Sarah Hamilton Fleischmann.[69] With support from Charles A. Dana, the front section (now the central part) of Dana Hall became a unit of the men's residential facilities in 1959, and the additions of East and West Dana completed this complex in 1967.[70]

Grover Hermann's gift made possible the construction of a new administration building, Hermann Hall, in 1964 as well as of a new college entrance, new streets, and walkways with lighting. Berry then acquired a thirty-three-acre plot of land near the new campus entrance that made the property completely contiguous.[71]

The addition of two sections to the Mothers' Building in 1966 created a new U-shaped classroom building named Trustees Hall (later Evans Hall). The addition of Kate Macy Ladd Student Health Center in 1967 moved health care from its disparate locations in the men's and women's dormitories to a centralized and well-managed operation west of Hermann Hall. The renovation of classrooms and laboratories, reconstruction of the interior of the Green Hall classroom building in 1969, and addition of new maintenance shops and warehouses improved students' learning and the work environments.[72]

Herman C. and Ellnora Krannert provided a gift that made possible the Krannert Center student activities building, completed in 1969. The renovation of Moon Building's interior in 1970 improved significantly for classroom use a facility that had originally housed the school store, the tearoom, and the grocery store. In 1971 the Jones Building, named in honor of Hubert Jones, longtime director of the physical plant, was constructed to provide space for warehousing, maintenance, and operations.

Modular housing units for female students set up in the pine forest west of Hermann Hall accommodated a sudden growth in female enrollment during the 1970s. O. Wayne and Grace Rollins made a substantial gift that enabled enhancements to the campus and the environment and built the Rollins Beef Research Center.[73]

In 1972, Mary Morton provided a gift that permitted the construction of the Martha Berry Museum, thereby expanding visitors' opportunities in the area of Martha Berry's home, Oak Hill, which also opened to the public that year.[74] Atlanta Hall on the Log Cabin Campus was renovated to make way for a model kindergarten, which opened in 1973 and

Hermann Hall, Berry's current administration building, c. 1964.

The Krannert Center, Berry's student activities building and home of the campus dining hall and post office, 1970s.

*Interior of Martha Berry Museum, which opened in 1974,
late 1970s.*

would become an important component of Berry's teacher-education program.[75] Fire destroyed Elizabeth Cottage, the largest of the guest cottages on the Log Cabin Campus, in 1975; reconstruction at a site across the street from the original location was financed by numerous gifts, especially that of Jewel Brooks Milner, in whose honor the replacement cottage was named.[76]

During this era, Berry also came to welcome the general public to its spacious campus, opening its cultural-events programs to area citizens, hosting civic and service meetings, and encouraging local residents to participate in the school's continuing-education programs. Sightseers, runners, cyclists, and others had long sought access to Berry's beautiful grounds.[77]

Others have often seen in Berry's landholdings the solution to various needs, either individual or collective. While Berry had sold a number of parcels, its landholdings had increased some thirty-three hundred acres since Martha Berry's death, and all recent acquisitions had increased and helped consolidate the main contiguous tract. In the early 1970s, the Georgia Power Company sought to obtain some two thousand acres of Berry land in the Rock Mountain area for a project. A private foundation offered a grant to cover the cost of a survey of Berry lands to determine their ecological significance and, if appropriate, to suggest areas where preserves and protected areas might be justified. Berry contracted with Richards Associates of Arlington, Virginia, to do the study, which Thomas W. Richards, former president of the Nature Conservancy, directed. Richards's "Environmental Analysis of Berry College Lands," presented to the board in January 1973, found that Berry's lands were not unique in the preservation sense but were significant because of the size of the holding in single, public-service-oriented ownership. The report suggested several land developments and mentioned such possibilities as golfing facilities and a recreation center. The proposed projects would not utilize land likely to be needed for expansion of either the college or the academy campus. Richards's environmental analysis indicated that Berry should be prepared to cooperate with other responsible organizations in making limited areas available by loan, lease, or sale, provided such cooperation served Berry's long-range interests.[78]

After Richards submitted his report, Berry resumed negotiations with Georgia Power regarding the company's "unusual power-generation project," in which water would be pumped up the mountain, generating electricity as it flowed down and forming a large lake to be used as a recreational area. In 1975, the deal was consummated, with Berry selling twenty-one hundred acres for $1,263,807, to be paid on February 25, 1976. In the interim, Georgia Power would pay semiannual interest at 8 percent. Berry reserved the right to harvest about one hundred acres of pulpwood on top of Rock Mountain before the lake was built. If Georgia Power subsequently bought land from others and paid more than $600 an acre, it was to pay Berry the difference between the higher price and what it had paid Berry.[79] Georgia Power also purchased an additional 440 acres from Berry, with the proceeds of the sale to go to the school's endowment.[80] In 1997, the Rocky Mountain Recreation Area opened, providing boating and fishing opportunities to the public year-round.

In June 1973, Berry leased the corner lot on Redmond Road and U.S. 27 North, valued at $150,000, to National City Bank for a period of twenty-five years.[81] The bank eventually became a branch of Wachovia, and the lease was extended to provide continued income to Berry.[82]

Members of the executive committee agreed in 1974 that all land in excess of that needed for campus and other educational purposes should be regarded as part of Berry's endowment and should be

The Old Mill, which became a campus tourist destination after the campus was opened to visitors, c. 1990.

Students assisting with forestry management on some of Berry's twenty-eight thousand acres, 1970s.

managed like any other investment.[83] Berry transferred to Florida Rock in 1975 the rock-quarry property on the west side of the campus, which Ledbetter Brothers of Rome had leased for some years. Florida Rock extended the lease, set to expire in 1990, to 2000, when it was allowed to lapse. In negotiations with the Berry board of trustees, Florida Rock increased the royalty paid to Berry on the rock used and continued tying the royalty to the wholesale commodity index. Guaranteed rent on the property increased from fifteen hundred dollars a year to fifty thousand dollars a year.[84]

Approaching the End of an Era

Bertrand observed at the end of his second decade that it would be good to pause and again to resolve that "Berry will be always and never the same; that we will continue to dedicate ourselves to the task of perpetuating our eternal values, and . . . of seeking at all times to strengthen our programs; and that we will continue to find sure ways of putting our principles and purposes and programs into action." He further noted that Berry entered its seventy-fifth

anniversary year "with full confidence in this vibrant institution and with unbounded determination to contribute our utmost to rewarding lives for our graduates. Their success and their service to others is our goal today and in the tomorrows ahead."[85]

The Berry Alumni Council passed a resolution of appreciation for Bertrand on January 17, 1976, stating, "we express to President Bertrand our appreciation and esteem for the inspired and inspiring way he has guided Berry through these twenty years, which included times that were smooth and times that were rough. To President Bertrand we pledge our support and help in his continuing years of leadership at Berry College and Berry Academy."[86]

By the late 1970s, faculty salaries had improved significantly, reaching an average for a full professor of $23,126 for 1979–80. In 1977, the board of trustees approved an ongoing professional-development program for faculty. The percentage of faculty members holding doctorates had grown from 15 percent in 1956 to 54 percent in 1977–78, and no regular teaching faculty held only bachelors degrees. Faculty promotions had placed 49 percent of faculty in the associate and full professor ranks, compared

Despite Berry's substantial changes since the first Mountain Day was held in 1914,
the 1976 celebration continued to tie the college to its roots.

Bertrand Way and the Shumard oaks, a gift of the Class of 1950 at its fiftieth reunion, 2000.

with 28 percent in 1956–57. The endowed and supported professorships and the faculty-development effort lent prestige to Berry's faculty and academic program.[87]

The Early Learning Center opened in 1977 as a primary school, a teaching and learning facility of the Department of Education and Psychology, and the college hosted its first visit from a NCATE committee. A new central dining facility opened in Krannert Center, the college established women's track and cross-country teams, and the library became a member of the Southeastern Library Network.[88] In 1977, the trustees approved a $2 million allocation toward a $3.8 million renovation and conversion of the Ford Buildings, Cook Building, Krannert Center, Blackstone Hall, Hoge Building, Ford Gymnasium, and some facilities at Berry Academy. All of these projects were well under way by the end of 1979 and were completed shortly thereafter.[89]

In 1978 Berry's teacher-education programs received NCATE accreditation, and a SACS reaffirmation team visited Berry following the completion of its self-study and subsequently reaffirmed Berry's accreditation for another ten years. The professional library staff grew to five with the addition of a librarian. The first December term offered three weeks of intensive study for students who wished to pursue a particular course or to move along in the completion of their programs. Berry's entering students brought average SAT scores of 963, well above the national average. By the fall of 1979, enrollment at the college had reached 1,542, with Berry subsidizing the educational expenses of each full-time student approximately $2,475 during the preceding academic year.[90]

In 1979 the Departments of Music and Home Economics moved into the renovated Ford recitation hall, which was larger and provided better facilities than their previous spaces. The Media Center relocated within Trustees Hall so it could provide its services to the broader community. The Mountain Campus shop building was converted to serve as the new middle school for Berry Academy and was renamed Inez Henry Hall.[91]

During Bertrand's long tenure, Berry mourned the death of numerous persons who had contributed much to the institution. Those of particular significance included E. H. Hoge, comptroller emeritus, who died in June 1959; G. Leland Green, president emeritus, who died on March 6, 1971; S. H. Cook, dean emeritus, who died on August 7, 1975; Grady Hamrick, former superintendent of the Foundation School, who passed away on December 10, 1975; and O. C. Skinner, former industrial manager, who passed away on May 9, 1979.[92]

John R. Bertrand retired as Berry's president on December 31, 1979, although he remained a consultant to the school for several months longer. Said the chair of Berry's board, William Bowdoin, "It's been a great privilege for me to serve 20 years of Dr. Bertrand's 24 years with him. I've known a lot of people in my career and a lot of places, but I've never known anyone more competent and more dedicated to the principles of Berry than Annabel and John Bertrand. It's been an inspiration to me."[93] In the spring of 2000, the college Class of 1950 planted fifty Shumard oak trees in Bertrand's honor, lining both sides of the avenue, later named Bertrand Way, connecting the flagpole with the Ford Buildings. Bertrand passed away on February 28, 2002, in Asheville, North Carolina, and was buried in Arlington Cemetery.[94]

During his more than twenty-three years at Berry, Bertrand had overcome some major deterrents to progress, mind-sets that had focused on past rather than future Berry. He had also removed the barriers to campus access for those beyond the immediate Berry community. He had achieved accreditation and integration, raised student qualifications for admission, and increased enrollment. He had established a number of endowed professorships, employed more faculty with terminal degrees from a broader range of institutions, and made good benefits available to faculty and staff. The enlarged and improved faculty had substantially strengthened the curriculum. Bertrand had also overseen considerable improvements and additions to buildings and grounds. He had laid the foundation for greater growth and for improvements in the institution's financial position.

The 1979 appointment of Gloria McDermith Shatto as Berry's president-designate, effective January 1980, brought publicity of a different sort. She was the first female president of a higher-education institution in Georgia and immediately drew attention by virtue of that distinction. As an economist, she focused on the school's financial stability and its recognition as one of the Southeast's outstanding colleges.

CHAPTER EIGHT

Polishing the Image

Entering a New Era

In February 1979, the Berry Schools' board of trustees selected Dr. Gloria Shatto, the George R. Brown Professor of Economics at Trinity University, in San Antonio, Texas, since 1977 and a Berry trustee since 1975, as president-designate of Berry College and Berry Academy.[1] Prior to her stint at Trinity, Shatto had served four years as associate dean and professor of economics at Georgia Tech's College of Industrial Management. She held a Ph.D. in economics from Rice University and had taught at the University of Houston as well as in the Houston public schools. Her husband, Robert, was a consulting electrical engineer.

The Shattos came to Berry on September 1, 1979, to learn more about the schools before she assumed the presidency the following January 1. She was inaugurated in a ceremony on April 19, 1980, at which Dr. Vernon Crawford, acting chancellor of

the University System of Georgia and vice president of Georgia Tech during Shatto's time there, was the featured speaker.

Shatto spent the fall 1979 semester familiarizing herself with the school. She studied official documents and got to know members of the Berry and Rome communities, who gave her insights that helped her select the approach to take when she officially assumed office. Shatto sought to build on John R. Bertrand's efforts to raise the schools' image by improving academics; faculty credentials, qualifications, and scholarly productivity; and the school's work and religion-in-life programs. To accomplish this goal, the institution needed to look closely at resources, to balance the operating budget and put Berry on sounder financial footing, and to adopt an approach to institutional planning that would involve all stakeholders.

Soon after taking office, Shatto made two crucial decisions regarding the faculty: she deferred

Gloria Shatto, Berry's president from 1980 to 1998, c. 1981.

in trust by others producing an annual income of about $750,000 for Berry. The school expected to receive another unrestricted $5 to $6 million from the Kate Macy Ladd Trust in 1983. Virtually contiguous land holdings included twenty-seven thousand acres, with twenty-three thousand acres of timber producing about $250,000 a year in income. A rock quarry generated another $250,000 a year, and a leased bank building returned approximately $50,000 annually. Berry carried no debt. Shatto also included among Berry's assets its mission as developed by Martha Berry: rigorous academic preparation, worthwhile work well done, ethical and moral values as a part of everyday life, and service to others. On the minus side of the ledger, Berry had challenges such as declining enrollment, an unwieldy administrative structure, and the existence of internal factions as a result of the recent legal strife.[4] Shatto clearly faced challenges that differed from those that Bertrand had confronted. She would move ahead to meet the issues of her time and to achieve "excellence," one of her goals. She launched a formalized planning process that enabled her to build on the worthy foundation she inherited and to pursue the goals of balancing the operating budget and achieving wide recognition for the college's high standards and accomplishments.

Planning for Growth

In 1981, Berry College received a grant from Inland Container to fund a two-year institutional-planning program, and the trustees participated in a 1983 planning retreat that produced a mission statement and eight institutional goals. Shatto then called for campus forums to examine the mission and purpose and determine planning priorities that would enable the college to address capital needs. A task force on mission and goals with four standing subcommittees—educational program, college

approval of promotions or tenure for the 1980–81 school year, and she decided not to make across-the-board salary increases to cover increases in the cost of living but instead to award merit increases only. The faculty received these announcements well. The fiscal year would end about as budgeted, with a deficit to be covered by unrestricted bequests, but the 1980–81 budget would have to be austere. As was the case at colleges nationwide, Berry's enrollment had been declining since 1975, to the tune of 19 percent among male students and 6 percent among female students. The resulting gender imbalance left a less-than-desirable social situation.[2]

In Shatto's view, Berry possessed "resources . . . so great that we must plan and manage boldly if we are to serve this region as it deserves."[3] A $21 million endowment was producing income of $1.77 million a year, with an additional $14 million in funds held communications, student work opportunity, and religion in life—worked to dissect and analyze the adequacy of each of these components. In 1985, the college created its Planning Council, a small group of faculty and administrators coordinated by the vice president for finance, to streamline the process by comparing data from institutions of similar enrollment and curriculum to evaluate Berry's greatest needs.[5]

Balancing the Budget and Building the Endowment

In early 1980, a faculty committee was developing an energy proposal to involve Berry and Georgia Tech in a joint project that would ultimately make Berry an energy self-sufficient community and would save the school hundreds of thousands of dollars yearly. The committee was seeking private funding for Berry's participation.[6] As a result of resource demands and economic slumps, the institution for a number of years had balanced its operating budget with funds from unrestricted bequests, a common practice among institutions at the time. Because of inflation's impact on Berry resources and the need to effect economies, increase income, and produce a balanced budget, Shatto convinced the board to eliminate Bertrand's plan that had guaranteed that an entering student's tuition would not be increased. To compensate for the deletion of that benefit, financial aid began to focus on scholarship funds and work opportunities. The college continued to operate under sound financial practices and at 4.48 percent had one of the nation's lowest student-loan default rates, far below the national average of 25 percent.[7]

In the spring of 1982, the board's investment committee looked at ways to generate more income from Berry's investments, and an important new alumni group was created, Young Alumni Building Berry Together. Completion of two challenges

in commemoration of Berry's eightieth anniversary produced $320,000 in new funds during that fiscal year.[8]

The board also decided to increase charges to academy students by about 17 percent and to raise college students' tuition by 14.5 percent and room and board by about 10.5 percent for 1982–83. As a cost-saving measure, Chaplain Larry Green would serve both the academy and the college in the religion-in-life program. Concerned about the continuing operating deficits, Shatto proposed that cuts be made in the next budget and called for a review of Berry Academy's viability.[9] Berry's administrators eliminated seven personnel positions, froze six, and eliminated or postponed budget requests to reduce potential expenditures by $1,270,761. The student-faculty ratio remained at 15.7 to 1, and some observers believed that the ratio could be comfortably increased to 18 to 1.[10]

To effect further savings, the institution deleted some programs for which study showed declining need, including the Infant-Toddler Center, the business education/office administration major, the secretarial science major, and the recreation major. Other programs needed strengthening; a computer science minor had existed for ten years and a major was under consideration; and instructors needed more computer support.

In the health-services area, the dean of students eliminated three positions for practical nurses and employed a new head registered nurse, concluded an agreement with Redmond Park Hospital for referrals, arranged to have a local physician visit for two hours a week, and established a preventive philosophy with workshops and a total orientation promoting wellness and physical fitness.[11] This new orientation to wellness significantly lowered the number of ill students and eliminated the need for the health center to function as a small hospital.

Gifts were crucial to the balancing of Berry's

Students Richard Montanaro and Melanie Smith in a production of Tartuffe *shortly after Blackstone Hall's renovation and reopening as the E. H. Young Theatre, 1984.*

budget. The purpose of the new Martha Berry Society was to target, by invitation from the board, selected people with a history of or potential for donating between two thousand and ten thousand dollars annually.[12] Alumnus E. H. Young of Greensboro, North Carolina, contributed $210,000 over a three-year period, the largest single gift ever made by an alumnus to that time, for development of a theater in the former Blackstone Dining Hall.[13] Trustee giving dropped somewhat, but foundation and personal gifts increased. The energy-conservation project engaged 150 students to insulate buildings. An automated management system acquired with the energy grant monitored building use of gas, oil, and electricity.[14]

Two major 1983 fund-raising projects involved $170,000 for the energy-management system and $90,000 to further develop the computer program. William Stokely Jr. made a $50,000 challenge gift to be matched with $100,000 annually of unrestricted endowment funds from alumni and friends for renovation and upkeep of the House o' Dreams.[15] To eliminate the need for short-term loans to cover cash-flow fluctuations, the trustees established a cash reserve by liquidating a portion of the quasi-endowment securities. In addition, the sale of five college-owned houses in Summerville Park brought $187,000.[16] The trust for the Kate Macy Ladd Fund was terminated, as scheduled, on May 21, 1983, resulting in $7.25 million for Berry's unrestricted endowment, with most of the money received in 1983 and 1984.[17]

After changing the name of the institution from the Berry Schools to Berry College in 1982 and reviewing the recommendation from the executive committee, the board members voted unanimously to close Berry Academy at the end of the 1982–83 school year.[18] It was a difficult decision necessary to balance the operating budget and to position Berry College for future success.[19] While the college and the high school had complemented each other for many years, the academy had become both an emotional and an economic drain, requiring resources disproportionate in relation to the number of students served. While most people then connected with the school agreed with the decision, the opponents were very vocal, creating an uncomfortable and perilous situation. Nonetheless, the closing of the academy opened the way for further growth of the college. Prior to the closing, the institution conducted placement efforts for academy faculty and staff, sent information to parents and other schools to aid the students' transition, and arranged for rising seniors to complete their high-school graduation requirements at Berry College in a summer program held after the academy closed.[20] Intent on preserving the memory of their school, alumni of the Mount Berry School for Boys and Berry Academy erected a bronze marker in a scenic spot by Swan Lake just west of Frost Chapel and dedicated it in January 1992, the ninetieth anniversary of Martha Berry's founding of the boarding schools.[21] Despite the academy's closing, Berry continued to operate its Early Childhood Education Center, established in 1977 with the aid of a Lilly Endowment grant, and the Berry College Middle School.

Shatto reminded board members on October 15, 1983, that twenty-five years previously, 50 percent of all college students had attended private

Marker placed at the Mountain Campus in 1992 to commemorate the Berry Academy, which closed in 1983.

institutions, compared with 20 percent in 1982. One hundred colleges and universities had closed in the past decade, with an additional two hundred closures predicted by the year 2000. Berry had great strengths: a unique mission; faculty, staff, and students committed to improving quality; a powerful board of trustees; significant ties to the business community and a strong board of visitors; strong alumni support; and recent national recognition, including the prestigious Freedoms Foundation Award for the Center for Economic Education and a teaching excellence award for the agriculture department. Quoting Father Theodore Hesburgh, the president of the University of Notre Dame, Shatto said, "The strong institutions might just get stronger, not by growing externally, but by promising frugality, integrity, and quality internally." All these strengths would ensure that Berry would survive.[22]

In October 1983, H. G. Pattillo, chair of the board's budget committee, proposed a comprehensive balanced budget for the 1983–84 fiscal year.[23] Because 115 fewer undergraduate students had enrolled that fall than in the previous year, income from tuition would be down considerably. However, this shortfall would be countered by seven hundred thousand dollars in projected net income from the sale of the modular-unit trailers, as well as some other real estate transactions and savings in energy consumption. Consequently, the board approved the balanced budget.[24]

The number of applications for the following fall rose considerably by February 1984, and Berry's financial future looked more optimistic.[25] In August 1984, following the annual audit, Vice President for Finance Joe Walton announced that the 1983–84 operating budget had resulted in the first net surplus since 1966–67.[26] Sharing this news in her 1983–84 *President's Report,* Shatto announced that the accomplishment was significant because it had not relied on tuition increases, and she added,

"For the future, Berry plans to continue living within its means."[27]

In December 1984, former president Bertrand took exception to what he felt was Shatto's disparagement of his running of the schools and wrote to her to express his concerns:

> For five years I have been troubled by some readily apparent efforts to remove from the record 23½ years of accomplishments at Berry. Now, in view of the thrust of many news stories, letters, and speeches during the past five years (including recent ones proclaiming that "for the first time in 17 years Berry operated with a balanced budget"), it seems important for me to counter the implication of irresponsible management and policy actions on the part of the Board of Trustees whose policies my associates and I administered from 1956 through 1979. For me to continue to remain voiceless about this matter would be unfair to the very able men and women who worked so fruitfully to move Berry ahead over the years.
>
> Berry trustees who served under Bill Martin and Bill Bowdoin from August 1956 to December 31, 1979, or any part of those years, know of the accomplishments as well as of the problems at Berry during those years. . . . Numbers of other persons may be less completely informed, and thus I shall probably quietly share information contained in this letter with other concerned persons in the future. . . . Never was the permanent endowment invaded as at numbers of colleges.[28]

Perhaps Shatto had not realized the apparent critical nature of her references to past deficits and their effect on Bertrand. Bertrand had followed the board's policies and guidelines, and Shatto served on that board for the last five years of Bertrand's presidency. Shatto's ideal of enhancing Berry's endowment by leaving unrestricted bequests intact was never fully reached, and had she been more tactful in recognizing the accomplishments of Bertrand and the trustees with whom he worked, this rift between the two presidents might never have arisen. Her references to the deficits seem subsequently to have diminished.

Early in 1985, the development team adopted new tactics, concentrating on unrestricted giving. The strategy included establishing a new board to promote giving by parents of Berry students, conducting a campaign among Berry seniors to get them in the habit of giving, simplifying the Martha Berry Society to admit anyone who donated one thousand dollars, opening all giving clubs to nonalumni donors, and creating a new Heritage Society to recognize those who added Berry to their wills or created unitrusts or annuities.[29]

The new fund-raising tactics produced results. The alumni phonathon raised an impressive $100,787 in 1983–84 and topped that amount by about 50 percent with more than $150,000 the following year. The Martha Berry Society had 168 members. Pattillo subsequently announced that all bequests would go to the endowment, with none used for operating expenses. He expected the balanced budgets to continue.[30] The endowment's market value increased from $25 million in 1979 to more than $46 million in 1985, gift support doubled in five years, and the percentage of alumni who gave to the school increased from 12.9 to 23.5 percent.[31]

In January 1986, rising maintenance and other costs caused the director of Oak Hill, Dan Biggers, to propose and initiate fees ($3.00 for adults, $1.50 for children, with group rates available) for admission to the home and to the Martha Berry Museum, a change that caused a dramatic decrease in the number of visitors.[32] Plans to attract adult groups, garden clubs, and school groups soon bore fruit, however, and the number of annual visitors to Oak Hill soon exceeded the earlier totals.[33] A 1988 face-lift of Oak Hill and major improvements in the gardens and grounds helped to attract still more visitors.[34]

With a tentative goal of fourteen million dollars, the "Berry Works" capital campaign began on June 1, 1985, seeking monies for renovations of the library, Memorial Gymnasium, and other campus buildings; instructional and laboratory equipment; and endowments of scholarships, lecture series, and student workships. The first, "silent," phase of the effort featured "A Day for Berry," November 12, 1985, when sixty volunteers engaged in a joint public-relations and development-office effort to increase support from Rome following a weeklong media blitz that sought to make city residents more aware of Berry's importance to the community.

By the time the campaign was officially announced in April 1986, $8.5 million had already been donated or pledged, including nearly $2.3 million from members of the board of trustees.[35] Six months later, 86 percent of the faculty and staff had contributed or pledged to the campaign, and the Student Library Fund had been created. Alice Richards pledged $737,000 from the estate of her husband, Roy Richards Sr., to renovate Memorial Gymnasium, which was renamed in his honor at her request.[36]

Although Berry Works was not scheduled to end until June 30, 1988, it surpassed its goal seventeen months earlier and ultimately raised $17.7 million. On May 16, 1987, in conjunction with a victory gala in Atlanta sponsored by the Young Alumni, Shatto announced that the goal had been reached and indicated that fund-raising would continue.[37] In addition to raising funds to improve facilities, the campaign had strengthened Berry's reputation and increased student enrollment and academic performance.[38]

In 1989, the John M. Olin Foundation denied Berry's request for funds for a science building, causing the school's administration to stop and reflect on its practices. The foundation questioned Berry's policy of holding onto land rather than selling it and investing the proceeds for a higher return. Berry viewed its land as part of the endowment but did not account for its real estate holdings as such. Olin also questioned the low level of tuition and the large amount of financial aid given to students. Ever conservative and mindful of Martha Berry's views regarding land, the trustees discussed all the issues and agreed that the school's policies concerning resources should not be changed.[39]

In 1990, Berry received a major gift from the Lettie Pate Evans Foundation, including $275,000 for improvements to the Westcott Building, which became the home of the agriculture program, and $225,000 for renovations to Trustees Hall, which was subsequently renamed Lettie Pate Evans Hall.[40]

Sales of timber had been an important source of income, producing between $600,000 and $750,000 a year in net general-purpose revenue. Seven million board feet were cut in 1987–88, and between 1984 and 1988, approximately three thousand acres of trees had been clear-cut and then replanted. Berry's forester recommended a switch to a policy of selective cutting that would reduce the amount harvested to match the annual growth rate. Thus, the number of board feet cut declined to 3.8 million, 2.8 million, and then to less than 1 million over the next three years, reducing the school's income in the short term but ensuring the sustainability of timber cutting as a source of funds over the long haul.[41]

The class-agent strategy, designed to increase alumni giving, identified agents for 50 percent of the classes to create a personalized approach that should result in increased giving. Shatto and selected development, alumni, and public-relations staffers focused on "Berry Days," a series of trips to alumni meetings, civic clubs, radio and television appearances, and meetings with current and prospective donors as well as corporations and foundations.[42]

A new giving group, the Viking Club, recognized donors of fifty dollars.[43] In spite of these efforts, fund-raising showed no increase in 1991–92.[44]

In August 1993, the Corrella and Bertram Bonner Foundation proposed endowing Berry's scholarship program with a gift of $4.92 million if the college could raise $1 million. The plan would help to fund Berry's work program by awarding scholarships for specified hours of community service. The board decided to use quasi-endowment funds to meet the college's commitment until other funds could be raised and to recognize donors of twenty-five thousand dollars or more to the Bonner Scholarship challenge.[45]

Between the fall of 1992 and the fall of 1993, undergraduate enrollment grew from 1,628 to 1,675, thereby increasing tuition revenue. Philanthropic support for Berry was twice the $1.5 million national average for private four-year colleges as a result of the school's "compelling mission, . . . committed Board of Trustees, and inspired presidential leadership," according to Chester A. Roush Jr., a member of the board of trustees.[46] Alumni giving increased as well, and a new group, the Berry Circle, was created to honor graduates from the past twenty years who donated five hundred dollars. Forty people, half of them new donors, joined. The Berry after Hours program was created; under it, after-work social gatherings were held in Atlanta to give alumni in that area an opportunity to maintain contact with one another and with the school. During the 1993–94 year, the college's bottom line reflected a $1 million improvement over the preceding year, and on August 31, 1994, the market value of the endowment exceeded $100 million.[47]

The Laura Berry Campbell Trust, established by J. Bulow and Laura Berry Campbell in 1925, provided more than fifty million dollars to Berry beginning in 1996. The board decided unanimously to dedicate all of this income to support the business school, which was renamed the Campbell School of Business.[48] Although the decision to devote all the money to the business school disappointed and angered faculty in other areas, the board decided not to divide up the funds because it wanted to make a significant impact and develop a top-quality business school.[49] This endowment enabled the college to renovate the Green Building, occupied by the Campbell School, in the late 1990s and to hire more faculty.

The Oak Hill Endowment Fund, valued at almost forty-two million dollars in December 1996, produced income beyond what was needed for Oak Hill's upkeep, and a judge granted clearance to use some of the earnings for academic purposes. The Historic Berry team was considering renovating the museum, and air-conditioning Oak Hill would be a major expense.[50] At the request of Columbia Seminary, another beneficiary under the Campbell Trust, SunTrust Bank petitioned the court to change the provisions of the trust agreement to allow the Campbell funds to be spent. Although Berry did not intend to spend the principal, the board authorized Shatto to execute agreements necessary to join in the court petition.[51]

Major capital improvements on the horizon included a new science building and renovation of the Cook Building to accommodate the School of Education. Trustee Glenn Cornell, a Berry College graduate, agreed to lead a new capital fund-raising campaign. The estimated cost of a new science building was $23.7 million; the Cook renovation, $4.9 million; and the board's instructions were to proceed with construction drawings for the science facility and a preliminary design for Cook. Cost-reduction efforts reduced administrative spending by $350,000 in 1996–97 and by $565,000 in 1997–98. Agriculture managers reduced the cattle herds;

administrators reduced the size of committees and, through careful management of costs, balanced the elementary school's budget.[52]

Growing with Students and Programs

Before Shatto took office, students had expressed interest in a Reserve Officers Training Corps program, under which students who completed all requirements would be commissioned as second lieutenants in the U.S. Army Reserves prior to graduation. A professor of military science at another institution had offered to set up a satellite program at Berry and staff it with one commissioned and one noncommissioned officer. Berry would provide office space and secretarial support as well as outside space for drilling. A survey of students and faculty found that 128 students and three-fourths of the faculty were interested in the program, which offered the possibility of increasing male enrollment.[53] Although overall enrollment had dropped 1.5 percent in the fall of 1981, seventy-nine men and women signed up for the new program.[54] In 1991, however, the government cut funding, ending the program at Berry.[55]

Berry Evening College began operating in the fall of 1981 to help adults and working young people to complete bachelors degrees. While late day and early evening classes had previously been offered from time to time, the new Berry Evening College promoted specific programs for older students, including a program in criminal justice and social science. Many Rome businesses paid all or part of their employees' tuition to support their completing a degree. Other 1981 additions included a bachelor of fine arts degree. By the early 1980s, six religious-life groups—the Baptist Student Union; the Methodist Wesley Foundation; the Catholic Students; the Episcopal Student Fellowship; and two interdenominational groups, the Fellowship of

Students from Berry's ROTC program, which ran from 1981 to 1991.

Christian Athletes and 60 Minutes—along with the campus chaplain and the church kept alive the second aspect of Berry's mission, the education of the heart.[56]

Since surveys on the subject began to be conducted in the early 1980s, Berry students have indicated commitments to traditional American values in the areas of belief in marriage, family, private enterprise, and personal responsibility that are significantly higher than those of freshman at other institutions of higher education. A 1984 survey indicated that students' reasons for attending Berry included its very good academic reputation, the availability of financial assistance, its special educational programs, alumni recommendations, and friends' recommendations. While many students had previously listed campus beauty as their main reason for choosing Berry, academic reputation became the pri-

mary factor, followed closely by financial assistance, although the campus retained its lovely setting.[57]

Students had five specialization opportunities under the master of education degree—early childhood education, industrial-arts education, learning disabilities, middle-grades education, and reading—and a sixth, home economics, was added in the summer of 1984. Exxon funds made possible a permanent venture-capital fund to provide financing to students who wished to launch business enterprises, with awards ranging from fifty to five hundred dollars, to be repaid with 5 percent interest.[58] Beginning in 1984–85, the Presidential Scholars program has brought to Berry many outstanding students: under the program, selected students with SAT scores of over 1,400 and high-school grade-point averages of 3.75 or higher receive full tuition.[59] In the mid-1980s, the college's honorary leadership society became a chapter of Omicron Delta Kappa, a national leadership society, whose membership includes students as well as faculty. Student members honor selected faculty and administrators by inviting them to join the group, which focuses primarily on community service.[60]

With students from thirty-one states and twenty-three foreign countries, Berry's total enrollment reached 1,528 in 1986.[61] The enhanced planning process resulted in a new enrollment target of 1,600 undergraduates, which the school approached in May 1987 when applications exceeded the number of students for whom accommodations could be provided.[62] That fall, Berry enrolled 1,734 men and women (including 150 graduate students), the largest number in the college's history. The dormitories were full, and the student-faculty ratio was 17 to 1. And the number of applications continued to rise the following year.[63]

In 1989, college leaders decided to convert from a quarter to a semester system to enhance the quality of instruction. Study-abroad programs were operating in England, France, Germany, and Spain. Chapel services had expanded the previous year to include faculty and students as speakers; this change, along with the introduction of the Staley Christian Scholar lectureship, produced an increase in chapel attendance.[64]

The Student Government Association constructed in the spring of 1982 a new physical-fitness course south of Memorial Gymnasium and named it in honor of Garland Dickey, the school's longtime athletic director, who died in 1981.[65] The Department of Health and Physical Education removed the fitness trail during the 1990s in response to changes in students' approach to physical fitness. In its place, the college erected the Berry Outdoor Leadership Development (BOLD) Adventure Challenge Course, which was dedicated to Dickey in September 2001 and is now known as the Dickey

Graduate student Adrian Perez on the BOLD Adventure Course (also known as the Dickey Adventure Challenge Course), 2002.

Adventure Challenge Course (DACC). At the end of Berry's first century, more than five thousand students in physical education courses and participants in corporate training groups were using the course each year.[66]

In 1982, Dr. Robert Pearson succeeded Dickey as Berry's director of athletics, serving through 1992 and again from 1994 to 1996. Under Pearson's leadership, the rich Viking sports tradition continued. The women's basketball team won one hundred games over the 1982–84 span. Women's soccer was added as a club sport and then given intercollegiate status in 1986, when it reached the National Association of Intercollegiate Athletics (NAIA) finals; a year later, the Lady Fury captured the national championship. The squad won two more national titles and hosted the NAIA women's soccer national championships in 1994 and 1995, and several members of the team received special recognition as NAIA Academic All-Americans. The women's tennis team won eight consecutive Georgia Intercollegiate Athletics Association (GIAC) championships between 1982 and 1989 and in 1992 won its first NAIA district title, made its third trip to the national tournament, and finished the season ranked thirteenth in the nation. In response to renewed interest and in hopes of attracting more male students, the college revived its intercollegiate baseball team in 1987, constructing a new field east of Mary Hall at the Ford Buildings and naming it the William R. Bowdoin Field in honor of the former chairman of the board of trustees.[67] Just two years later, the baseball team won the GIAC championship and advanced to the NAIA regional tournament. Viking Crew, established as a club sport in 1991, attracted students interested in developing and demonstrating their rowing skills on local and other rivers. Men's intercollegiate golf was reinstated and in 1998 won its first NAIA national championship. Women's volleyball became a club sport in 2000, and in 2003 both women's volleyball and golf became intercollegiate sports. In 1996, Berry left the GIAC and joined ten other prestigious schools from Alabama, Georgia, and Tennessee in the TranSouth Conference.[68] In 2003, the college decided to affiliate with the Southern States Athletic Conference, formerly the Georgia Conference, the same group with which Berry had been affiliated prior to joining the TranSouth Conference. Returning to the NAIA-affiliated Southern States Conference shortened travel times and reduced student-athlete class absences.[69]

The 1991 graduating class was Berry's largest to date, with 444 students. Additional majors adopted in 1990–91 included biomolecular science, designed to prepare students for careers in medicine or graduate studies in such fields as biochemistry or molecular biology; hotel and restaurant management, a joint venture between the Department of Business and the Department of Consumer and Family Sciences (formerly home economics) that prepared students for positions in the hospitality industry, at the time the second-largest worldwide; and international studies, combining political science, history, foreign languages, business, and economics in an interdisciplinary program preparing students for business and government careers requiring an understanding of economic and cultural perspectives.[70]

Students in Free Enterprise, an arm of the Center for Economic Education, spoke to civic groups on economic issues, taught personal economics to the probationers at the Rome Diversion Center, and developed a video presentation commemorating the two hundredth anniversary of the Bill of Rights. The team at various times returned its winnings from regional competitions to the college for further community and outreach programs, such as publishing and distributing throughout the community brochures on opportunities for volunteer service. Executive Round Table, a student-led organization

Berry's 1988 women's soccer team, which won the NAIA national championship just two years after the sport was added to the school's intercollegiate athletics program.

that also included faculty and business leaders, brought prominent businesspeople and successful entrepreneurs to campus and provided an opportunity for students to engage in networking and to enhance their communication skills. Biology and chemistry majors demonstrating unusually strong abilities in their fields could compete for a scholarship newly endowed by Becton Dickinson, an international health-care technology company.

Over the years Berry students have produced excellent publications. The Georgia College Press Association selected the *Campus Carrier* as Georgia's best small-college newspaper for eight consecutive years in the late 1980s and early 1990s, and the paper won twenty-three awards from the Georgia College Press Association in 1996–97. Berry's literary magazine, *Ramifications*, won first place in

its division as judged by the American Scholastic Press Association in 1990–91 and 1991–92, and the Society of Collegiate Journalists deemed *Ramifications* the best literary magazine in the nation the following year. Also in 1991–92, the *Cabin Log* won a first-place rating from the Columbia Scholastic Press Association, which judges college and university yearbooks nationwide.

Students have studied public speaking since the creation of Berry College, and the establishment of a forensics team in 1986 offered an opportunity to demonstrate their rhetorical prowess. In 1990–91, the Berry team won Florida State University's Seminole Classics Forensics Tournament and placed fourth in the national tournament for colleges with fewer than five thousand students. Over the next twelve years, Berry speakers won 2,048 awards.

Student at work in the dairy, late 1980s.

Competing against all of the nation's schools, regardless of size, the Berry forensics team placed in the Top 10 in 1992, 1994, and 1997. At Interstate Oratory, the country's oldest and most prestigious speech tournament, Berry students served as Georgia's two representatives every year between 1990 and 2002. In seven of those years, a Berry student placed among the top six in the nation, and in 2001 and 2002, both Berry speakers placed in the top twelve.[71]

Veterinary medicine, one of the most competitive fields for admission into graduate study, had long been an avenue pursued by Berry graduates. In 1991–92, schools of veterinary medicine in five states accepted the college's graduates, and over the previous five years, more than 85 percent of Berry's applicants to vet schools had gained admittance, a record of success that has continued.

To prepare students in education to meet the challenge of a multicultural student mix, Berry developed an English for Speakers of Other Languages program in collaboration with the Northwest Georgia Regional Educational Service Area. The program attracted educators from across the state as well as Berry students and became one of Berry's best-known offerings in education. As of 1992–93, the School of Business has encouraged all students to demonstrate awareness of global dimensions by completing an international course, studying a foreign language, or studying abroad.[72]

During the Shatto era, the Berry choir performed at New York City's Carnegie Hall and in other notable places. Senior Joanna Grant received a Rhodes scholarship for study during 1994–95 at Oxford University in England. By the mid-1990s, students were also becoming involved in faculty research, especially in the sciences, and it subsequently became a common practice for students and professors to deliver and publish papers jointly. With support from the United Parcel Service, the "Teaching Pathways" program, a pilot effort that encouraged minority children in the local community to aspire to teaching careers, engaged a minority Berry student to recruit teacher-education candidates.

In her 1990–91 annual report, Shatto stressed that as a consequence of student participation in community-service initiatives, the "threefold educational mission of study, work, and worship established by Martha Berry at the turn of the century [is] as relevant in 1990–1991 as it was in 1902." Faculty, staff, and students challenged each other to volunteer for community service as part of a yearlong celebration of the institution's ninetieth anniversary, awarding certificates of recognition to those who performed ninety hours of community service with a variety of organizations, including local nursing homes and Habitat for Humanity. Thus, Shatto noted, the ethical and moral dimensions of religion in everyday life were "explored both within and outside the classroom."

Other evidence of Berry's commitment to community service could be seen in the 1992–93 creation of a chapter of Alpha Kappa Tau, a national collegiate honor society recognizing community service, and in the Symposium on Community Service, sponsored by the Joseph E. Mertz Memorial Educational Foundation of Indianapolis and held at the college in 1992.[73] The symposium's events included a community-service fair and a workshop on preparing for community service, and student organizations and individuals alike subsequently increased their level of community-service activity to reach more of the Berry community as well as the larger Rome community. On Annual Hunger Cleanup Day, a national one-day work-a-thon, students raised more than three thousand dollars from community sponsors. Members of the Berry Chapter of Habitat for Humanity spent spring break building houses for low-income families.

In 1993, Georgia initiated its Helping Outstanding Pupils Educationally (HOPE) Scholarships, which required students to achieve a B average in high school and to be Georgia residents. The HOPE scholarships require students to maintain a B average in college and to enroll full time; in exchange, students at private, degree-granting institutions receive three thousand dollars per academic year. The scholarships have increased the number of Georgia residents attending Berry, so that they now make up 85 percent of the student body.[74] As a result of these scholarships and of studies and efforts undertaken by the Berry administration, Berry's student-retention and graduation rates have grown significantly, from less than 40 percent during the early 1980s to about 60 percent in 1994–95.[75] Established in 1995, the Freshman Center works to help first-year students adjust to college and oversees the freshman-seminar program, which includes approximately twenty seminar groups of around twenty students each in the fall term. As a result of such efforts, the freshman retention rate topped 76 percent between the 1997 and 1998 academic years.

Berry's first full-time director of work opportunity brought greater structure and strength to that program. During the 1980–81 year, 88 percent of the graduates had worked voluntarily on campus during their days at Berry to help pay their college costs. Also in 1980, Berry students participated in cooperative work programs at Alston and Bird, Bell-South, Delta Air Lines, Georgia Power Company, Northwest Georgia Regional Hospital, Rock-Ten Company, and Siemans-Allis.[76] In 1983, O. Wayne and Grace Rollins pledged one hundred thousand dollars a year for ten years to support of the student work program.[77] In 1982–83, President Shatto reported that more than 90 percent of Berry students worked on campus during their careers at Berry, although the number of students on the work scene fluctuated from semester to semester.[78] More than

95 percent of the school's 1988 graduating class met the requirements of the O. Wayne Rollins Educational Trust with regard to student work.[79]

In 1985, under the guidance of alumnus Billy Smith, Berry graduates established Alumni Work Week, demonstrating both their strong work ethic and their devotion to their alma mater. An unheard-of event for a college, Work Week made headlines in the *New York Times* in 1989, and in 2001, 256 former students returned to campus to spend the week before the annual alumni meeting working at carefully assigned tasks and contributing their special skills toward important maintenance and campus-enhancement efforts that might otherwise have been delayed as a result of lack of staff or funds.[80] In 1994, the Saturday before Work Week became designated as Work Day for those with young families who had difficulty being away for a week; by 2000, more than one hundred alumni participated in Work Day.

Enhancing Faculty and Related Programs

Berry boasted its best-qualified faculty ever in 1982, with 69 percent holding doctorates; however, 90 percent remained the goal. Forty-six percent of the faculty were tenured, and the student-faculty ratio was slightly under 16 to 1.[81] During the 1980s, student evaluations and faculty development and scholarly efforts became increasingly important in decisions regarding promotion, tenure, salary adjustments, contract renewal, and termination. Under a program of small grants for faculty development approved by the board almost ten years previously, twenty-four faculty submitted grant proposals, seventeen of which received funding.[82] The establishment of a faculty-research office spurred an increase in the quality and quantity of articles and books published by the faculty and in papers presented at scholarly meetings.[83] Faculty members have been engaging in international travel, study, and research

since 1999, when benefactors established funds for that purpose.

Several special grants and awards by donors have also helped faculty and inspired achievement. In each of four years during the 1980s, Shell Oil selected an academic department to receive two thousand dollars to inspire innovation and strengthen the department. The Mary S. and Samuel Poe Carden Award provides one thousand dollars to a faculty member for outstanding teaching and service; the first recipient was Dr. Julian Shand, physics professor, in the spring of 1985.[84] Three other special faculty awards were established to recognize excellence in teaching, scholarship, and advising. Faculty qualifications continued to rise, and by the fall of 1986, 76 percent of the faculty held doctorates from universities in twenty-three states and England. This broad geographic representation meant a richer resource for the development of Berry students' understanding and outlook.[85]

By 1990, both faculty and students wanted more communication with administrators and greater involvement in administrative decisions and in long-range planning. Faculty members wanted to know what percentage of their peers received salary increases, while students wanted to know that their class evaluations were being considered in promotion and tenure decisions. Such increased involvement came about as faculty and student representatives began regularly to attend meetings of the board's personnel committee and to voice their opinions about changes made without their involvement.

In the spring of 1990, the Equal Employment Opportunity Commission scheduled an investigation of Berry College to determine its compliance with the Equal Pay Act of 1963, which required equal pay for men and women. The school was found to be in compliance with the law.[86]

The restructuring of the academic program in 1991–93 allowed the faculty to devote more time

G. C. Miller, Harold Jones, and Maurice Thompson recondition a door during Alumni Work Week, 1987.

to students rather than administrative duties. Four schools—Business; Education and Human Sciences; Humanities, Arts, and Social Sciences; and Mathematical and Natural Sciences—each headed by a dean, grouped together similar disciplines to effect closer planning and collaboration in teaching, research, and related activities, thereby helping to overcome traditional barriers among the disciplines and to draw faculty to work together.[87] Of significance to Berry's professors was Berry's 1996 ranking by *U.S. News and World Report* as first among the South's liberal-arts colleges in commitment to high-quality teaching.

In the wake of the board's decision to devote all of the Campbell funds to the school of business, board members decided that for economic, internal-relations, and public-relations reasons, efforts should begin to find funds to help the other three schools. The Berry science faculty were already working with a facilities and campus-planning consultant on specifications for the science space in the new campus plan under design toward a forthcoming capital campaign.[88]

In 1997, an assistant professor of biology filed a lawsuit against Berry and certain administrators on the basis of religious discrimination in the granting of promotion and tenure. The professor, who was Jewish, left Berry, and the school settled with him to avoid a costly legal fight. No such issues have been raised by Berry's other Jewish faculty members.[89]

Improving Facilities and Managing the Land

When the board decided to close Berry Academy, the executive committee established guidelines for the use of the former academy facilities. Use had to be compatible with Berry College and its mission and should be reimbursed by an outside agency, not operated by Berry. Income for this use should cover all costs of services and maintenance provided by Berry as well as allowance for depreciation. Preferably, use would involve college faculty, staff, and students on a mutually beneficial basis. The facilities were definitely not for sale.[90]

In the winter of 1983–84, Truett Cathy, an Atlanta entrepreneur and founder of Chick-fil-A who had visited Berry a number of times since 1981, proposed a major new scholarship program. Employees of Chick-fil-A who met Berry's admission requirements were recommended for the program, under which the company provided half of an eight thousand dollar scholarship and the remainder came from the college's general fund.[91] Berry would offer student work and other financial aid. If fifty or more students were recruited for the fall 1984 quarter, Chick-fil-A would have use of certain former academy facilities for a "Leadershape Campus." Male students were to reside in Pilgrim Hall and female students in Friendship Hall, and they would attend classes on the college campus. Projected additional net revenue to Berry with fifty students was $84,365; with seventy-five students, $153,138. The committee agreed to the plan on a trial basis, and Cathy paid for the renovation of the buildings. The agreement was completed in January 1984, and seventy-five Chick-fil-A scholars enrolled in the fall. The partnership proved successful and has continued under the name WinShape Centre.[92]

When Cathy expressed an interest in housing foster children on the WinShape campus, he received authorization to renovate and enlarge Woodbury Cottage, former home of the academy's headmaster, to house eight children and two adults.[93] Cathy also built a home for eight to ten boys and girls and two house parents near the site of the former store on the mountain campus. WinShape funded these with the agreement that the houses would become Berry's property should the agreement with WinShape terminate. All WinShape projects had to be compatible with Berry's mission.[94] In the early 1990s, the WinShape Centre completed cabins and a pavilion for primary use by summer Camp WinShape participants. The cabins have provided accommodations for various groups throughout the year, and the pavilion has become home to many gatherings, including the Mountain Day barbecue lunch preceding the Grand March.[95]

The college also improved facilities and equipment on the main campus during these years. Blackstone Dining Hall was converted into a theater and classrooms appropriate for drama study and production and was renamed the E. H. Young Theatre.[96] A new language laboratory enhanced the learning of foreign languages; a new computer center for the business department and a new computer and terminals for the math–computer science laboratory increased activity in those areas; a campus cable television system was installed in each residence hall and featured a local channel for campus communication and educational programs; and a Pew grant brought new science equipment.[97]

In 1985, while looking at Berry's library needs, the Facilities Planning Committee decided to renovate and enlarge the existing structure at a cost of approximately $3.5 million rather than build a new library at a cost of approximately $7.3 million, and the renovated building was dedicated on May 19, 1989.[98] From its beginnings as bookshelves in the Cabin and in Brewster Hall, Berry's library had moved to the Recitation Hall in 1905 and to an area of Blackstone Dining Hall in 1915. In 1926, Macy Memorial Library opened, and it had been expanded three times over the ensuing sixty years. With each expansion, workmen carefully removed and reinstalled the historic cathedral windows, and the original panes still overlook the chapel to the rear of the library.[99]

Berry also undertook an extensive renovation of Barnwell Chapel, part of Berry's historic district recorded in the National Register of Historic Places. The renovation effort won Berry an award from the Georgia Trust for Historic Preservation.[100] By 1987, plans were in place for a student housing complex to replace the modular housing units west of Hermann Hall, near the Ladd Center. Designed by architect Tom Spector, a Berry Academy graduate, sixteen permanent town houses were constructed on the site over the next three years, providing structures that could be used for a variety of housing purposes as needed.[101]

Good facilities and equipment were necessary to support the goals of academic instruction. Renovation of the dining hall in the Krannert Center updated that facility and brightened the students' dining environment.[102] In 1990–91, the college used approximately $2.8 million in gifts and proceeds from recent land sales to finance the installation of air-conditioning in residence halls at the Ford Buildings and on both the upper and main campuses as well as of a new heating system at Ford. Contributions from private foundations and donors made possible a $300,000 academic computer project that included the creation of three new computer laboratories, greatly expanding faculty access to improved technology.[103] The same year, the board's executive committee approved a plan submitted by a committee of students, faculty, and staff for naming campus streets to reflect the institution's heritage and natural environment.[104]

In 1996, Art Lidsky of Dober, Lidsky, Craig, and Associates of Belmont, Massachusetts, studied the extent of Berry's landholdings, the city of Rome's impact on the campus, the layout of the campus and walking distances between major buildings, the uses of the major buildings, parking, traffic flow, and the locations of sinkholes and then prepared a status report on Berry's master-planning effort. He compared Berry with thirteen other colleges and found an immediate need for more space and improved facilities, particularly with regard to the science departments. Planners considered the expansion and renovation of Cook for the sciences against advantages of a new facility in another area, and the college sought architectural advice regarding the project and costs of the alternatives. A new building was eventually constructed, and Cook was renovated to house the Charter School of Education and Human Sciences. Lidsky also advised that the college needed

an athletic and recreation center to provide space for events such as commencement, visiting speakers, sports, and student activities.[105]

The executive committee authorized the college to begin renovation of Green Hall in the summer of 1997. Other renovation projects included improving and expanding the guest cottages, moving admissions offices to the Ford Buildings, moving computing and technology offices to Hermann Hall, and making improvements in the college chapel. Work on Pilgrim Hall on the mountain campus was also on the agenda.[106]

When Martha Berry died in 1942, Berry's landholdings totaled 27,400 acres. In the ensuing thirty-nine years, Berry acquired 9,000 acres through purchase or gift but sold 8,000 acres, resulting in a net increase of just 1,000 acres by 1981. When land was sold, the income went into the endowment fund or the building fund. Timber covered 80 percent of Berry's property, and its value had more than tripled over that span, rising from $2.9 million to $9.0 million.[107] The remainder of the land had various uses: 10 percent in agriculture; 7.2 percent for campus/scenic purposes; and 2.8 percent leased for mining or agriculture.[108] The forests represented a valuable resource, producing income for operating costs not covered by student payments or gifts.

Beginning in the early 1980s, Berry engaged in a series of land transactions both large and small, sales and purchases, with a goal of achieving contiguity and meeting community needs where possible. During the early 1980s, the state Department of Transportation began planning for a north Rome bypass through Berry College property. After holding public hearings and negotiating with the college, construction began along a route that intersected with U.S. Highway 27 near the Gate of Opportunity and cut across the south end of the campus. As part of the deal, the department agreed to provide two new gates similar to the Oak Hill gate—an entrance gate on the south side of the north Rome connector where it crossed the winding driveway to Oak Hill and an exit gate on the east side of U.S. Highway 27 opposite Charlton Street, near the south line of the Oak Hill property.[109] Visitors to Oak Hill began using these gates in 1986.

In 1983, Berry agreed to allow the city of Rome to annex between seven hundred and eight hundred acres of Berry land—a strip on the southern edge of Berry's large contiguous tract lying west of the rock quarry. The city would build a road through the property and provide water and sewer services as needed for development of what became Technology Parkway and the Berry Corporate Center. Students became concerned that the development of heavy industry on the parcel would disrupt Berry's peace and tranquility; in response, the executive committee decided to give consideration to aesthetic and environmental factors and work to have the park house clean industry rather than heavy industry. The Chamber of Commerce and its director of economic development are actively marketing the park, and its current tenants include Legacy Marketing, a call center; Suzuki, a four-wheeler assembly plant; and Neaton, a manufacturer of plastic auto parts.[110]

In 1989, the Crown American Corporation of Johnstown, Pennsylvania, purchased Berry property located between the Three-Mile Road and Old Dalton Road on U.S. 27 North for the construction of the Mount Berry Square Mall.[111] In May 1992, the city of Rome purchased approximately 100 acres north of the campus and created the Stonebridge Golf Course, which opened on October 17, 1994. After discussing its development options, the college selected a plan for the construction of homes on its land in the vicinity of Stonebridge, and by April 1998, thirty-four of the sixty-two lots available in the first phase of the Berry Forest housing development had been sold. By early 2005, all of the 105 lots in Berry Forest had been sold, 96 homes

had been finished, and three were in various stages of construction. The group is now developing the Fairways, where 40 of 114 lots have been sold. The development should be complete by 2012.[112]

During the 1990s, the Berry campus was plagued by sinkholes, which had been detected during the schools' early years but had not been a problem for decades. A study conducted by Law Engineering concluded that the sinkholes might be caused by Florida Rock's quarry, and in 1992 the college asked Florida Rock to find a new location for the quarry operation so that the present quarry could be closed. Although the quarry was not closed until Florida Rock's lease expired in 2000, the company worked with Berry to attempt to minimize the number of sinkholes and paid for half the cost of some major repairs to Berry facilities necessitated by the sinkholes. Geologists reported that the problem would persist for the foreseeable future, and concerned about the safety of its employees and students as well as about unfavorable publicity, Berry's executive committee established a consulting bank of geologists, including two experts from elsewhere in the state along with Berry's consulting geologist, Richard Fountain, to guide Berry in adding to its current piezometer warning system, using state-of-the-art technology. They would look at all aspects of the situation and advise on reducing the threat of sinkholes on campus, both near term and long term. The plan also included the expansion of a campuswide safety and communication plan that would be crucial to Berry's future.[113]

Reaping the Rewards

Berry achieved national recognition in 1984–85 with its listing in *The Best Buys in College Education,* which featured 221 high-quality, low-cost colleges, as well as its listing as one of America's best undergraduate colleges in the November 1985 issue of *U.S. News and World Report. U.S. News* has subsequently continued to give Berry high marks, including a ranking of first among the South's comprehensive colleges in 2001 and as one of the "Best College Values in the South" from 1999 to 2002. Since 1985, Berry has also been recognized by *USA Today;* the *Wall Street Journal; Peterson's Competitive Colleges; Money* magazine; and Barron's *Profiles of American Colleges,* among many others. [114]

Although her health had begun to fail, Shatto continued her work on Berry's behalf and was named as one of *Georgia Trend* magazine's "100 Most Powerful and Influential Georgians" in 1996. [115] She retired at the end of the 1997–98 school year, after more than eighteen years at the school's helm, and was honored at a trustee-sponsored dinner held in Atlanta on May 6, 1998. [116] She continued to work on writing projects in an office in the Campbell School of Business, and she attended the April 1999 inauguration of her successor, Scott Colley, before she died on June 13. [117]

In his April 9, 1999, inaugural address, Scott Colley used as his theme "A Heritage of Hope—A Vision for the Future." Speaking of Martha Berry's vision, the college today, and its outlook for the future, Colley brought encouragement and renewed enthusiasm to the Berry community. Colley expressed his commitment to strengthening an institution that, guided by this mission for nearly a century, had grown into an outstanding small liberal-arts college. In his first five years, he would carry the college confidently into its second century.

CHAPTER NINE

Into the Second Century

Berry's Seventh President

On February 21, 1998, Berry's board of trustees unanimously selected Dr. John Scott Colley, provost and dean of the faculty at Hampden-Sydney College in Virginia, as Berry's seventh president. H. G. Pattillo, chair of the board, said that Colley's "exemplary experience as a faculty member, a researcher, and an administrator make him uniquely qualified to hold this position at this important juncture in Berry's history. He is a creative leader with strong academic credentials."[1]

In addition to his administrative duties at Hampden-Sydney, Colley had taught freshman writing courses, surveys of literature, humanities, and Shakespeare. He had taught in the English department at Vanderbilt University from 1968 to 1988 and had served as an associate dean and as department chair. At both Vanderbilt and Hampden-Sydney, Colley received awards for excellence in teaching and in leadership. He held a bachelors degree from Randolph-Macon College and a masters and a doctorate from the University of Chicago. His wife, Dr. Christine Colley, was an art historian and artist.[2]

Colley's presidency has seen much progress and many positive changes at Berry College, particularly in such areas as strategic planning, fund-raising, facility improvements, and faculty development and governance. In addition, under Colley's stewardship Berry has significantly enhanced its integrated education of the head, the heart, and the hands, and in 2002, the Berry community enjoyed a yearlong salute to the centennial of the school's founding, the Celebration of a Century.

Transitions

Berry's board of trustees experienced two leadership changes between 1998 and 2003. On June 30, 2000, Pattillo retired from active board membership after thirty years as a board member and five years as chair. Pattillo had served on the search committee that brought Colley to Berry and was, as Colley stated, "at every step thereafter a confidant, guide, tutor, colleague, and friend" to the new president.[3]

William B. Johnson of Atlanta took over as the board's chair on July 1, 2000, and served until May 2002. While his time at the helm was relatively brief, it was a period of tremendous progress and in-depth strategic planning for Berry's future. Johnson was succeeded by William B. Stokely III of Knoxville, Tennessee, who had served on the board since 1986. In February 2001, under Johnson's leadership, the board of trustees amended the bylaws and charter to increase the maximum number of members to twenty-three and to designate the chair of the college's board of visitors as a trustee ex officio, the same representation on the board of trustees enjoyed by the alumni association.[4]

The college's administrative leadership and structure experienced some significant changes during this period. Shortly after assuming the presidency, Colley appointed Bettyann O'Neill, assistant dean and director of external relations for Berry's Campbell School of Business, as vice president for institutional advancement. Over the next several years, O'Neill worked to enhance alumni relations, public relations, and fund-raising operations to create significant long-term support for the college.

Changes in academic affairs included the 1999 appointment of Dr. Kathy McKee, professor of communication, to succeed Dr. Ouida Dickey as dean of academic services and the 2000 appointment of Dr. Thomas Dasher, dean of the College of Arts and Sciences at Valdosta State University, to succeed Dr. Doyle Mathis as provost. Mathis had led academics at Berry College for twenty-five years and was designated provost emeritus and subsequently professor of government emeritus. Dickey retired after serving the school in a variety of capacities for forty-three

John Scott Colley, Berry's president since 1998, 1998.

years and was designated dean of academic services and professor of business emerita. In 2003, responsibility for admissions was transferred to the dean of academic services, and the admissions office began a variety of initiatives to reach out to prospective students.[5] McKee added the role of associate provost to her other duties in the spring of 2001. Also in 2003, Brian Erb, associate vice president for financial systems and services and associate treasurer of Gettysburg College, succeeded Joe Walton, who had served Berry at various levels for thirty-five years, as vice president for finance and corporate treasurer.[6]

Strategic Planning

In 2000, the board of trustees' Strategic Planning and Resources Committee, chaired by Thomas Fanning, became engaged in a collaborative effort with Berry's Planning Council, chaired by McKee, to chart the college's course for the next decade.[7] The 2002–12 strategic plan, *Renewing Our Mission,* was drafted with input from all segments of the Berry community—faculty, staff, students, and alumni—and after approval from the Planning Council and the Faculty Assembly, the board officially adopted the plan in December 2001.[8] *Renewing Our Mission* included redrafted mission, purpose, and values statements as well as a vision statement for the future that spoke of achieving "national distinction for a balanced and integrated education of the head, the heart, and the hands that provides students a solid foundation for life and the inspiration to serve others." The revised mission statement, incorporating elements of earlier ones, added new focus on community and civic betterment: "Berry College is a comprehensive liberal-arts college with Christian values. The college furthers our students' intellectual, moral and spiritual growth; proffers lessons that are gained from worthwhile work done well; and challenges them to devote their learning to community and civic betterment. Berry emphasizes an educational program committed to high academic standards, values based on Christian principles, practical work experience and community service in a distinctive environment of natural beauty. It is Berry's goal to make an excellent liberal-arts education accessible to talented students from a wide range of social and economic backgrounds."[9]

Fanning well articulated the college administration's approach to the future: "One of the opportunities presented before us now, at the advent of Berry College's next 100 years, is to celebrate and build upon the great foundation laid by the ideals of head, heart, and hands. At the same time, we must project those ideals forward into a contemporary setting. Our challenge is to retain what is distinctive about Berry while embracing an ever-more diverse world that requires us to think and act on an ever-broadening scale."[10]

Renewing Our Mission includes twelve goals that fall within six basic areas: international learning for faculty and students; a student-centered culture of personal and intellectual growth; ethnic and geographic diversity in an open and welcoming environment; technology; financial and physical asset management; and fund-raising in support of strategic objectives.[11] In May 2002, the board approved benchmarks to help measure progress in achieving the goals and objectives of the strategic plan, and a year later the college launched a Web site to chart publicly the school's progress toward those benchmarks.[12]

Fund-Raising

In 1998, Barnes and Roche of Rosemont, Pennsylvania, conducted a feasibility study that found that Berry College was unprepared to enter a fund-raising campaign of the magnitude required to support college needs. A restructured advancement division showed promise, however, and on July 1, 1999, Berry College began the silent phase of a fund-raising campaign of yet-to-be-determined scope.

Following the implementation of the strategic plan, immediate priorities for fund-raising were clarified. The Campaign Executive Steering Committee was formed, chaired by alumnus W. Glenn Cornell, chair of the board of trustees' advancement committee. In 2002, reassessment of the college's ability to raise significant funds produced a positive result, and in August of that year the campaign committee voted to go public on October 5 with a $100 million campaign, an effort of unprecedented size and scope for Berry College. A total of $60 million in gifts and pledges was already in hand when the Century Campaign was announced at an elegant dinner on the grounds of Oak Hill.[13] Contributions to this first phase included $10 million from an anonymous foundation for the science center, $5 million from an anonymous donor to renovate the Cook Building to serve as the new home for the Charter School of Education and Human Sciences, $9.4 million from the Ford Motor Company Fund for renovation of the Ford Buildings, and $3.2 million from an anonymous donor for international learning initiatives.[14]

Campaign priorities included building renovations and construction, technology enhancements, and endowed funds in support of international learning, diversity, a lecture series, and extracurricular learning opportunities. The priorities also included increased support for student scholarships and the student work program. The two largest projects were a twenty-five million dollar student athletic and recreation center and a twenty million dollar endowment for the college's new math and science building.[15]

Faculty Expansion and Empowerment

Between 1997–98 and 2002–3, Berry's full-time equivalent faculty increased from 130.3 to 166.1, and the student-faculty ratio decreased from 15 to 1 to 11.8 to 1. Over that span, the percentage of full-time teaching faculty in the professorial ranks (the top three ranks) holding doctorates increased from 93.5 percent to 95.3 percent. These data demonstrate Colley's and the institution's focus on the faculty and students as prime areas for achieving the goals of academic excellence.[16]

During the first year of Colley's term, a committee of faculty met regularly with the president, the provost, and the deans to exchange ideas for becoming the best educators possible. Administrators and faculty alike felt that morale among the faculty reached an all-time high.[17] The Faculty Council had been disbanded toward the end of Gloria Shatto's presidency, and faculty were searching for a way to reconstitute a faculty forum. At the end of the 1998–99 academic year, faculty members charged their

executive committee with drafting a new constitution for a faculty senate. Although the senate idea was not approved, discussions led to the creation of the Faculty Assembly, which the faculty and president approved. The change gave a voice to all faculty members, including adjuncts, librarians, and administrators, and resulted in a 14 percent reduction in the number of college committees.[18] To provide a forum at which faculty members could discuss issues of concern without administrators' involvement, faculty colloquiums were instituted. The minutes for these colloquiums are circulated with all comments unattributed so that participants can freely express their opinions.[19]

Reestablishment of department-chair positions, which had been eliminated in the early 1990s, represented another significant change during the first years of Colley's presidency. One faculty member observed that department chairs would know their faculty's needs, and Dasher, in his first year as provost, thought that having someone in that role would bring about a greater sense of collegiality and mutual support, thereby benefiting students.[20] The board of trustees approved the concept, and it was implemented in August 2001.[21] Faculty members in twenty departments selected chairs to serve three-year terms, working with the deans and the faculty in curriculum development, faculty evaluation and mentoring, and academic governance.

Innovative ways to support faculty members were implemented over the 1998–2003 period. In 2000, for example, faculty summer international travel/research grants were initiated and have since received additional support through the generosity of an anonymous donor. More than two dozen faculty members have spent a month abroad through this program, and all returned excited about the experience, determined to infuse that excitement into their teaching and research, and able to advance individual research projects.

Thus, the hallmarks of the Colley administration have been the stabilization of the faculty, the establishment of an effective shared-governance system, and support for faculty development as members of the Berry and professional communities. Through effective, consistent evaluation and strong communication, faculty and staff across the campus have become much more committed to the institution's mission and to maximizing educational opportunities for all students.

Improving Facilities

Some of the most dramatic changes at Berry during Colley's first five years have been improvements in physical facilities. Two new structures have been added to the campus, several existing buildings have undergone extensive renovations and repairs, and productive new uses have been found for historic structures.

Already in progress when Colley arrived were renovations of Green Hall and the Martha Berry Museum. Between 1997 and 1999, Green Hall, home of the Campbell School of Business, was totally refurbished and provided with state-of-the-art technology. The extensive museum project produced exhibits that carry visitors from Martha Berry's early life to Berry College today.[22]

In June 1999, the college broke ground for a science building, the first new structure on Berry's campus in three decades. The need was so great that for the first time in Berry's history, the board of trustees decided to use bond funding to construct a new academic building. The 130,000-square-foot structure, opened for use in January 2001, was designed to support a discovery-based, hands-on curriculum that strongly emphasizes student-faculty collaboration. The facility features thirty faculty-student team laboratories; nineteen lecture classrooms; eighteen laboratory classrooms; a two-hundred-seat multimedia auditorium; three greenhouses; a robotics lab; specialized laboratories for aquatics, tissue culture, and microscopy/image analysis; and specialized instrumentation.[23]

The opening of the science building paved the way for renovation of the Cook Building, former home of math and science, as the dedicated facility for the Charter School of Education and Human Sciences. The improvements were designed to complement and support the school's new technology-enhanced curriculum and included large classrooms that enable team teaching and/or observation, small seminar rooms, and two classrooms for use by sixth-, seventh-, and eighth-graders at Berry College Middle School.[24] Renovations were completed in time for the fall semester of 2002.

After the relocation of all education and psychology faculty, staff, and classes into the Cook Building, Evans Hall again provided dedicated space for the Evans School of Humanities and Social Sciences. This move fulfilled a goal of having a central facility to serve as a foundation for learning for each of Berry's four schools.[25]

Announced on Founder's Day 2001, the $9.4 million grant from the Ford Motor Company Fund represented the largest grant in Berry's history and powerfully reaffirmed the historical ties between the schools and the Ford Motor Company.[26] The project started in mid-2001 and was completed in 2004 and included many structural repairs and improvements, with stonework performed by Ronald Cescutti of Rome; his son, Ronald Cescutti Jr.; and an apprentice, Jody Gordon. The Cescuttis are the descendants of the original stonemasons, Antonio and Ettori Cescutti, whom Henry Ford brought from Italy to construct the Ford Buildings.[27]

As part of the Ford renovations, the first-floor wing to the right of the Ford Buildings' main archway became the Berry Alumni Center, an elegant, fourteen-thousand-square-foot center made poss-

Joe Walton, vice president for finance, in front of the state-of-the-art Science Building at the time of its opening in 2001.

ible by donations from two alumni families.[28] Opened officially on Founder's Day 2003, the center includes a variety of meeting rooms as well as graceful living, dining, and sitting areas. It is furnished with antiques from the Martha Berry Museum collection.[29]

An unexpected renovation began in 1999 when sinkholes were discovered under the north end of the Krannert Center. Damage caused by the sinkholes was extensive, and repairs were long and difficult. The college took the opportunity to refurbish the entire structure, creating a modern, first-class student center.[30]

In 2001, the Rollins Center was renovated and renamed the Rollins Center for Ruminant Research, bringing all dairy, beef cattle, and sheep operations together. The project included the creation of a so-phisticated, computerized dairy and supported curricular changes designed to emphasize research in dairy science rather than production.[31]

These changes in the animal-science program left the historic Normandy Buildings on the Mountain Campus largely unused. In April 2001, however, the college and the Chick-fil-A-sponsored WinShape Foundation announced plans to redevelop the Normandy Buildings into a retreat facility, with funding provided by the foundation.[32] Phase 1 of the project transformed the complex into a seventy-eight-thousand-square-foot, three-hundred-person retreat facility that hosts marriage-enrichment, church, and corporate retreats during Berry's academic year and the WinShape summer camp for girls when school is not in session. In addition to renovation of the dairy structures, two new buildings that were part of Martha Berry's original plans for the complex but were never built were also constructed. Phase 2 of the project will focus on improvements to the retreat center's grounds and recreational areas and will include the construction of a new auditorium.[33] The college and the WinShape Foundation also shared expenses for a covered arena at the Gunby Equestrian Center and a paved walking/biking path that runs parallel to the three-mile road connecting Berry's main and mountain campuses.[34]

The final building project of Colley's first five years was a new residence hall, which opened in the fall of 2003. The 58,800-square-foot structure houses 122 students in apartment-like suites.

Educating the Head

Berry's undergraduate academic program in 2002–3 included bachelor of arts, bachelor of music, and bachelor of science degrees. Thirty-eight majors were offered with minors in thirty-seven areas. Also available were dual-degree programs with the Emory University School of Nursing, Georgia Tech, and the Mercer University School of Engineering. Graduate programs offered masters degrees in business administration and education and an educational specialist degree.[35]

In 2003, *U.S. News and World Report* ranked Berry among the South's best small colleges for the seventeenth time in eighteen years. Berry was ranked second among undergraduate comprehensive colleges in the twelve-state southern region, a drop from Berry's first-place finish in 2002. *U.S. News* also listed Berry third among its "Best Values."[36] In 2002, the college received approval to establish a chapter of Phi Kappa Phi, one of the largest and most prestigious U.S. honor societies, recognizing individuals in all disciplines who exemplify academic excellence and good character.[37]

In 1998–99, Berry received high marks in its accreditation review conducted by the Commission on Colleges of the Southern Association of Colleges and Schools. Also that year, the Campbell School of Business began the five-year process of accreditation by the Association to Advance Collegiate Schools of Business, the blue-ribbon accrediting organization for business programs. The Campbell School implemented a new curriculum in 1997–98 that stressed business ethics and global management issues. Twenty-one northwest Georgia business leaders were recruited for a new executive advisory council that would help identify ways the school could meet the area's business community's needs.[38]

In 1998–99, Berry's writing and rhetoric program, begun ten years earlier as Writing across the Curriculum, underwent revisions and received renewed emphasis as a writing-intensive program to promote excellence in writing and thinking. A new interdisciplinary major in environmental sciences blended traditional science courses with economics, political science, and environmental ethics and utilized the college campus as a learning laboratory.[39] The agriculture department offered a major and a minor in animal science, with a new curriculum unveiled in January 2001; a curriculum in preveterinary medicine; and a developing curriculum in plant science.[40] Although programs in family and consumer sciences and athletic training were no longer offered to incoming students at the end of 1998–99, child-development and coaching minors were available.[41] Family sciences ultimately became a minor, blending family, business, psychology, and sociology courses. Health and physical education began to focus only on teacher preparation as a major and coaching as a minor.[42]

The Charter School of Education and Human Sciences spent 1998–99 redefining its approach to teacher education, thanks to three-year funding from the BellSouth Foundation. The school then launched a new curriculum designed to prepare teachers for the twenty-first century.[43] The Atlanta-based Goizueta Foundation aided the Charter School's efforts to help teachers excel in a multi-cultural environment with a $1.5 million grant to provide scholarships for Hispanic and Latino students and with funds to incorporate instructional-technology improvements.[44] The Charter School's accreditation by the National Council for Accreditation of Teacher Education was reaffirmed in 1999–2000. The program received a strong vote of confidence when the head of the council's visiting team remarked that he had never encountered a better teacher-preparation program.[45]

In the spring of 2000, Berry unveiled a new core course required for all students. "*E Pluribus Unum: Moments in American Democracy*" was designed to take students on a journey to discover the foundations of American civilization in all its diversity.[46]

The following spring, the Council on Student Scholarship sponsored the first annual Symposium on Student Scholarship to highlight and encourage student scholarship at Berry. Student representatives from all departments presented papers, posters, and performances. The two-day symposium was popular and became an annual event, with more than seventy participants in 2002 and more than eighty a year later.[47]

In 2001, the Center for Teaching Excellence was created to support teaching and learning by hosting discussions among faculty, offering presentations on innovations in teaching, and offering summer grants for course development.[48] The same year, the Academic Support Center was created to work with the Counseling Center to help students with special needs by offering student workshops, coordinating tutorials, and assisting physically disabled students with necessary accommodations, such as wheelchair-accessible doors.[49]

During the early part of Colley's tenure, participation in study-abroad programs grew dramat-ically from 53 students in 1999–2000 to 130 in 2002–3.[50] In addition to traditional semester-abroad experiences in a wide variety of countries, May-term programs have become popular. The biology department now offers alternating summer-term programs in Costa Rica and Belize; education majors take part in required cultural-immersion experiences in countries such as Costa Rica, Greece, Italy, and Mexico as well as in cultural-pocket areas of the United States; and an exchange program with the Women's University of Seoul, Korea, has been initiated. Teacher-education students also have opportunities to perform student teaching abroad through the Consortium for Overseas Student Teaching.[51]

Educating the Heart

In 2003, a full-time chaplain and thirteen student organizations supported the college's religion-in-life emphasis. Concerns over a Berry College Chapel program involving speakers of various faiths after the September 11 terrorist attacks in 2001 gave rise to what will no doubt be a continuing debate on Berry's role as a Christian institution in a diverse community. The 2002–3 establishment of the Interfaith Council had its basis in the 2002–12 strategic plan, which stated, "The college remains dedicated to the interdenominational Christian values on which it was founded and welcomes individuals of diverse backgrounds into the campus community."[52]

Through an adjunct to the chaplain's office, the Office of Volunteer Services, the college encourages all sanctioned student organizations to participate in community service. An annual Freshman Service Day was inaugurated in 1998–99 as a way to introduce Berry's newest students to the college's commitment to service and its motto, "Not to be ministered unto, but to minister." More than four hundred students, faculty, staff, and alumni spent a Saturday volunteering with Rome-area service agencies.[53]

Students Becky Stoll and Gina Croft on Freshman Service Day, 1999.

One student group that received local, regional, and national attention in 2002 was Berry College Viking Athletes Bettering the Community. The club's service-day projects were highlighted on the Web sites of the National Association of Intercollegiate Athletics (NAIA) and the TranSouth Conference as well as in the *Rome News-Tribune*.[54] Another group, Students in Free Enterprise, whose major focus was service through business education, finished in first place in regional competition in 2001, 2002, and 2003 and was first runner-up in the nationwide competition in 2003.[55]

In 2002–3, 150 Berry students volunteered as mentors for local schoolchildren, and more than 130 students spent a portion of their Saturdays staffing the Berry Community Kitchen, Rome's only weekend free-lunch program, which Berry students started in 2001. In addition, hundreds of students annually have taken part in Make a Difference Day and other special projects, such as Potato Drop 2002, in which Berry students bagged and loaded thirty-five thousand pounds of potatoes for distribution to local food pantries.[56]

In 2003, through ongoing support of the Bertram F. and Corella Bonner Foundation, Berry College established the Bonner Center for Community Service. In addition to overseeing the work of the Bonner scholars, who receive scholarships based on their ongoing dedication to community service and who perform nearly forty thousand hours of such service each year, the Bonner Center began coordinating all of the college's community-service efforts. Early areas of focus included working with Berry faculty to explore how community-service efforts could be more fully integrated into the college's curriculum and working with student activities staff to develop a program to train students in leadership development.[57]

Educating the Hands

While Berry's work-opportunity program remains a source of financial aid and of workers for campus operations, important changes have been made. Two goals of the 2002–12 strategic plan directly address work at Berry, calling for improved work opportunities that would allow students to learn from an increasing variety of hands-on experiences and about work's roles in self and society. These goals also stress high standards for student-work performance and emphasize expansion of work opportunities related to areas of academic concentration.[58]

Throughout this period, increasing numbers of students held work positions that provided direct experience in their areas of study. For example, the Berry Information Technology Students program, which was piloted in 1998 and launched in 1999 with donor assistance, provides valuable training and practical work experience by having information-technology students provide computer support to the campus community.[59] Equally important, the college sought to expand the number of work positions that coincided with students' interest in service. Students work as directors of volunteer services, linking Berry students with community agencies in need.

At any given time, the college continues to provide work to approximately 80 percent of its students in approximately 120 job classifications. Students who work ten or more hours a week for at least half of their semesters at Berry receive certificates of work along with their diplomas. Each spring, those students who demonstrate an outstanding work ethic receive the O. Wayne Rollins Work Award. The Founder's Work Program, designed to meet the needs of students from middle-income families by alternating terms of full-time work with full-time study, enables these students to finish their education in five years free of tuition debt.[60]

From their earliest years, the mission of the Berry Schools and Berry College has been based on academics, religion, and work. Established during the Progressive Era, the precollegiate schools supported Progressive ideals such as character, honor, and service.[61] Despite the fact that the college still gives special attention to a service or heart component and certainly has placed increasing importance on academic excellence in recent decades, for much of its history Berry has been recognized primarily for its work program. If Berry may be said

Make a Difference Day, part of Berry's emphasis on community service, 2002.

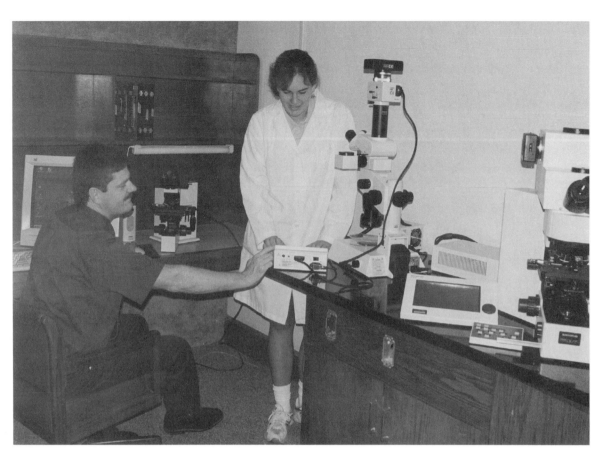

Student Eve Raburn with Dr. Bruce Conn in biology research laboratory, 2001.

to have an organizational saga as described by Burton Clark in his study of Antioch, Reed, and Swarthmore, the on-campus work program represents just one component.[62]

In 1987, the Ford Foundation sponsored self-study conferences for Alice Lloyd, Berea, Blackburn, the School (now College) of the Ozarks, and Warren Wilson, at the time the nation's only four-year colleges requiring on-campus labor for all undergraduate students. Work earnings help keep student costs low, and the mandatory nature of the work programs minimizes class distinctions. The work colleges are viewed as lamps of educational opportunity for disadvantaged rural students.[63] These five colleges have continued their mandatory on-campus work programs into the early twenty-first century.

Berry, which had a mandatory on-campus work program for more than six decades, dropped its work requirement in the 1960s, although most undergraduates continue to participate in the program for at least a part of their college careers. Berry is unique among the traditional work colleges because it has continued to emphasize on-campus work while shifting from a mandatory to a quite successful voluntary work program.

Another study of college student-work programs conducted in the early 1980s included these five colleges as well as Berry College and Alabama's Oakwood College. The criteria for inclusion on this list were a work program in operation for more than half the life of the institution and a majority of enrolled students participating in a work program with an educational mission. This study concluded that the work programs generally began out of economic necessity but now contribute significantly to students' education.[64]

The members of the Work Colleges Consortium, the current work-college association headquartered at Berea, include Alice Lloyd; Berea; Blackburn; College of the Ozarks; Sterling, a Vermont college with fewer than one hundred students established in the latter part of the twentieth century; and Warren Wilson. Deep Springs College, founded in California early in the twentieth century but now with only about two dozen students, is an associate member. The consortium lists Berry College and Knoxville College of Tennessee as institutions sharing the culture and benefits of work colleges, although they do not belong to the organization.[65]

Campus Life

A wide variety of activities and involvements continue to challenge Berry students and encourage them to develop their full potential. Berry students have excelled in activities including athletics, forensics, the College Bowl, the Model Arab League, the Model United Nations, the student newspaper, Students in Free Enterprise, and equestrian competitions.

In 1999, Michelle Abernathy received her twelfth NAIA All-American award at the NAIA Outdoor Track and Field National Championships in Florida, becoming the most decorated athlete in Berry history. In 2000–2001 Berry athletes claimed numerous individual and team honors as well as academic honors, including ten Academic All-Americans and three NAIA All-Americans. Kurt Swanbeck, men's soccer coach, became the winningest coach in Viking soccer's thirty-eight-year history.[66] During 2002–3, eight Berry teams won TranSouth Conference titles and participated in

NAIA national championship tournaments. For the first time in the college's history, Berry sent five women's teams to championship tournaments—cross country, soccer, basketball, golf, and tennis—and won the TranSouth Conference all-sports trophy.[67]

The Berry campus provided the setting for parts of several major motion pictures, including *Remember the Titans* in 1999 and *Sweet Home Alabama* in 2001. The presence of the movie crews provided excitement as well as valuable experience for students fortunate enough to secure working positions on the productions.

Celebrating a Century

In the spring of 1999, Colley appointed a committee, cochaired by Ouida Dickey and Scott Breithaupt and including faculty, staff, student, alumni, and trustee representatives, to begin planning for Berry's centennial. The yearlong celebration was kicked off by a gala dinner on January 12, 2002, at the Ritz Carlton in Atlanta. A special Founder's Day service and activities followed on campus the next day.

A variety of on- and off-campus events were held throughout the year. The Centennial Road Show, headlined by Colley, shared historical exhibits, speakers, and a video on the twenty-first-century Berry with alumni and other friends of the college in twenty-five southeastern U.S. cities. Several individual alumni and classes developed a gallery of portraits of Berry's seven presidents and two acting presidents to hang in the front of the Berry College Library.

A generous alumnus sponsored a student essay contest on the question, "How should Berry's threefold mission to educate the head, the heart, and the hands be realized in the college's second century?" Winners included Autumn Hostetter's "Keeping the Gate of Opportunity Open: Berry College in the

Berry tennis player Sven Plass (shown here in 2002), a native of Darmstadt, Germany, was named NAIA National Senior Player of the Year by the Intercollegiate Tennis Association in 2004.

Twenty-first Century" (first place), Michael Morrell's "Sailing the Great Ship Berry: Steady Waters and Changes from One Century to Another" (second), Michael Rupert's "Educating the Souls of Tomorrow" (third), and John Coleman's "Ministering in a New Millennium" (fourth).[68]

The centennial program also included a spring "Appalachia in Context" speakers series; a fall "Humanitarianism in Context" speakers series; regilding of the library dome; a wildflower beautification project along Martha Berry Highway (U.S. 27) by the Mount Berry Garden Club in cooperation with the Georgia Department of Transportation; a U.S. Post Office postal cancellation issued on January 13, 2002; production of the original multimedia musical *Martha!* by alumnus James Way; and a wide variety of other events on campus and in the local commu-

nity. Dr. Stanley Pethel, fine-arts department chair, composed a centennial anthem, "I Will Lift Up My Eyes," which debuted on Founder's Day 2002.

The centennial celebration ended on Founder's Day 2003. In recognition of the year's events, the college subsequently received a silver medal in the Council for Advancement and Support of Education's National Circle of Excellence Awards in the special events category for institutional relations.[69]

Continuing the Vision and the Hope

At Berry, 1998–2003 constituted a period of growth and positive movement toward the goal of academic excellence. Writing to faculty and staff in January 2003, Colley pointed out, "no one would deny that we have challenges of our own. We also have our

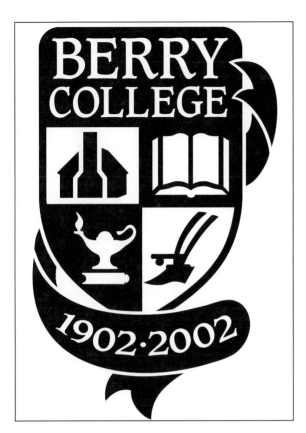

Berry's centennial logo.

triumphs." Citing a sterling reputation, new facilities, growing international-studies programs, and speakers and special programs that contribute to the campus's remarkable cultural and intellectual vitality, the president observed, "it is a grand time for us and the college."[70]

Berry College's goal of making an excellent liberal-arts education accessible to talented students from a wide range of social and economic backgrounds has become a reality. During the first hundred years of its existence, the institution became competitive with other private institutions in the South while strengthening its threefold mission of educating the head, the heart, and the hands of every student for a life of worthwhile service.[71] In her 2002 remarks to the College Board National Forum, First Lady Laura Bush cited Martha Berry as an example of someone who believed that all children should have an opportunity to go to school and who dedicated her life to that belief. Educators, said Bush, should "reaffirm the hope of Martha Berry that education will always be the right of every man, woman and child who lives in the promise of America and for the promise of a greater tomorrow."[72] With its firmer-than-ever foundation, Berry College is carrying that hope into a new century.

Important Dates in the Life of Martha Berry and the Development of Her Schools

1821	September 21, Thomas Berry (father) born in Tennessee.
1838	July 30, Frances Margaret Rhea (mother) born in Alabama.
1860	April 11, Thomas Berry and Frances Margaret Rhea marry in Alabama, live in Turkeytown area of Cherokee County (now Etowah County), Alabama.
1866	July 23, Thomas Berry buys first real estate in Floyd County, Georgia, on Howard Street (now Second Avenue). October 7, MB born in Alabama (according to MB; some sources put her birth in 1865).
1871	July 7, Thomas Berry purchases property including original part of house now known as Oak Hill.
c. 1900	MB begins Sunday schools and day schools in Rome area.
1902	January 13, Boys Industrial School founded on Lower Campus.
1903	Boys Industrial School incorporated by order of the judge of the Superior Court of Floyd County; MB deeds eighty-three acres of land to Boys Industrial School.
1908	Corporate charter amended, legal name changed to the Berry School; alumni association established.
1909	Thanksgiving Day, Martha Berry School for Girls opens on Log Cabin Campus.
1910	President Theodore Roosevelt visits Berry.
1914	First Mountain Day.
1916	School for boys started on Mountain Campus at foot of Lavender Mountain.
1917	Corporate charter amended, legal name changed to the Berry Schools.
1920	MB receives honorary doctor of pedagogy degree, University of Georgia.
1922	Berry Schools accredited by Southern Association of Colleges and Secondary Schools.
1923	Henry and Clara Ford first visit the school.
1924	MB elected to the National Institute of Social Sciences; MB named distinguished citizen of the state by the Georgia General Assembly.
1925	MB receives Roosevelt Medal, Roosevelt Memorial Association, presented by President Calvin Coolidge.
1925–31	Ford Buildings completed.
1926	Berry Junior College established with G. Leland Green as first president.
1927	MB obtains remaining ownership of Oak Hill; MB deeds Oak Hill to the Berry Schools.
1928	First junior-college class, twelve students, graduates.

1929	Berry Junior College accredited by Southern Association of Colleges and Secondary Schools.
1930	Berry (senior) College established; MB receives honorary doctor of laws degree, University of North Carolina; MB included on Ida Tarbell's list of America's fifty greatest women.
1931	MB voted one of America's Twelve Greatest Women, *Good Housekeeping* magazine contest.
1932	MB appointed to Board of Regents, University System of Georgia; first senior-college class, seventeen students, receives degrees.
1933	MB receives Eleanor Van Rensselaer Fairfax Biennial Medal for patriotic service to America, Colonial Dames of America; MB receives honorary doctor of laws degree, Bates College; MB receives honorary doctor of humanities degree, Berry College.
1934	MB received at the Court of St. James's by King George V and Queen Mary.
1935	MB receives doctor of public service degree, Oglethorpe University; MB receives doctor of laws degree, Duke University.
1936	MB receives doctor of letters degree, Oberlin College.
1937	MB receives doctor of laws degree, University of Wisconsin; MB appointed member of Georgia State Planning Board.
1939	MB receives American Institute of Social Science Medal.
1942	February 27, Martha Berry dies, Saint Joseph's Hospital, Atlanta; M. Gordon Keown becomes acting director of the Berry Schools.
1944	Dr. William Jesse Baird becomes Berry's second president.
1946	Dr. James Armour Lindsay becomes Berry's third president.
1951	Dr. Samuel Henry Cook becomes Berry's acting president.
1953	Dr. Robert Stanley Lambert becomes Berry's fourth president.
1955	William McChesney Martin Jr., chairman of the board of trustees, becomes Berry's acting president.
1956	May, High School for Girls closes. Dr. John R. Bertrand becomes Berry's fifth president.
1957	Berry College accredited by Southern Association of Colleges and Schools.
1959	First international student admitted.
1961	Board approves modification of the two-day work requirement; day students allowed to enroll.
1962	Calendar changed to quarter system; student uniforms abolished.
1964	First African American students enroll; name of Mount Berry School for Boys changed to Berry Academy.
1968	First meeting of board of visitors held.
1969	Chapel attendance requirement abolished.
1971	Girls first enroll at Berry Academy as day students.
1972	Master of education degree instituted.
1973	Master of business administration degree instituted.
1980	Dr. Gloria Shatto becomes Berry's sixth president.
1981	Martha Berry's portrait hung in Georgia State Capitol's Gallery of Distinguished Georgians.
1983	Berry Academy closes.
1984	Chick-fil-A/Berry College partnership established; WinShape Centre established on Mountain Campus.
1985	Berry College first listed in national college rankings by such publications as *U.S. News and World Report* and the *New York Times;* Alumni Work Week tradition established; education specialist program instituted.
1989	Calendar changed to semester system.
1991	Berry named to *Peterson's Guide to Competitive Colleges;* Berry College reorganized into four academic schools.

1992	Martha Berry inducted into Georgia Women of Achievement Hall of Fame.
1993	Berry's first Rhodes Scholar named.
1996	School of Business endowed through the Laura Berry Campbell Trust; Berry serves as site of summer 1996 International Olympic Youth Camp.
1998	Dr. Scott Colley becomes Berry's seventh president.
2000	MB named one of "100 Georgians of the [Twentieth] Century" by *Georgia Trend* magazine.
2002	MB inducted into University of Georgia's Agriculture Hall of Fame.

Berry Trustees

Chairmen

John J. Eagan, 1902–24
Robert C. Alston, 1924–38
John Bulow Campbell, 1938–40
John A. Sibley, 1940–55
William McChesney Martin Jr., 1955–73
William R. Bowdoin, 1973–83
James M. Sibley, 1983–89
H. Inman Allen, 1989–95
H. G. Pattillo, 1995–2000
William B. Johnson, 2000–2002
William B. Stokely III, 2002–

Members

Martha Berry, 1902–42
Thomas Berry, 1902–29
J. Paul Cooper, 1902–21
John J. Eagan, 1902–24
John H. Reynolds, 1902–11
Henry L. Higginson, 1909–19
Moses R. Wright, 1902–25
Hoke Smith, 1906–10
Frank R. Chambers, 1908–42
Henry S. Johnson Sr., 1908–23
Joseph K. Orr, 1908–39
V. Everit Macy, 1909–15
Albert Shaw, 1909–47

George W. Perkins, 1910–20
Robert F. Maddox, 1911–57
Marion M. Jackson, 1914–33
James R. McWane, 1914–33
Walter G. Ladd, 1916–24
Hamilton Steward, 1916–26
G. Lister Carlisle Jr., 1917–54
M. Gordon Keown, 1921–56
M. Standish Meacham, 1921–35
William L. McKee, 1921–47
W. W. Orr, 1921–27
Robert C. Alston, 1923–38
Harcourt A. Morgan, 1923–50
J. Bulow Campbell, 1924–40
Valentine E. Macy Jr., 1924–35
Robert W. Woodruff, 1924–67
R. Fulton Cutting, 1928–34
S. F. Boykin, 1935–54
Sam Finley, 1935–42
John A. Sibley, 1935–55
George W. Winship, 1936–56
W. Warren Moise, 1937–59
Harmon W. Caldwell, 1940–67
Nelson Macy Jr., 1940–64
Lamar Westcott, 1940–71
Virginia Campbell Courts, 1943–77
Philip Weltner, 1943–56
William McChesney Martin Jr., 1946–77

James G. K. McClure, 1952–56

John C. Warr, 1952–69

Inez Wooten Henry, 1957–79

Pollard Turman, 1957–58

William R. Bowdoin, 1960–84

Richard Edgerton, 1960–82

L. Johnson Head, 1960–2001

Howell Hollis, 1960–91

A. W. Ledbetter, 1960–64

John W. Maddox, 1960–70

Arthur N. Morris, 1960–85

Lee Price Jr., 1960–62

Alex P. Gaines, 1964–90

Walter H. Mann, 1964–81

Julian McGowin, 1964–73

John J. McDonough, 1965–83

Harold Clotfelter, 1967–79

James M. Sibley, 1967–90

H. G. Pattillo, 1970–2000

Benjamin F. Wardlow, 1970–81

Frank Barron Jr., 1971–2002

O. Wayne Rollins, 1973–83

Bernard Storey, 1973–84

Roy Richards, 1974–85

Gloria Shatto, 1975–80

Robert E. Shaw, 1977–2002

H. Inman Allen, 1978–96

Clinton G. Ames Jr., 1978–92

Gaynelle Grizzard, 1978–92

Helen S. Worden, 1980–92

Chester A. Roush Jr., 1982–93

David C. Garrett Jr., 1983–86

R. Randall Rollins, 1983–92

A. Worley Brown, 1984–94

Percy Marchman, 1984–93

Bernard M. Fauber, 1985–92

J. Paul Ferguson, 1985–

William B. Johnson, 1985–

R. Earl Roberson, 1985–98

Edward L. Addison, 1986–95

L. P. Roberts, 1986–

William B. Stokely III, 1986–

Joel R. Wells Jr., 1987–91

Joseph E. Antonini, 1988–95

James H. Blanchard, 1991–94

Chester W. Diercks Jr., 1992–97

Edward P. Gould, 1992–97

John A. Williams, 1992–94

Kenneth W. Cannestra, 1993–99

Alice Richards, 1993–2002

Paul J. DeNicola, 1993–99

W. Joseph Biggers, 1994–99

Drayton Nabers Jr., 1994–2001

W. Glenn Cornell, 1995–

Carl Swearingen, 1995–2003

Gregory T. Baranco, 1998–

Karen Holley Horrell, 1998–

Robert W. Browning, 1999–2002

Thomas A. Fanning, 1999–

Terry A. Graham, 1999–

Burl T. Horton, 2000–

William H. Rogers Jr., 2000–

Dan T. Cathy, 2001–

Martha Berry Walstad, 2001–

G. Bert Clark, 2002–

J. Barry Griswell, 2003–

Steven J. Cage, 2003–

Harold Kilpatrick, 2005–

Chief Administrative Officers and Chief Academic Officers

Chief Administrative Officers

Martha Berry, director, 1902–42

G. Leland Green, president, 1926–44

M. Gordon Keown, acting director, 1942–44

William Jesse Baird, president, 1944–46

James Armour Lindsay, president, 1946–51

S. H. Cook, acting president, 1951–53

Robert S. Lambert, president, 1953–55

William McChesney Martin Jr., acting president, 1955–56

John R. Bertrand, president, 1956–79

Gloria Shatto, president, 1980–98

Scott Colley, president, 1998–

Chief Academic Officers

G. Leland Green, 1926–44

S. H. Cook, 1944–57

O. N. Darby, 1957–59

Robert C. Whitford, 1959–60

John R. Timmerman, 1960–69

Thomas W. Gandy, 1969–71

William C. Moran, 1971–75

Doyle Mathis, 1975–2000

Thomas E. Dasher, 2000–

Berry Alumni Association Presidents

W. Clayton Henson (1904H), 1908–15

M. Gordon Keown (1905H), 1915–23

Walter A. Johnson (1912H), 1923–26

B. W. Romefelt (1917H), 1927

Eugene Gunby (1919H), 1928

Allen J. Ammons (1909H), 1929

Haskell C. Stratton (1921H), 1930

Starrett D. Copeland (1908H), 1931

Charles H. Higgins Sr. (1910H), 1932

Chelsie H. Barker Jr. (1930C), 1933

Thomas H. Wheelis (1929H), 1934–35

Clarence N. Walker (1914H), 1936

Bryan L. Brown (1924H), 1937

J. Theodore Phillips (1929H, 1933C), 1938

Starling S. Smith (1915H), 1939

Henry W. Gheesling (1937C), 1940

Mack G. Hicks (1921H), 1941–43

Neil Andrews (1914H), 1944

Sam W. Gray (1924H), 1945–46

Harvey F. Roberts (1936C), 1947

John C. Warr (1937C), 1948–49

Walter L. Russell (1942C), 1950–51

H. G. Hamrick (1912H), 1952

Reavis Sproull (1930JC), 1953–54

Thomas W. Gandy (1939H, 1942C), 1955–56

L. Johnson Head (1933H, 1938C), 1957–58

J. Battle Hall (1938C), 1959–60

John C. Warr (1937C), 1961–62

Hal Smith (1931H, 1935C), 1962–64

Milton S. McDonald (1938C), 1964–66

Lloye L. Whitfield (1938H), 1966–68

Walter A. Johnson (1912H), 1968–70

J. T. Parker Jr. (1937H), 1970–72

Brainerd G. Kidder (1938C), 1972–74

Earl W. Williams (1941C), 1974–76

Randolph B. Green (1937H, 1941C), 1976–78

Eloise Taylor Smith (1943C), 1978–80

J. Mitchell Elrod Jr. (1937H, 1941C), 1980–82

Percy T. Marchman (1947C), 1982–84

Leland R. Dean (1941C), 1984–86

Anne Smith Johnson (1953C), 1986–88

Thomas A. Bowen (1955H), 1988–90

Edward England Jr. (1957C), 1990–92

G. Bert Clark Jr. (1982C), 1992–94

Earl E. Tillman (1952H), 1994–96

Glynn R. Gaulding (1964C), 1996–98

Martha Wyatt Bowen (1955H, 1959C), 1998–2000

Timothy R. Howard (1982C), 2000–2002

Edward England Jr. (1957C), 2002–4

Ouida W. Dickey (1950C), 2004–6

C = Berry College

H = Berry high schools

JC = Berry Junior College

Alumni Awards

Distinguished Achievement

General George A. Carver, 1928JC	1969
Dr. John L. McDaniel, 1939C	1969
Dr. Thomas W. Gandy, 1939H, 1942C	1970
Dr. T. Latham Smith, 1912H	1970
Dr. Theodore Phillips, 1929H, 1933C	1971
J. K. East, 1935C	1972
J. A. Shropshire, 1930H	1972
J. T. Parker Jr., 1937H	1973
Dr. Reavis C. Sproull, 1930JC	1973
Dr. Clayton C. O'Mary, 1943C	1974
Dr. Dale Purcell, 1938H	1974
E. Grant Fitts, 1934H	1975
J. Dewitt Purcell, 1931H, 1936C	1976
Charles T. Ray, 1948C	1977
Ann Fite Whitaker, 1961C	1978
Herman A. Watson, 1924H	1979
Roy Richards, 1930H	1980
Amilee Chastain Graves, 1929H	1981
Dr. Horace D. Brown, 1939C	1982
Dr. Milton S. McDonald, 1938C	1983
David E. Estes, 1939C	1984
Dr. Kenneth Whitten, 1953C	1985
Dr. Betty Whitten, 1960C	1985

A = Berry Academy

C = Berry College

G = Berry graduate programs

H = Berry high schools

JC = Berry Junior College

Admiral Lewis A. Hopkins, 1939C	1986
John Lie-Nielson, 1954H	1987
Leland R. Dean, 1941C	1988
Dr. E. Kay Davis Dunn, 1957C	1989
W. Joseph Biggers, 1945H	1990
Dr. Quincey L. Baird, 1952C	1991
Norman D. Burkett, 1946C	1992
Dr. Koji Yoda, 1965C	1993
Reba Shropshire Wilson, 1935C	1994
Dr. Ouida Word Dickey, 1950C	1995
Dr. James R. Scoggins, 1952C	1996
Dr. James K. Miller, 1953C	1997
Dr. Jerry W. Young, 1957C	1998
Dr. Natholyn Harris, 1961C	1999
B. Leon Elder, 1954C	2000
Dr. L. Doyle Mathis, 1958C	2001
Dr. E. Dwight Adams, 1953C	2002
W. Buford Jennings, 1958C	2003
Dr. Philip D. Whanger, 1959C	2004

Distinguished Service

H. Grady Hamrick Sr., 1912H	1969
Dr. Inez Wooten Henry, 1921H	1970
John C. Warr, 1937C (posthumous)	1970
Walter A. Johnson, 1912H	1971
Mary Alice Barnes, 1918H	1972
Eugene P. Gunby, 1919H	1972
Dr. George C. Young, 1935C	1973

Sam Gray, 1924H	1974
Raymond E. Henderson, 1923H	1975
Dr. Garland M. Dickey, 1942C	1976
Benjamin F. Wardlow, 1935C	1977
Martha Page Cousins, 1937C	1978
A. B. "Gus" Jarrett, 1931JC, 1933C	1979
Kankakee Anderson, 1925H	1980
Wallace Hopkins, 1939C	1981
Frankie Usher Hopkins, 1939H, 1943C	1981
Mildred McWhorter, 1951C	1982
Talmadge R. Tucker, 1935C	1983
Leary Bell Doss Finley, 1944C	1984
Paul E. Smith, 1948C	1985
J. Noble Finley, 1942C	1986
Geneva Craig Jarrett, 1931H, 1936C	1987
Mary Sheffield Banks, 1936H	1988
Dr. Herchel H. Sheets, 1948C	1989
Albert Lawton Dean, 1939C	1990
Earl Williams, 1941C	1991
G. Monroe Guyton, 1930H	1992
W. Carl Paul, 1936C	1993
Virginia Webb, 1944C	1994
John R. Lipscomb, 1940H, 1944C	1995
Ellen McGehee Doughtery, 1952C	1996
W. Milton Chambers, 1978A, 1982C	1997
Earl D. Tillman, 1952H	1998
Lillian C. Farmer, 1942C	1999
Frances Denney Barnett, 1949C	2000
Linnie Lane Gibson, 1951C	2001
Nettie Ruth Brown, 1952C	2002
Tim Howard, 1982C	2003
Carolyn T. Smith, 1953C	2004

Outstanding Young Alumni

Karen Holley Horrell, 1974C	1987
Elise Alewine Baggett, 1981C	1989
G. Bert Clark, 1982C	1990
D. Frank Pitts, 1976C	1991
Timothy R. Howard, 1982C	1992
Patty J. Etchison, 1977C	1992
Gregory R. Hanthorn, 1982C	1993
Dante L. Tomaselli Jr., 1985C	1994

Leigh E. Patterson, 1986C	1995
Dr. William R. Holcomb, 1986C	1996
Kendra D. Grimes, 1993C	1997
M. Scott Breithaupt, 1991C, 1996G	1998
Bart Cox, 1992C	2000
Allen Bell, 1995C	2001
Jason E. McMillan, 1998C	2004

Entrepreneurial Spirit

Smith Foster, 1949A	1990
Forrest H. Ingram, 1939C	1991
R. Wayne Shackelford, 1955C	1992
T. Mack Brown, 1982C	1994
Harold D. Kilpatrick, 1960C	1995
Arthur E. Pugh, 1952H, 1956C	1997
Fontaine McFerrin Souther, 1971C	1998
Frances Richey-Goldby, 1983A, 1987C	2000
Richard E. Pickering, 1984C	2001
Faye Junkins Gibbons, 1961C	2002
Karen Christensen Fenaroli, 1983C	2003
Steven J. Cage, 1974C	2004

Loyalty/Generosity (special award)

Ehrman H. Young, 1920H	1982

Service in Alumni Leadership (special award)

Billy Smith, 1939H	1994

Notes

Abbreviations

AcAffC	Board of Trustees Academic Affairs Committee
AdvC	Board of Trustees Advancement Committee
BAQ	*Berry Alumni Quarterly*
BCA	Berry College Archives, Memorial Library
BCC	*Berry College Catalog*
BIS Advance	*Boys Industrial School Advance*
BOTM	Board of Trustees Minutes, Board of Trustees Record Group
BSB	*Berry Schools Bulletin*
BS ExCM	Berry Schools Executive Committee Minutes
BS ExCS	Berry Schools Executive Committee Series
CC	*Campus Carrier*
ExCM	Board of Trustees Executive Committee Minutes, Board of Trustees Record Group
FSRG	Berry Faculty and Staff Record Group
GLG	G. Leland Green
GS	Gloria Shatto
HH	Hermann Hall, Berry College
JJE	John J. Eagan
JRB	John R. Bertrand
MB	Martha Berry
MBN	*Mount Berry News*
MGK	M. Gordon Keown
PR	President's report/newsletter (published under various titles)
RNT	*Rome News-Tribune*
RTH	*Rome Tribune-Herald*
SH	*Southern Highlander*
WJB	William Jesse Baird
WMM	William McChesney Martin Jr.

Introduction

1. Susan Asbury, "Foreword," in Kane and Henry, *Miracle in the Mountains*.

2. Robert H. Adams, "The Widening Circle," *SH*, Jan.–Feb. 1909, 11–13; *BAQ*, Feb. 1926, 7, Mar. 1928, 24; J. R. McCain to GLG, Feb. 28, 1942, GLG Series.

3. "Miss Berry's Last Letter to Alumni," *BAQ*, Mar. 1942, 3; "The Last Message of Miss Berry to the Faculty," *Staff Member's Handbook*, n.d., 3–4; "Miss Berry's Last Message," *Worker's Handbook*, 1943–44, 3–4; Kane and Henry, *Miracle in the Mountains*, 306.

4. Cook, *Half Century at Berry*, 1.

One. Origin of a Vision

1. Dorothy Orr, *A History of Education in Georgia* (Chapel Hill: University of North Carolina Press, 1950), 19–68; Kenneth Coleman, ed., *A History of Georgia* (Athens: University of Georgia Press, 1977), 121.

2. Orr, *History of Education*, 69–103, 116–78; Coleman, *History of Georgia*, 121, 146, 176, 197.

3. Orr, *History of Education*, 263–64; Coleman, *History of Georgia*, 239–41.

4. Irvine S. Ingram, "Development and Significance of the District Agricultural and Mechanical Schools in Georgia," in *Studies in Georgia History and Government*, ed. James C. Bonner and Lucien E. Roberts (Athens: University of Georgia Press, 1940), 172; Orr, *History of Education*, 132.

5. Ingram, "Development," 173; Orr, *History of Education*, 133.

6. Frederick Rudolph, *The American College and University: A History* (Athens: University of Georgia Press, 1990), 217–18; Spright Dowell, *A History of Mercer University, 1833–1953* (Macon, Ga.: Mercer University, 1958), 84. For other work colleges, see P. David Searles, *A College for Appalachia: Alice Lloyd on Caney Creek* (Lexington: University Press of Kentucky, 1995); Elisabeth S. Peck and Emily Ann Smith, *Berea's First 125 Years, 1855–1980* (Lexington: University of Kentucky Press, 1982); Glenn L. McConagha, *Blackburn College, 1837–1987: An Anecdotal and Analytical History of the Private College* (Carlinville, Ill.: Blackburn College, 1988); Helen Godsey and Townsend Godsey, *Flight of the Phoenix: A Biography of the School of the Ozarks—A Unique American College: The First 75 Years* (Point Lookout, Mo.: School of the Ozarks, 1984); Mark T. Banker, *Toward Frontiers Yet Unknown: A Ninetieth Anniversary History of Warren Wilson College* (Swannanoa, N.C.: Warren Wilson College, 1984).

7. *Georgia Laws* (Atlanta: Franklin-Turner, 1906), 72–75; Orr, *History of Education*, 133, 148–49.

8. Searles, *College*, 4.

9. For the Moonlight Schools, see http://kentucky stewarts.com/WilliamG/CoraWilsonStewartArticle.htm.

10. Gaylord William Douglass, "The Mount Hermon of the South," *Mount Hermon Alumni Quarterly*, Mar. 1906, 36–38; *BIS Advance*, Oct. 6, 1906, 10–11.

11. *BIS Advance*, Mar. 25, 1905, 10–11, 19; *Mount Hermon Alumni Quarterly*, Mar. 1906, 36–38, Mar. 1907, 74, June 1907, 93, Sept. 1915, 14–15, Sept. 1927, 10–11.

12. Information on the early members of the Berry family in America as well as the general background and migration of the Scots-Irish appears in Jim Jackson, Carol Vass, Marie Loughlin, and Donna Fischer, "Genealogy of the Berry and Associated Families of Augusta, Rockbridge, and Washington Counties, Virginia," available at http://freepages.genealogy.rootsweb.com/~berry/. Additional sources on the Berry family include William F. Boogher, "The Lineage of Miss Martha Berry," typescript, 1910, BCA; Mathis and Dickey, *Martha Berry*, 4; Berry family Bible, MB Museum, Berry College; MB Collection.

13. *Jacksonville (Ala.) Republican*, Jan. 28, 1857, 2; *Chattanooga Free Press*, Dec. 31, 1995, 24; Zella Armstrong, *The History of Hamilton County and Chattanooga Tennessee* (Chattanooga: Lookout, 1931), 1:299.

14. Chattooga County, Ga., deed book B, 12, Chattooga County Courthouse, Summerville, Ga.

15. MB Collection; Aztec Club of 1847, Mexican War officers search page, http://www.aztecclub.com/search.asp.

16. The party arrived in a gold-mining area about eighty miles east of Sutter's Fort on August 25, 1849, after traveling primarily by boat to Independence, Missouri, and from there by mule and wagon through Fort Laramie to California. Their voyage is recorded in several letters written by a member of the group; see Alexander Thornton Harper to mother, Mar.–Aug. 1849, MB Collection. Berry was in Calaveras County at the time of the 1850 Census (U.S. Census, 1850, Calaveras County, Calif., 78).

17. Marriage certificate, MB Collection.

18. U.S. Census, 1860, Cherokee County, Ala., 218; Slave Schedules, U.S. Census Index, 1860, Cherokee County, Ala., first district, 373. The estimated increase in the consumer price index is used to convert historic dollars to 2003 dollars. $1.00 in 1860 was equivalent to approximately $20.39 in 2003.

19. Persons associated with Berry College have sometimes suggested that Thomas Berry commanded a unit of men from the Rome area and that the Berry Infantry, a Floyd County unit, was named for him. It was actually named for his brother, James (*Rome Weekly Courier*, Sept. 20, 1861, 1). Records of Confederate soldiers are in record group 109, National Archives. The MB Collection contains numerous records relating to Thomas Berry's war experiences.

20. Floyd County, Ga., deed book O, 642, Floyd County Courthouse, Rome, Ga.

21. Floyd County, Ga., deed book K, 779. The purchase price of Oak Hill was equivalent to $137,650 in 2003.

22. *Rome Tri-Weekly Courier,* Mar. 7, 1871, 2. Bill Arp was the pseudonym Smith used to write humor columns that appeared in several southern newspapers.

23. Calhoun County, Ala., deed book K, 535, deed book L, 1, deed book M, 323–24, deed book X, 65–66, Calhoun County Courthouse, Anniston, Ala.

24. Personal papers of Captain and Mrs. Thomas Berry, MB Collection.

25. The 1870 Census (Floyd County, Ga., 202), the first after her birth, lists Martha Berry as Mattie, age five. Since all accounts agree that she was born on Oct. 7 and

the census was taken in June, the 1870 Census suggests that she turned five on Oct. 7, 1869, in which case she was born in 1864. The 1900 Census (Floyd County, Ga., ED 117, sheet 9) states that she was born in 1864 in Alabama. Some area residents have suggested that Martha was born at Oak Hill, but, as mentioned earlier, her father did not buy that property until July 1871. On an application to the Daughters of the American Revolution, MB wrote that she was born on Rhea Plantation in Etowah County, Alabama. The 1880 Census (Floyd County, Ga., ED 62, sheet 73), lists her as Mattie, age fourteen, suggesting that she was born in 1865. The record of her baptism on Apr. 2, 1881, in St. Peter's Episcopal Church in Rome, shows that she was born near Gadsden, Alabama, on Oct. 7, 1865. The record of her October 29, 1882, confirmation at the same church lists her age as seventeen, again indicating that she was born in 1865 (parish register, vol. 1, 1877–87, 50, 80). In the back of a Berry family Bible (MB Museum, Berry College), Thomas Berry apparently listed the births of his first three children (J for Jennie, M for Martha or Mattie, and I for Isaac) but not the others. This entry gives MB's birth date as Saturday evening, 7 Oct. 1865. Thus, MB was very likely born before 1866.

26. Berry family Bible, MB Museum, Berry College; Mathis and Dickey, *Martha Berry, 32.*

27. Brewster, "Martha Berry"; Frances Berry Bonnyman typescript statements on Berry family, 1956, MB Collection.

28. Bonnyman typescript statements; Thomas Berry to MB, April 31 [*sic*], 1885, MB Collection. The Berry Boys attended Proctor's Boys School in Rome; Bingham Military Academy near Raleigh, North Carolina; and then the University of the South in Sewanee, Tennessee.

29. Will of Thomas Berry, personal papers of Captain and Mrs. Thomas Berry, MB Collection. Thomas had purchased 83 acres from Seaborn Wright for $1,100 in 1881 and an adjacent 160-acre tract from William T. Trammell for $1,200 the same year (Floyd County, Ga., deed book AA, 284, 286). Martha Berry deeded the first tract to her newly incorporated Boys Industrial School in 1903.

30. Bonnyman typescript statements.

31. For Georgia history, see Coleman, *History of Georgia;* Numan V. Bartley, *The Creation of Modern Georgia* (Athens: University of Georgia Press, 1983).

32. Bartley, *Creation of Modern Georgia,* 16, 20, 38, 145.

33. Robert C. Puth, *American Economic History,* 3d ed. (Orlando, Fla.: Dryden, 1993), 330; Gary M. Walton and Hugh Rockoff, *History of the American Economy,* 6th ed. (Orlando, Fla.: Harcourt Brace Jovanovich, 1990), 307.

34. Coleman, *History of Georgia,* 227.

35. Ibid.; Puth, *American Economic History,* 333–35, 338.

36. John C. Campbell, *The Southern Highlander and His Homeland* (New York: Sage, 1921), 195–225.

37. Ibid., 176–94.

38. Ibid.

39. R. L. Watson to Henry F. Cutler, Feb. 22, Apr. 14, 1902, FSRG.

Two. Sharpening the Focus

1. MB, "Uplifting Backwoods Boys in Georgia," 4986; also in Mathis and Dickey, *Martha Berry,* 189–98. Other written accounts describing the early years of the institution founded by MB include MB, "Story of the Berry School"; Brewster, "Chronicles of a Flatwoods School"; Brewster, "Beginning of the Berry School"; *Story of Berry Schools,* reprinted in Mathis and Dickey, *Martha Berry,* 89–108. Unless otherwise noted, these works are the sources for events described in this chapter.

2. "Roman Recalls First Class Held in Berry School Cabin," *RNT,* Aug. 16, 1953, 1. The exact year is not known, although it seems to have been either 1896 or 1897. Phillips recalled the meeting as having taken place in 1897. MB, "Uplifting Backwoods Boys in Georgia," gives the date as 1896. *Rome Tribune,* May 28, 1902, 4, stated in "Noble Educational Work," "Some six years ago Miss Berry began a Sunday school . . . in an abandoned cabin near her home." The *Boys Industrial School Catalog,* 1903–4, 3, BCA, indicated that the school had begun six years earlier. The *BIS Advance,* Mar. 15, 1904, 5, placed the beginning about seven years earlier.

3. MB, "Story of the Berry School" (Dec. 1915), 180.

4. Mary Ruth Beams Camp, "Memories of Seventy-two Years Ago," typescript, BCA.

5. *RNT,* Aug. 16, 1953, 1; *BIS Advance,* Apr. 15, 1904, 10.

6. Floyd County Board of Education minutes, 1888–1907, Feb. 27, 1899, 88, Feb. 5, 1901, 127, Rome and Floyd County Records Center, Rome, Ga.

7. Ibid., Feb. 14, 1900, 104.

8. Ibid., Jan. 8, 1901, 123–24.

9. Brewster, "Why and How."

10. *Rome Tribune,* Jan. 22, 1902, 5; *SH,* Jan.–Feb. 1912, 41.

11. MB to Henry F. Cutler, Jan. 10, 1902, MB Collection; Richard L. Watson to Henry F. Cutler, Feb. 22, 1902, FSRG.

12. *BAQ,* Feb. 1914, 11.

13. Boys Industrial School financial statement, May 14, 1904, BCA.

14. Brewster, "Beginning of the Berry School," 13–14.

15. Richard L. Watson to H. F. Cutler, Apr. 14, 1902, FSRG.

16. *Rome Tribune,* Sept. 2, 1902, 8.

17. Brewster, "Chronicles," 19, 21.

18. BOTM, May 2, 1905.

19. Albert S. McClain to Henry F. Cutler, Aug. 20, 1904, Dec. 2, 1910, Jan. 9, 1911, FSRG.

20. See the traditional story of wash day in Mathis and Dickey, *Martha Berry,* 201.

21. Brewster, "Chronicles of a Flatwoods School," 19–24; *BIS Advance,* Apr. 15, 1904, 8; *SH,* Nov. 1908, 173.

22. JJE to MB, Dec. 29, 1904, MB Collection.

23. *Boys Industrial School Catalog,* 1902–3, cover, 1–2, BCA.

24. Ibid., 1903–4, 5–8, 1904–5, 9.

25. Ibid., 1903–4, 12, 1905–6, 23.

26. *BIS Advance,* Feb. 15, 1904, 9, Apr. 15, 1904, 8; *Boys Industrial School Catalog,* 1906–7, 37, BCA.

27. *Boys Industrial School Catalog,* 1903–4, 11–12, 1904–5, 27, 1906–7, 17–19, 28, BCA.

28. Letters from deans or presidents of these institutions to Robert H. Adams, Apr. 1908, Office of the Principal Collection.

29. Gaylord William Douglass, "The Mount Hermon of the South," *Mount Hermon Alumni Quarterly,* Mar. 1906, 36–38.

30. A listing and brief biographies of the Berry trustees from 1902 to 1960 appear in Cook, *Half Century at Berry,* 41–76.

31. Floyd County, Ga., marriage book H, 131, Floyd County Courthouse, Rome, Ga.

32. Cook, *Half Century at Berry,* 50; *Boys Industrial School Catalog,* 1904–5, 7, BCA.

33. The head of the Berry board was referred to as president during most of the time Eagan held that position and was later known as chairman. The most complete information on Eagan appears in Robert E. Speer, *John Eagan* (Birmingham, Ala.: privately printed, 1939).

34. *SH,* July 1924, 4.

35. The deed from MB to the Boys Industrial School was recorded on Apr. 4, 1903, Floyd County, Ga., deed book OOO, 200, Floyd County Courthouse, Rome, Ga.

36. The text of the original charter and a brief history of amendments to it appear in Mathis and Dickey, *Martha Berry,* 109–12.

37. BOTM, Apr. 3, 1903.

38. Ibid., Apr. 30, 1907, Apr. 28, 1908.

39. Ibid., May 2, 1905.

40. Floyd County, Ga., deed book OOO, 200, deed book UUU, 431, deed book ZZZ, 554, 739.

41. The best description of campus buildings appears in O. Dickey and Higgins, *Berry Trails.* Another useful discussion of the early campus buildings appears in Cook, *Half Century at Berry.*

42. *Rome Tribune,* May 11, 1902, 6. This structure was later called the Roosevelt Cabin. Today it is the oldest extant building constructed for the schools.

43. *BIS Advance,* Jan. 25, 1905, 6.

44. Floyd County Board of Education minutes, 1888–1907, Feb. 4, 1902, 144, May 6, 1902, 147, Oct. 7, 1902, 153, Dec. 1, 1903, 181, Dec. 6, 1904, 204, Feb. 5, 1907, 279; Floyd County Board of Education minutes, 1908–

11, Sept. 8, 1908, *35;* Mar. 15, 1910, 81; Oct. 2, 1911, 108.

45. Floyd County Board of Education minutes, 1888–1907, Mar. 3, 1903, 164.

46. Ibid., Oct. 7, 1902, 153.

47. MB Collection.

48. MB to Clayton Henson, Nov. 13, 1902, MB Collection.

49. MB, "Story of the Berry School" (Apr. 1916), 8–11.

50. Boys Industrial School financial statements, BCA.

51. George Foster Peabody to Andrew J. Ritchie (copy to MB), Apr. 19, 1907, MB Collection.

52. Albert S. McClain to M. J. Miller, Apr. 3, 1904, FSRG; *Mount Hermon Alumni Quarterly,* Mar. 1906, 36–38, Mar. 1907, 74, June 1907, 93, Sept. 1915, 14–15, Sept. 1927, 10–11; *BIS Advance,* Oct. 6, 1906, 10–11.

Three. Growing Pains

1. *Martha Berry School for Girls Catalog,* 1917–18, 9, BCA.

2. William Loeb Jr. to MB, June 12, Oct. 25, 1905, MB Collection.

3. William Loeb Jr. to MB, Apr. 6, 1907, Isabella L. Hagner to MB, Mar. 21, 1907, Edith Roosevelt to MB, Sept. 17, 1907, letter and White House luncheon invitation card from Roosevelt's secretary to MB at Washington hotel, Apr. 18, 1908, MB Collection.

4. Theodore Roosevelt to MB, Jan. 1, 1909, July 13, 1910, MB Collection; Theodore Roosevelt speech, Oct. 10, 1910, in Mathis and Dickey, *Martha Berry,* 202–9.

5. For the Log Cabin Campus, as the original area of the girls' school is now known, see O. Dickey and Higgins, *Berry Trails,* 51–55; Cook, *Half Century at Berry,* 18–22; *Martha Berry School for Girls Catalog,* 1923–24, 17, BCA; *BAQ,* Feb. 1926, 12–13.

6. *RTH,* Nov. 6, 1909, 1; BOTM, May 10, 1910.

7. *SH,* summer 1923, 19.

8. MB to Ida Tarbell, Feb. 26, 1916, Ida Tarbell to MB, Mar. 29, 1917, MB Collection.

9. MB to Henry Ford, Feb. 7, Mar. 21, Mar. 28, 1922, MB Collection; Roberts, "Berry Schools," 184.

10. Clara Ford to MB, Jan. 8, 1923, MB to Clara Ford, Jan. 18, 1923, MB to Henry Ford, Feb. 10, Mar. 23, 1923, Clara and Henry Ford to MB (telegram), Apr. 6, 1923, MB Collection.

11. *BSB,* Nov. 1914, 3–8, 22–23.

12. John R. Angell to MB, June 8, 1921, MB Collection.

13. *Berry School News,* Dec. 12, 1912, 1; *BAQ,* Nov. 1921, 12.

14. For information on the buildings of the mountain campus, see O. Dickey and Higgins, *Berry Trails,* 58–65; Cook, *Half Century at Berry,* 25–27; *SH,* Apr. 1916, 33; *BSB,* Nov. 1920, 24.

15. J. B. Murray (head of academic department, Foundation School), annual report, Apr. 30, 1923, BCA.

16. *Student Handbook,* 1910, 9, 1915–16, 8, 1916–17, 43.

17. *SH,* winter 1926, 18.

18. For more on the campus church, see Evelyn Hoge Pendley, "A History of the Mount Berry Church," typescript, 1987, BCA.

19. For more on the Berry chapels, see O. Dickey and Higgins, *Berry Trails,* 22–23; Cook, *Half Century at Berry,* 7–8; Pendley, "History of the Mount Berry Church."

20. Cook, *Half Century at Berry,* 35–37; *Martha Berry School for Girls Catalog,* 1909–10, 11, BCA; report of the industrial manager, May 1915, Board of Trustees Record Group; report of the principal and registrar, May 1923, GLG Series, BCA.

21. *BSB,* 1920.

22. MB to GLG, Mar. 2, 1925, MB Collection.

23. MB to GLG, Nov. 12, 1925, MB Collection.

24. For more on athletics at Berry, see Bandy, *Viking Tradition;* Cook, *Half Century at Berry,* 22, 29.

25. Ouida Dickey, "A Brief History of the Berry Alumni Association, 1908–2002," typescript, 2002, BCA; *BAQ,* May 1922, 21, Aug. 1922, 10–11.

26. BOTM, Nov. 23, 1921; MB Collection, box 215.

27. Application and letters, 1910, personnel files, Office of the Principal Collection; Samuel Henry Cook to E. Herman Hoge, Jan. 20, 1920, BS ExCS.

28. *BAQ,* summer 1975, back cover.

29. BS ExCM, May 14, 1920.

30. MB to JJE, March 22, 1921, MB Collection; *BAQ,* May 1921, 3.

31. JJE to W. C. Atkins, E. Herman Hoge, and D. W. Densmore, Apr. 28, 1916, BS ExCS.

32. BS ExCM, Mar. 8, 14, 1921.

33. *BAQ,* Mar. 1927, 10; Floyd County, Ga., deed books, Floyd County Courthouse, Rome, Ga.; Cook, *Half Century at Berry,* 13.

34. *BAQ,* Dec. 1926, 8.

35. Annual report of the Industrial Department, May 1916, Board of Trustees Collection; *Berry News,* Dec. 12, 1922.

36. *BAQ,* Nov. 1920, 3–5, Mar. 1927, 15; O. Dickey and Higgins, *Berry Trails,* 24–25.

37. Unless otherwise noted, the following description of this controversy is taken from the MB Collection, boxes 1, 210.

38. *RTH,* Aug. 3, 1909, 1.

39. Unsigned proposed deposition, MB Collection, box 1.

40. *RTH,* Aug. 3, 1909, 1, Aug. 7, 1909, 1, Aug. 10, 1909, 1, 8, Aug. 13, 1909, 8.

41. Ibid., Aug. 12, 1909, 1, Aug. 15, 1909, 1; BOTM, May 10, 1910; *Berry School v. Rome and Northern Railroad Company,* Floyd Superior Court, civil subpoena docket, 1:338, civil issues docket, vol. 5, Jan. term 1910, case 4, p. 82. The right-of-way property was transferred from the school to the railroad through several Sept. 1909 deeds, but the transfers were not recorded until 1912 and 1915 (Floyd County, Ga., deed book 84, 162–63, deed book 91, 603–4).

42. MB to George Foster Peabody, Sept. 30, 1909, MB to R. G. Peters, Sept. 27, 1909, R. G. Peters to MB, Oct. 8, 1909, MB Collection.

43. *RTH,* Nov. 3, 1916, 1, 3.

44. Floyd County, Ga., deed book 122, 555–60.

45. MB to L. A. Downs, Jan. 23, May 25, June 25, 1925, L. A. Downs to MB, Jan. 31, 1925, boxes 45, 210, MB Collection.

46. O. Dickey and Higgins, *Berry Trails*, 54; Cook, *Half Century at Berry*, 20.

47. Petitions by Butler and her father and demurrers and answers by Berry in *Miss Wilma Butler by Her Next Friend, O. M. Butler v. Berry School, a Corporation*, case 231, and *O. M. Butler v. Berry School, a Corporation*, case 232, Dec. term 1917, civil record, City Court, Floyd County, Ga., S:298–305.

48. MB to JJE, July 13, 1917, MB Collection; Civil record, City Court, Floyd County, Ga., S:298–305.

49. MB to JJE, July 23, Aug. 11, 18, 1917, MB to Lula Ray, May 20, 21, 1918, MB Collection.

50. Civil record, City Court, Floyd County, Ga., S:298–305.

51. City Court, Floyd County, Ga., minutes, 21:141; MB to Lillie Mae Tillery, Sept. 28, 1920, MB Collection; Cook, *Half Century at Berry*, 20.

52. MB to JJE, Sept. 1, 1917, MB Collection; *Berry School News*, Sept. 11, 1917, 1.

53. Unless otherwise noted, the following description of this controversy is taken from MB Collection, box 213.

54. MB to JJE, July 13, July 23, 1917, MB Collection.

55. *Georgia Laws, 1917* (Atlanta: Index Printing, 1917), 39–41; *Georgia Laws, 1919* (Atlanta: Byrd Printing, 1919), 82–83.

56. MB to JJE, Nov. 2, 7, 1921, MB Collection.

57. *BAQ*, Nov. 1921, 3, 5; *RTH*, Nov. 8, 1921, 1, Nov. 13, 1921, 1–2, Nov. 18, 1921, 1.

58. *RTH*, Nov. 16, 1921, 2.

59. BOTM, Nov. 23, 1921; MB to JJE, Nov. 26, 1921, JJE to MB, Nov. 29, 1921, MB Collection.

60. *RTH*, Nov. 19, 1921, 1; MB to J. O. Martin, Dec. 3, 1921, JJE to G. E. Maddox, Jan. 9, 1922, MB Collection; *BAQ*, Feb. 1922, 3.

61. James Becham to Samuel H. Bishop, July 22, 1905, MB Collection.

62. R. A. Franks to MB, Apr. 19, 1907, MB to Louise Whitfield Carnegie, Mar. 24, 1909, MB to Andrew Carnegie, Dec. 6, 1909, James Becham to MB, Dec. 15, 1909, MB Collection; *RTH*, Oct. 31, 1909; BOTM, Apr. 27, 1909.

63. Andrew Carnegie to MB, Dec. 9, 1912, Olivia Sage to MB, Feb. 14, 1913, MB Collection.

64. John D. Rockefeller to MB, July 11, 1908, MB Collection.

65. BOTM, Nov. 6, 1915, Apr. 26, 1917; James Becham to MB, June 30, 1919, MB Collection.

66. John R. Angell to MB, June 8, 1921, MB Collection; BOTM, May 1, 1923.

67. Cook, *Half Century at Berry*, 6–8, 12–17, 30, 39, 53.

68. Ibid., 4, 61; Floyd County, Ga., deed book 129, 122–24, Floyd County Courthouse, Rome, Ga.; Kate Macy Ladd Trust file, Advancement Office, Berry College; *BAQ*, Mar. 1927, 5, Mar. 1928, 6.

69. Cook, *Half Century at Berry*, 4–5, 61; Kate Macy Ladd Trust file, Advancement Office, Berry College.

70. *BAQ*, June 1925, 12.

71. MB to JJE, Dec. 29, 1916, Nov. 2, 1921, MB Collection.

72. For Berea College, see Shannon H. Wilson, "Window on the Mountains: Berea's Appalachia, 1870–1930," *Filson Club History Quarterly* 64 (July 1990): 384–400; for Alice Lloyd College, see P. David Searles, *A College for Appalachia: Alice Lloyd on Caney Creek* (Lexington: University Press of Kentucky, 1995); for mountain stereotypes and efforts to change Appalachian culture, see J. W. Williamson, *Hillbillyland: What the Movies Did to the Mountains and What the Mountains Did to the Movies* (Chapel Hill: University of North Carolina Press, 1995); David E. Whisnant, *All That Is Native and Fine: The Politics of Culture in an American Region* (Chapel Hill: University of North Carolina Press, 1983).

73. MB to E. G. Maddox, Nov. 21, 1919, MB Collection.

74. BS ExCM, July 4, 1923.

75. *BAQ*, Nov. 1923, 7–8; BS ExCM, Sept. 25, 1923.

76. Report of the comptroller, Mar. 31, 1925, E. H. Hoge Series.

77. Report of the principal and registrar, Mar. 5, 1925, GLG Collection.

78. MB to GLG, Nov. 14, 1925, MB Collection.

79. Cook, *Half Century at Berry*, 41–76.

80. BOTM, Apr. 14, 1915.

81. *RNT*, Oct. 5, 1925, 1; *BAQ*, Nov. 1925, 1–3, June 1925, 8–11.

1. Report of the principal and registrar, May 5, 1925, GLG Series.

2. *BAQ,* Feb. 1926, 18.

3. Report of the principal and registrar, May 1923, GLG Series; *BAQ,* Feb. 1923, 21.

4. *BSB,* 1928–29, 29, 49–62; *BAQ,* Sept. 1926, 13, 15, July 1928, 6, 20; alumni directory, 1904–34, 30–31, BCA.

5. *BSB,* 1928–29, 47–48; *BAQ,* Dec. 1926, 6.

6. *BAQ,* Dec. 1929, 3, Mar. 1930, 4; *MBN,* Jan. 6, 1930, 1.

7. *BSB,* 1928–29, 30–33.

8. Report of the principal and registrar, May 1931, GLG Series; *BAQ,* Oct. 1930, 10.

9. Mathis and Dickey, *Martha Berry,* 111–12, 225; M. L. Duggan to GLG, Nov. 24, 1931, GLG to M. L. Duggan, Nov. 28, 1931, GLG Series; alumni directory, 1904–34, 32; *BSB,* June 1931, cover.

10. Report of the principal and registrar, May 1931, GLG Series; *BAQ,* Jan. 1931, 14–15.

11. MB address to Southern Association of Colleges and Secondary Schools, Dec. 16, 1933, MB Collection; W. P. Few to MB, May 16, 1933, MB Collection.

12. Robert L. Kelly to MB, Nov. 14, 1934, J. R. McCain to Alice Logan Wingo, Jan. 22, 1935, MB Collection; president's report, May 25, 1936, GLG Series; *BAQ,* Apr. 1936, 8.

13. *BSB,* 1935–36, 57–59, 88, 97, 99.

14. Ibid., 1939–40, 40, 44.

15. West, "Sweatshops in the Schools," 216.

16. Along with Myles Horton, West later cofounded the Highlander Folk School near Monteagle, Tennessee, which became a center for labor activity and then for the civil-rights movement. In 1965 West and his wife, Connie, founded the Appalachian South Folklife Center, located in West Virginia. Critics accused both institutions of having communist ties.

17. *BAQ,* Mar. 1932, 11–12, May 1932, 12, 22; *SH,* summer 1933, 28–29.

18. Don West to MB, Apr. 15, 1932; *BAQ,* May 1932, 22.

19. West, "Sweatshops in the Schools," 216.

20. Charles Proctor to National Student League (written but not mailed), Oct. 18, 1933, MB Collection.

21. Committee for Student Rights in Berry High School, *Berry Students Demand Justice,* MB Collection.

22. Basso, "About the Berry Schools," 208; Charles Proctor to *New Republic* (written but not mailed), Oct. 18, 1933, MB Collection.

23. BS ExCS.

24. Dunbar, *Against the Grain,* 53–54.

25. MB to Emily Vanderbilt Hammond, Oct. 9, 1933, MB Collection.

26. *New Republic,* Oct. 25, 1933, 292.

27. Committee for Student Rights in Berry High School, *Berry Students Demand Justice,* MB Collection; Basso, "About the Berry Schools," 207–8.

28. "Protest of Berry Students against False Propaganda Being Spread about Them by Don West and Others," MB Collection.

29. Subject files, Don West incident, MB Collection; *New Republic,* Oct. 25, 1933, 292; Basso, "About the Berry Schools."

30. MB to Emily Vanderbilt Hammond, Oct. 9, 1933, MB Collection. A lengthy discussion of the controversy appears in Guthrie, "Education and the Evolution of the South," 81–102.

31. Catherine McDonald, interview by Ouida Dickey and Doyle Mathis, May 1, 2003.

32. David E. Whisnant, *All That Is Native and Fine: The Politics of Culture in an American Region* (Chapel Hill: University of North Carolina Press, 1983); P. David Searles, *A College for Appalachia: Alice Lloyd on Caney Creek* (Lexington: University Press of Kentucky, 1955).

33. MB to GLG, Sept. 14, 1939, MB Collection.

34. BS ExCM, Dec. 28, 1932, Mar. 8, 1933, Feb. 27, 1935; *BAQ,* winter 1977, 4.

35. MB to Berry Schools executive committee, Feb. 28, 1926, Jan. 26, 1931, BS ExCS; BS ExCM, Jan. 27, Feb. 3, 1931, Dec. 28, 1932.

36. MB to GLG, Sept. 14, 1939, in Mathis and Dickey, *Martha Berry,* 297; Elena Moore, interview by Ouida

Dickey and Doyle Mathis, Oct. 31, 2002; *Past Times* (News Publishing Company), Aug. 2002, 4; *BAQ,* Jan. 1936, 32.

37. Cook, *Half Century at Berry,* 6–7, 12–13, 17, 39, 53; O. Dickey and Higgins, *Berry Trails,* 18–19, 33–34, 39–41.

38. *SH,* summer 1933, 12–13, 28–29; *BAQ,* Mar. 1927, 16, May 1933, 3, Sept. 1933, 3, 5, Dec. 1933, 5.

39. *BAQ,* Nov. 1937, 8, Dec. 1940, 8.

40. Mount Berry Garden Club Yearbook, 2002–3, BCA.

41. Daughters of Berry Yearbook, 2002–3, BCA; *BAQ,* Dec. 1939, 6.

42. *BAQ,* Dec. 1929, 5, June 1934, 1, 8.

43. BS ExCM, Dec. 5, 1927; MB to Berry Schools Executive Committee, Apr. 24, 1934, BS ExCS.

44. *BSB,* 1939–40, 39–40.

45. *BAQ,* Oct. 1939, 29, Mar. 1940, 8.

46. Lawrence E. McAllister, *Dr. Mac: A Brief Autobiography of Dr. Lawrence E. McAllister of Berry College,* ed. Alexander W. Whitaker III (Mount Berry: Berry College, 1975).

47. BS ExCM, Sept. 7, 1926, Dec. 30, 1930, Apr. 11, 1934; MB to Berry Schools executive committee, Dec. 27, 1930, BS ExCS.

48. BS ExCM, Apr. 21, 1934.

49. Ibid., Sept. 19, 1934; Berry Schools executive committee resolution, Oct. 26, 1934, BS ExCS.

50. McDonald interview.

51. *BSB,* 1939–40, 126.

52. Ibid., Dec. 1942, 43–44.

53. MB to Berry Schools executive committee, Jan. 26, 1931, BS ExCS; BS ExCM, Dec. 17, 1934, Feb. 13, 20, 1935; *Student Handbook,* 1941–42, 65.

54. Teachers' schedules, 1942, GLG Series.

55. "Staff Rules at Berry," *Worker's Handbook,* 1943–44, 10–16.

56. Ibid.

57. *Worker's Handbook,* 1943–44, 17.

58. "Special Advantages, Health," *BSB,* Dec. 1942, 20.

59. "Industrial Course," *BSB,* Dec. 1942, 25.

60. "Boys' Athletics" and "Athletics," *Student Handbook,* 1941–42, 72, 52, 56.

61. "Permissions and Excuses" and "Miscellaneous," in ibid., 63, 65, 72–73.

62. "Scholarship" and "Buildings," in ibid., 65–66, 69.

63. "Uniforms," in ibid., 67.

64. G. L. Eberhardt to MGK, Sept. 27, 1943, MGK to G. L. Eberhardt, Oct. 5, 1943, MGK Series.

65. "Uniforms," *BSB,* Dec. 1942, 28–29.

66. "Attendance," in ibid., 66–67; "Uniforms," *Student Handbook,* 1941–42, 67.

67. Minutes of faculty meetings, 1942, GLG Series.

68. GLG to "Dean, Industrial Manager, or Principal," Feb. 29, 1942, GLG to Sophie Payne Alston, Aug. 13, 1942, GLG Series.

69. "The Berry Code," *Student Handbook,* 1941–42, 76–77; copy of the code in Inspirational Writings file, BCA.

70. *BAQ,* June 1930, 4, Jan. 1936, 3.

71. Ibid., Mar. 1932, 10; *Student Handbook,* 1941–42, 24–25, 37–38, 61; "Excelsior and Honor Clubs," *Cabin Log,* 1949, 40; "Excelsior Club," *Cabin Log,* 1950, 74.

72. "Daily Schedule of Bells," *Student Handbook,* 1941–42, 45.

73. BS ExCM, Jan. 2, 1929, May 6, 1932; Byers, *For the Glory,* 67–71, 75–80, 126, 139–43; Sophie Payne Alston to Ethel A. Adams, Oct. 22, 1937, Sophie Payne Alston Series; *BAQ,* Dec. 1936, 33.

74. *BAQ,* June 1941, 21.

75. Ibid., Mar. 1938, 3, Nov. 1940, 5, Dec. 1940, 19; Cook, *Half Century at Berry,* 44–75; Mathis and Dickey, *Martha Berry,* 185.

76. *BAQ,* Dec. 1940, 4, Oct. 1941, 3.

77. BOTM, Sept. 13, 1941.

78. Mathis and Dickey, *Martha Berry,* 41–42; Evelyn Hoge Pendley, "A History of the Mount Berry Church," typescript, 1987, 34, BCA.

79. *New York Times,* Feb. 27, 1942, 17, Mar. 6, 1942, 14; Mathis and Dickey, *Martha Berry,* 40–55; "Marble Slab on Miss Berry's Grave Unveiled," *BAQ,* July 1942, 8.

80. *BAQ,* Mar. 1942, inside front cover, 3; Mathis and Dickey, *Martha Berry,* 48–49.

81. Cook, *Half Century at Berry,* 60; "Successor to Miss Berry Named by Her; Mr. Keown Becomes Acting Director," *BAQ,* Mar. 1942, 30.

82. *BAQ,* Jul. 1942, 2–3.

83. President's report, May 1942, GLG Series.

84. Comptroller's report, May 1943, E. H. Hoge Series.

85. "Miss Berry's Last Letter to Faculty," *Staff Member's Handbook,* n.d., 3–4; Martha Berry, "Dear Friends," *Worker's Handbook,* 1943–44, 3–4.

86. Burton R. Clark, *The Distinctive College* (New Brunswick, N.J.: Transaction, 1922).

87. Kane and Henry, *Miracle in the Mountains,* 306.

Five. Challenges and Changes

1. Mildred Johnston to MGK, Apr. 16, 1942; MGK to Mildred Johnston, Apr. 28, 1942; Frank F. Berry to MGK, Sept. 30, 1942; MGK to Frank F. Berry, Oct. 5, 1942, MGK Series.

2. GLG, "Report to the Board of Trustees," May 25, 1942, GLG Series.

3. Floyd County, Ga., deed books; document prepared by Berry Land Resources, 1981, GS Series.

4. *United States of America, Petitioner v. 160 Acres of Land in Floyd County, Georgia (Rome General Hospital, Georgia), Berry Schools, et al., Defendants,* civil action 432, Nov. term 1942, U.S. District Court, Northern District of Georgia, Rome Division.

5. Floyd County, Ga., deed book 194, pp. 349, 354, deed book 198, pp. 192, 228.

6. GLG to Emory Q. Hawk, Apr. 9, 1942, GLG Series.

7. John Warr to Francis J. Brown, "Data Regarding Male Enrollments and Deferments," Mar. 15, 1943, GLG Series.

8. "Request for Funds to Resume Possum Trot Community School," 2, Dec. 1945, Possum Trot file, BCA.

9. "Report to Acting Director and the Board of Trustees," May 24, 1943, Board of Trustees Record Group.

10. ExCM, Feb. 12, 1943.

11. Irene Owens Large, Grace Moore Johnson, and Dewey Large, interview by Ouida Dickey, May 29, 2003.

12. "A.A.F. Training at Berry," *BAQ,* spring 1943, 4.

13. William Dick to GLG, Apr. 9, 1942, GLG Series.

14. Pirkle, *Lectures,* 297.

15. "Report to Acting Director and Board of Trustees," May 24, 1943, Board of Trustees Record Group.

16. ExCM, May 10, 1944; "Report to Acting Director and Board of Trustees," May 24, 1943, GLG Series.

17. "Berry Men Make Excellent Record in Service," *BAQ,* spring 1943, 2.

18. "They Also Serve," *BAQ,* summer 1943, 2; Walter Johnson, "Berry Alumni Association," typescript, c. 1947, 1, in 1989–90 alumni scrapbook, BCA.

19. Walter Johnson, "Berry Alumni Association," typescript, ca. 1947, 1, in 1989–90 alumni scrapbook, BCA.

20. "The Berry People in the Armed Forces of America," "Bonds for Berry," and "Report of Committee to Study Plans for War Bonds Campaign," *BAQ,* Oct. 1942, 9–13, 20–24, 4–5.

21. GLG, "The Task Ahead," in *Worker's Handbook,* 1943–44, 5–9.

22. W. Morrison McCall to GLG, Sept. 22, 1942, GLG Series.

23. M. C. Huntley to GLG, June 8, 1942, GLG Series.

24. GLG, Berry College Oral History Collection, 19640611-01, June 11, 1964, BCA.

25. Pendley, *Sixty Years of Education for Service* (1963), 20–21.

26. Philip Weltner to GLG, Samuel Henry Cook, Sophie P. Alston, and O. C. Skinner, Aug. 5, 10, 1943, GLG Series.

27. Ibid.

28. Pendley, *Sixty Years of Education for Service* (1963), 24–27.

29. GLG, "Dear Men and Women of Berry," *BAQ,* summer 1944, 3.

30. Charles T. Morgan to MGK, Dec. 31, 1943, President's Office Collection.

31. Charles T. Morgan to the executive committee of the board of trustees, Dec. 15, 1943, President's Office Collection.

32. WJB, "To the Former Students and Graduates of the Berry Schools," *BAQ,* summer 1944, 2.

33. "William Jesse Baird Assumes Duties of New Office," *BAQ,* summer 1944, 5.

34. WJB, "My Gallup Poll," *SH,* fall–winter 1944, 12–13.

35. Spring 1944 college roster, Student Rosters, vertical file, BCA; *Cabin Log,* 1945, 10; Pirkle, *Lectures,* 310–11; WJB to G. Lamar Westcott, Oct. 6, 1945, WJB Series.

36. Pendley, *Sixty Years of Education for Service* (1963), 28–29.

37. Ibid., 30.

38. Ibid., 30, 33; Pirkle, *Lectures,* 319, 320, 330.

39. Pendley, *Sixty Years of Education for Service* (1963), 31.

40. Pirkle, *Lectures,* 323–24.

41. WJB to Archibald Barrow, Jan. 1, 1945, WJB Series.

42. WJB to E. A. Sutherland, May 25, 1945, WJB to Leigh R. Scott, Aug. 7, 1945, WJB Series; "In Memoriam: Miss Alice Logan Wingo," *SH,* fall–winter 1945–46, 18–19.

43. "In Memoriam: Mrs. Walter G. Ladd," *SH,* fall–winter 1945–46, 19.

44. "Berry Welcomes Vets Back to Campus," *MBN,* Feb. 7, 1946, 1.

45. "Berry as Seen by a College Senior," *SH,* spring 1946, 4.

46. *MBN,* Feb. 7, 1946, 4.

47. "Religious Education at the Berry Schools," *SH,* spring 1946, 11.

48. "Do You Know Berry's Needs?" *SH,* fall–winter 1945–46, 8–9.

49. *BSB,* Dec. 1946, 33–35, 63–68.

50. "Berry Schools Observes Forty-fourth Commencement," *BAQ,* summer 1946, 6–7.

51. "Dr. W. J. Baird, Berry President, Resigns Position," *Cedartown (Ga.) Standard,* June 11, 1946, n.p.; "Dr. William Baird Elected Head of Morehead College," *Maysville (Ky.) Independent,* Aug. 7, 1946, n.p.; Pirkle, *Lectures,* 331.

52. Tracy Byers to JRB, Aug. 21, 1965, JRB Series.

53. Assessment of Baird's presidency in this and the following paragraphs is from Pirkle, *Lectures,* 311–32.

54. Ibid., 326–30, 335.

55. "Dr. Lindsay, Well-Known Citizen Here, New Berry President," *Dalton North Georgia Citizen,* June 13, 1946, n.p., James Armour Lindsay Series.

56. "Dr. James Armour Lindsay Becomes President of Berry," *BAQ,* summer 1946, 2.

57. Pirkle, *Lectures,* 339–40, 345.

58. "Summer Convocation," *BAQ,* summer 1946, 2–3, 15.

59. *SH,* fall–winter 1946–47, inside back cover.

60. "Flood Scenes," *SH,* spring 1947, 11.

61. "Urgent Needs," *SH,* summer 1946, 15.

62. "A Fund for Our Faithful Workers," *SH,* fall–winter 1946–47, 4–5; "Needed BA Retirement Fund for Our Faithful Workers," *SH,* spring 1947, 6–7; "Needed BA Retirement Fund," *SH,* fall 1947, 9.

63. Susan J. Bandy, "100 Years of Sport at Berry," typescript, Mar. 20, 2001, 2, BCA.

64. "Berry Plays Oglethorpe Wednesday," *MBN,* Dec. 8, 1947, 4.

65. "Christmas at Berry," *SH,* winter 1947, 5.

66. "Old Railway Station Converted to Picnic Center by Garden Club," *MBN,* Apr. 10, 1948, 1.

67. Pendley, *Sixty Years of Education for Service* (1963), 37.

68. Ibid., 38–39.

69. "Inflation Hits Grades," *MBN,* Jan. 13, 1949, 1.

70. "New Courses Offered," *MBN,* Jan. 13, 1949, 4.

71. Pendley, *Sixty Years of Education for Service* (1963), 40–43. The following discussion is drawn from this work.

72. Ibid., 39–42.

73. Ibid., 42.

74. Ibid., 43.

75. "Clarence Walker (1914) Named Business Manager and Director of Finance," *SH,* spring 1948, 3.

76. "Skinner Heads School at Rabun Gap," *MBN,* Dec. 16, 1948, 1.

77. Pendley, *Sixty Years of Education for Service* (1963), 45.

78. "Needed: Possum Trot Grammar School Reopened: About 40 Children Eager to Attend," *SH,* fall 1947, 19.

79. "Possum Trot Is Having Its Face Lifted," *SH,* spring 1949, 3–4.

80. Pirkle, *Lectures,* 346–47.

81. "Henry Ford Is Dead at 83 in Dearborn," *New York Times,* Apr. 8, 1947, 1.

82. "Beloved Trustee Dies," *SH,* fall 1947, 11.

83. "In Memoriam," *SH,* summer 1949, inside front cover, 6–7.

84. "Miss Alice B. Warden Dies," *MBN,* Mar. 25, 1950, 1.

85. "In Memoriam," *SH,* Oct. 1950, inside front cover.

86. Pendley, *Sixty Years of Education for Service* (1963), 46.

87. Ibid.; "Berry's Dr. Lindsay Placed on Inactive Status," *RNT,* June 10, 1951, n.p.; Pirkle, *Lectures,* 365–66.

88. "Deaths: Dr. James Armour Lindsay," *BAQ,* Oct. 1954, 14; Pirkle, *Lectures,* 366.

89. Pirkle, *Lectures,* 346, 348, 366.

90. "Dean S. H. Cook Promoted to Presidency," *BAQ,* July 1951, 2.

91. Pirkle, *Lectures,* 375.

92. Pendley, *Sixty Years of Education for Service* (1963), 48.

93. Pirkle, *Lectures,* 385–86.

94. *SH,* Sept. 1951, 3.

95. "The Golden Year," *SH,* Mar. 1952, 3, 11.

96. "Mrs. Hammond Awarded Certificate by Daughters of Berry," *SH,* Mar. 1952, 11; "Mrs. Hammond Delivers Address at Commencement," *SH,* Mar. 1952, 8.

97. Pendley, *Sixty Years of Education for Service* (1963), 49–51.

98. "General Education Exam—Incentive to Learn?" *MBN,* Feb. 18, 1952, 2.

99. *SH,* June 1953, 5.

100. Pendley, *Sixty Years of Education for Service* (1963), 52.

101. "Record Crowd Attends Commencement," *MBN,* June 24, 1937, 1; "Building a New Life," *SH,* summer 1949, 11.

102. "Dr. Lambert Named President of the Berry Schools," *BAQ,* July 1953, 6.

103. Pirkle, *Lectures,* 402; "President and Mrs. Lambert Honored," *BAQ,* Oct. 1953, 21.

104. "A Letter from Dr. Lambert," *BAQ,* Oct. 1953, 3.

105. "The President's Letter," *BAQ,* Jan. 1954, 3.

106. Pendley, *Sixty Years of Education for Service* (1963), 57–68; Pirkle, *Lectures,* 414–15.

107. Pirkle, *Lectures,* 402–3.

108. "Dr. Lambert's Engagements," *BAQ,* Apr. 1954, 5.

109. Jack Jones to Ouida W. Dickey (e-mail), Jan. 19, 2003.

110. Pendley, *Sixty Years of Education for Service* (1963), 53–54. Pendley provides more detail regarding actions at board meetings, for which reports were available when she wrote her administrative history in 1963. Those reports from this interim period following Berry's death were not available at the time of this writing.

111. Ibid., 56, 57–58.

112. Ibid., 68; *BSB,* Dec. 1954, 67.

113. Pirkle, *Lectures,* 410–11.

114. *BSB,* Dec. 1954, 62–71.

115. "Berry Retirement Fund," *BAQ,* July 1955, 11.

116. Pendley, *Sixty Years of Education for Service* (1963), 69.

117. "Morton Hall Dedicated," *SH,* Mar. 1955, 4.

118. "Accreditation," *BAQ,* Apr. 1955, 6.

119. "Standards for Degrees Changed by Faculty," *MBN,* May 1955, 1.

120. Pendley, *Sixty Years of Education for Service* (1963), 69.

121. Tom Gandy to Robert S. Lambert, June 23, 1955, Robert S. Lambert file, HH.

122. Pirkle, *Lectures,* 424–25.

123. *RNT,* June 10, 1955, 1.

124. Tracy Byers to JRB, Sept. 9, 1965, JRB Series; "Mr. Martin Brings Inspiring Message," *SH,* Sept. 1955, inside front cover; "Mr. Sibley Welcomes New Students

and Staff at First Joint Chapel," *SH*, Sept. 1955, 14. During the 1960s, Inez Henry told journalist Tracy Byers, "Dr. and Mrs. Lambert gave a cocktail party in Oak Hill for some friends from Rome. Of course, we had to get rid of them" (Tracy Byers to JRB, Sept. 9, 1965, JRB Series).

125. http://www.rich.frb.org/research/treasury/bios/martin.html; http://www.tennisfame.org/enshrinees/william_martin.html.

126. WMM to Garland Dickey, Aug. 4, 1955, WMM Series; Mathis and Dickey, *Martha Berry*, 179.

127. "Mr. Martin Brings Inspiring Message," *SH*, Sept. 1955, inside front cover.

128. "Mr. Sibley Welcomes New Students and Staff at First Joint Chapel," *SH*, Sept. 1955, 14.

129. *BSB*, Sept. 1955, 74; *The Torch*, 1956, 25–38.

130. "$150,000 Fire Destroys H.S. Building," and "Schedule Continues with No Classes Missed," *MBN*, Dec. 1955, 1.

131. Pendley, *Sixty Years of Education for Service* (1963), 74–75.

132. "Biography of William McChesney Martin, Jr. (1906–1998)," http://www.rich.frb.org/research/treasury/bios/martin.html.

Six. Foundation for the Future

1. Philip Weltner to JRB, Mar. 12, 1953, handwritten note, "Telephoned Invitation Resulted in My Visiting the Berry Schools at Their Expense on May 18, 19, 20, 1953," JRB Series.

2. "Dr. John Bertrand Is Elected as New President by Trustee Board," *BAQ*, July 1956, 6.

3. WMM to JRB, Mar. 15, 1956, JRB Series.

4. JRB, notes for use in discussion with WMM, May 1956, JRB Series.

5. P. Stewart, S. Shaw, and J. Jarvis to WMM, Apr. 23, 1956, JRB Series.

6. WMM to JRB, May 25, 1956, JRB Series.

7. Report to Southern Association of Colleges and Secondary Schools, May 21, 1951, Accreditation Reports, MB Collection.

8. Robert E. Lee, interview by Ouida Dickey and Doyle Mathis, Aug. 1, 2001.

9. Donald C. Agnew to WMM, Mar. 13, 1956, JRB Series.

10. Berry College Faculty 1956–57, JRB Series. Two administrative staffers also held earned doctorates.

11. Report to Southern Association of Colleges and Secondary Schools, Dec. 1, 1956, Accreditation Reports, MB Collection.

12. Report to Southern Association of Colleges and Secondary Schools, Oct. 1, 1957, Accreditation Reports, MB Collection.

13. Donald C. Agnew to JRB, Dec. 11, 1957, JRB Series.

14. Samuel Henry Cook to JRB, June 11, 1956, JRB Series.

15. JRB to Inez Henry, June 5, 1956, JRB Series.

16. JRB, "The Berry Schools—Past, Present, and Future," typescript, Sept. 3, 1956, 2–6, JRB Series.

17. Ibid., 9–10.

18. JRB to staff members, Sept. 8, 1956, JRB Series.

19. "The President's Message," *BAQ*, Oct. 1956, 4.

20. BOTM, Nov. 24, 1956; JRB to staff members, Dec. 10, 1956, JRB Series.

21. "Confidential Survey of Opinions of Staff Members," fall 1956, JRB Series.

22. JRB to WMM, Feb. 1, 1957, JRB Series.

23. Berry College News Service, 1977, JRB Series.

24. BOTM, May 25, 1957.

25. "Some Bench Marks in Two Decades at Berry—1956–76," PR, fall 1976, 4.

26. O. N. Darby to faculty, Sept. 4, 1957, JRB Series.

27. Minutes of staff meeting, Nov. 11, 1957, JRB Series.

28. "Personal Notes for Use in Discussion with [Dean of Women] in 1957," JRB Series.

29. JRB, "Problems Provide Opportunities for Berry," May 24, 1958, 1–3, JRB Series.

30. Ibid.

31. Ibid.

32. "Comparison of 1962–1963 Average Salaries,

Nine Months' Basis, at Selected Colleges," BOTM, June 23, 1962.

33. "Comparison of 1962–1963 Average Salaries, Mount Berry School for Boys with Composite Scale (Approximate Midpoint between Salary Scales of Westminster and Rome City Schools), Including Value of Perquisites," BOTM, June 23, 1962.

34. Ibid.

35. Pendley, *Sixty Years of Education for Service* (1963), 106–7.

36. Ibid., 107–10; reports of 1958 study committees to president, JRB Series.

37. "Berry Looks toward the Future: President's Report to Board of Trustees," December 6, 1958, JRB Series.

38. Ibid., 2.

39. Ibid., 3.

40. Ibid., 3–4.

41. BOTM, Dec. 6, 1958.

42. JRB to C. Clement French, Feb. 11, 1959, JRB Series. Bertrand's agenda for meeting with WMM, Feb. 21, 1959, JRB Series; see also other letters from this time period, JRB Series.

43. Clarence N. Walker, motion to alumni association, Feb. 7, 1959, Clarence Walker to J. Battle Hall, Feb. 9, 1959, JRB Series. Bertrand's notes on the copy of the motion say that many of the statements were unfair, but the motion nevertheless passed. Walker was working directly with Sibley and Robert Woodruff at Coca-Cola (Geraldine Gebbie Bellinger to JRB, Mar. 9, 1959, JRB Series).

44. JRB to Geraldine Gebbie Bellinger, Mar. 2, 1959, JRB Series.

45. BOTM, Feb. 28, 1959.

46. President's special report to board of trustees, Feb. 28, 1959, JRB Series.

47. "Making History at Berry," *BAQ,* Apr. 1959, 25–29; Pendley, *Sixty Years of Education for Service* (1963), 125.

48. WMM to JRB, Apr. 13, 1959, JRB Series.

49. JRB to WMM, Apr. 17, 1959, Carl Collins to JRB, Apr. 19, 1959, JRB Series.

50. Tracy Byers to JRB, Aug. 21, 1965, JRB Series.

51. JRB to WMM, Apr. 20, 1959, JRB Series.

52. JRB to WMM, May 29, 1959, JRB Series.

53. "Special Committee Reports on Recommendations," *BAQ,* Oct. 1959, 3–4.

54. J. Battle Hall to WMM, June 2, 1959, JRB Series.

55. J. H. Scarborough to JRB, June 9, 1959, JRB Series.

56. JRB, "Preliminary Notes to William McChesney Martin, Jr., in Lieu of Opportunity for Personal Discussion," July 25, 1959, JRB Series.

57. Summary of conference between WMM and JRB, Washington, D.C., Oct. 6, 1959, JRB Series.

58. Ibid.

59. Ibid.

60. JRB to Lamar Westcott, Oct. 16, 1959, JRB Series.

61. JRB to Charles Fleming, Oct. 19, 1959, JRB Series.

62. JRB to WMM, Dec. 11, 1959, JRB Series.

63. John A. Sibley to WMM, Dec. 10, 1959, JRB Series.

64. Cook, *Half Century at Berry,* 43–47; "Trustees of the Berry Schools 1962–Present [1988]," Board of Trustees file, BCA; Alan Storey, executive assistant to the president, telephone conversation with Ouida Dickey, Feb. 11, 2005.

65. PR, winter 1968, 1.

66. JRB, "Announcement to Students," July 10, 1957, "Uniforms for Male Students," Oct. 2, 1957, "Changes in Policy on Student Privileges," announced at meeting of student body on Oct. 2, 1957, to become effective Oct. 11, 1957; "Costume Parties," Nov. 11, 1957, Student Life Council; "Regulations Concerning Smoking," Dec. 18, 1957, Administrative Council; JRB to all staff members, with uniform regulations for women, Jan. 13, 1958, JRB Series.

67. *Handbook for Women,* 1957–58, 54–56.

68. JRB to staff members and students, Sept. 12, 1957, JRB Series.

69. "A Voyage through 75 Years," *BAQ,* winter 1977, 7.

70. Ibid.; "Changes in Policy on Student Privileges," Oct. 2, 1957, JRB Series.

71. "A Voyage through 75 Years," *BAQ*, winter 1977, 7.

72. Ibid.

73. Ibid.

74. BOTM, Nov. 23, 1974.

75. "Bench Marks of Progress for Berry College," Sept. 18, 1965, JRB Series; "Some Bench Marks in Two Decades at Berry—1956–1976," PR, fall 1976, 4.

76. Mathis and Dickey, *Martha Berry*, 62.

77. "A Voyage through 75 Years," *BAQ*, winter 1977, 7–8.

78. Ibid.

79. "Some Bench Marks in Two Decades at Berry—1956–1976," PR, fall 1976, 5.

80. Kennesaw began classes in 1966, Dalton in 1967, and Floyd in 1970. Kennesaw progressed to four-year status in 1978, added graduate studies in 1985, and achieved university status in 1996. Authorized to begin a baccalaureate program in 2000, Dalton became Dalton State College (www.georgiaencyclopedia.org/nge/Education/HigherandPostsecondary).

81. John W. Maddox, report to board of trustees, BOTM, Nov. 16, 1968.

82. BOTM, Nov. 29, 1969.

83. ExCM, Nov. 16, 1973.

84. Sidney Tickton, remarks to board of trustees, Nov. 17, 1973, BCA.

85. Senator J. Battle Hall, comments at hearing, Cartersville, Ga., June 11, 1965, JRB Series. Paul Smith, a 1948 Berry College graduate and state representative on the Transportation Committee, indicated in a February 11, 2005, telephone conversation with Ouida Dickey that a decision on the point at which the connector will join I-75 would be made in the next few weeks. The road should be built by around 2010.

86. "Some Bench Marks in Two Decades at Berry—1956–1976," PR, fall 1976, 7.

87. "Vikings and Valhalla," JRB Series.

88. Bandy, *Viking Tradition*, 51–52.

89. "A Voyage through 75 Years," *BAQ*, winter 1977, 7–8.

Seven. Triumphs and Tribulations

1. *Oberlin College Bulletin*, Apr. 1965, 7; Wiggins, *Desegregation Era in Higher Education*, 12. Oberlin also became the world's first coeducational institution of higher learning.

2. Roy Reed, "Blue Grass Music Comes to Berea College," *New York Times*, Oct. 19, 1971, 26.

3. Wiggins, *Desegregation Era in Higher Education*, 1; Reed, "Blue Grass Music," 26.

4. *BSB*, 1908–9, 1909–10, 1953–54.

5. Ibid., Mar. 1954, 15.

6. JRB to Fred Loveday, Feb. 3, 1964, JRB Series.

7. "Negroes of South Gain in Colleges," *New York Times*, Sep. 3, 1950, 25.

8. Benjamin Fine, "Education in Review," *New York Times*, Dec. 30, 1956, E7.

9. *Brown v. Board of Education* (1954), 347 U.S. 483.

10. Kenneth Coleman, *Georgia History in Outline* (Athens: University of Georgia Press, 1978), 112.

11. JRB, "Events in Berry's Race Relations since 1959," Apr. 29, 1961, JRB Series.

12. Ibid., 3.

13. *Campus Carrier*, May 13, 1961, 3.

14. Ibid., June 1964, 3.

15. Michelle Brattain, *The Politics of Whiteness: Race, Workers, and Culture in the Modern South* (Princeton: Princeton University Press, 2001), 201–32; E. Blythe Hatcher notes, Mar. 29, 1963, JRB Series.

16. JRB, "College Is Helpful but Not Essential to Success," Nov. 7, 1963, JRB, "Freedom within the Law," Nov. 7, 1963, 3–5, JRB Series.

17. JRB, "Freedom within the Law," Nov. 7, 1963, 3–5, JRB Series.

18. Ibid., 6–7.

19. JRB, notes on address to students and staff, Sept. 23, 1964, JRB Series; *Boys Industrial School Catalog and Historic Sketch*, 1903–4, 7.

20. Ben A. Franklin, "Schools in South Integrate to Bar Loss of U.S. Aid," *New York Times*, Mar. 7, 1965, 1.

21. JRB, "Without Regard to Race," *BAQ*, fall 1964, 6–7.

22. Ibid., 8.

23. "Berry College Admits Negroes without Incident," *Atlanta Journal,* Dec. 31, 1964, 3; "3 Negroes Attending Berry College," *Atlanta Journal and Atlanta Constitution,* June 1, 1965, 8-A.

24. JRB, "Message from the President of Berry College to All New Students Accepted for Admission for Fall Quarter 1965," JRB Series.

25. JRB to Sam P. Wiggins, Jan. 19, 1966, Southern Study in Higher Education file, JRB Series.

26. Ibid., 51–56.

27. Wiggins, *Desegregation Era in Higher Education,* 50, 51–56.

28. Kenneth Heineman, *Put Your Bodies upon the Wheels: Student Revolt in the 1960s* (Chicago: Dee, 2001); John K. Wilson, "In Review of the Literature: The History of Academic Freedom," available at www.collegefreedom .org/bibguide.htm, 9. Heineman reported that "between January 1969 and April 1970 radicals bombed five thousand police stations, offices, military facilities, and campus buildings across America; 26,000 students were arrested and thousands injured or expelled while engaged in protest activities" (3).

29. Herman Higgins, telephone conversation with Ouida Dickey, Feb. 12, 2005.

30. Burl Horton, telephone conversation with Ouida Dickey, Feb. 14, 2005.

31. BOTM, Nov. 19, 1969.

32. "Some Bench Marks in Two Decades at Berry—1956–76," PR, fall 1976, 3–6.

33. Academic Council minutes, Sept. 11, 1973.

34. *BCC,* 1976–77, 32–35.

35. Academic Council minutes, Sept. 14, 1976.

36. JRB, "Comments to Trustees of the Berry Schools," Apr. 3, 1965, JRB Series.

37. "Cowperthwaite Fund, 1969–70," Ouida Dickey Series.

38. Henry W. Littlefield to JRB, Nov. 14, 1966, Dana Professorships file, President's Office Collection.

39. William C. Moran, report on sabbatical program, ExCM, July 5, 1974.

40. Jorge A. González, "Report on Foreign Student Work," Sept. 28, 1976, Ondina González and Jorge González to Ad Hoc Committee on Recruitment of Students Abroad, Jan. 18, 1978, Jorge González Series.

41. "Student Profile," PR, fall 1977, 4.

42. Doyle Mathis to board of trustees, July 24, 1976, Board of Trustees Collection.

43. "NCATE Team Visits Berry," *CC,* Nov. 4, 1977, 5.

44. "NASM Self-Study Report for Renewal of Full Membership for Berry College," June 10, 1994, Accreditation Reports, MB Collection.

45. *The Berry Schools, Petitioner, Cross-Respondent, v. National Labor Relations Board, Respondent, Cross-Petitioner; N. Gordon Carper, Joyce Carper, Petitioners, v. National Labor Relations Board, Respondent,* 627 F.2d 692, 700; BOTM, Mar. 30, 1974.

46. *Berry Schools v. National Labor Relations Board,* 700.

47. BOTM, July 13, 1974.

48. *Berry Schools v. National Labor Relations Board,* 701.

49. Ibid., 702.

50. Ibid., 695.

51. Ibid.

52. BOTM, Apr. 5, 1975.

53. *Berry Schools v. National Labor Relations Board,* 696.

54. BOTM, July 12, 1975.

55. *Berry Schools v. National Labor Relations Board,* 696, 699.

56. Ibid., 704, 705.

57. BOTM, Dec. 6, 1975.

58. *Berry Schools, Petitioner, Cross-Respondent, v. National Labor Relations Board, Respondent, Cross-Petitioner,* 653 F.2d 966, 968, 969, 970.

59. Ibid., 971, 972.

60. H.R. 1040, Georgia House of Representatives, Feb. 14, 2000; *Berry Dispatch,* Mar. 6, 2002, 1, BCA.

61. James D. Maddox to JRB, Dec. 1, 1975, JRB to Booth McCain, Mar. 30, 1977, JRB Series.

62. ExCM, May 9, 1975.

63. "Munn's Appeal Rejected," *CC,* Sept. 19, 1975, 1.

64. Some details of this case's journey through the court appear in Issues Docket, Floyd Superior Court, vol. 28, Case 10539, *Richard Munn v. Berry Schools*, 226, and microfilm roll 5–05, Records Room, Floyd Superior Court; *RNT*, Dec. 21, 1975, 1-B.

65. Lee R. Clendenning to JRB, Nov. 13, 1975, JRB Series.

66. Bobby Venable, security report, 8, 1978, JRB Series.

67. JRB to interested persons, July 18, 1978, JRB Series.

68. For more detail on Berry's vast facilities and their history, see O. Dickey and Higgins, *Berry Trails.*

69. "New Fleischmann Addition to the College Library," *SH*, fall 1957, 3.

70. "A Challenge and a Dormitory," *BSB/SH*, Mar. 1959, 4–6; "Berry, as Always, Is Building for the Future," *Berry College Bulletin/SH*, Mar. 1966, 6–7.

71. "Benchmarks of Progress for Berry College," *SH*, Sept. 1965, 2–5; "Some Bench Marks in Two Decades at Berry—1956–76," PR, fall 1976, 5.

72. "Some Bench Marks in Two Decades at Berry—1956–76," PR, fall 1976, 5.

73. Ibid.

74. "A Voyage through 75 Years," *BAQ*, winter 1977, 8.

75. ExCM, June 22, 1973.

76. Ibid., Feb. 17, 1975; O. Dickey and Higgins, *Berry Trails*, 54.

77. "Some Bench Marks in Two Decades at Berry—1956–76," PR, fall 1976, 6.

78. Board of trustees executive committee, draft report to board, Jan. 16, 1973, Board of Trustees Collection.

79. BOTM, Nov. 23, 1974.

80. ExCM, Apr. 4, 1975.

81. Ibid., June 22, 1973.

82. Frank George, telephone conversation with Ouida Dickey, July 16, 2003.

83. ExCM, Feb. 22, 1974.

84. Ibid., Aug. 26, 1975.

85. "Some Bench Marks in Two Decades at Berry—1956–76," PR, fall 1976, 4.

86. "Resolution of the Berry Alumni Council," Jan. 17, 1976, JRB Series.

87. "Some Benchmarks at Berry . . . 1956–1980," PR, fall 1979, 8.

88. "Ten-Year Chronology," in Berry College's report to the Southern Association of Colleges and Schools, 1988, 1–4–1–5, BCA.

89. JRB, "Some Bench Marks in Two Decades at Berry College, 1956–1957 to 1977–1978," typescript, JRB Series.

90. Ibid., 1; "Some Benchmarks at Berry . . . 1956–1980," PR, fall 1979, 8.

91. "Some Benchmarks at Berry . . . 1956–1980," PR, fall 1979, 9.

92. "In Retrospect," *BSB/SH*, June 1959, 2–3; "Leland Green, Former Berry Head, Succumbs," GLG folder, vertical file, BCA; *BAQ*, summer 1975, front cover, winter 1976, 8; O. C. Skinner folder, vertical file, BCA.

93. William R. Bowdoin, excerpts from closing remarks at 1979 General Convocation, PR, fall 1979, 6.

94. J. Thomas Bertrand, Diana B. Williams, Karen Bertrand Wilson, and J'May B. Rivara to "Beloved Friends and Family of John and Annabel Bertrand," Mar. 13, 2002, in possession of the authors.

Eight. Polishing the Image

1. BOTM, Feb. 17, 1979.

2. ExCM, Feb. 8, 1980.

3. GS to Robert N. Kreidler, May 29, 1980, GS Series.

4. BOTM, Oct. 18, 1980. At the Oct. 18, 1980, board meeting, the following funds and their returns were reported: General Endowment, $20,318.961, 7.7 percent; Oak Hill Endowment, $2,578,994, 6.8 percent; Current Restricted Fund, $475,314, 5.7 percent; Unexpended Plant Fund, $856,156, 4.1 percent; and Current Fund $188,512, 5.6 percent. The annual operating budget was $11–$12 million. A large part of Berry's endowment was in Coca-Cola stock.

5. "Background Information on Long-Range Planning Forums," c. 1988, GS Series.

6. ExCM, Feb. 8, 1980.

7. Ibid., Oct. 15, 1982, GS Series.

8. BOTM, Feb. 20, 1982.

9. Ibid., May 15, 1982.

10. ExCM, Sept. 22, 1982.

11. AcAffC report, Oct. 16, 1982, Board of Trustees Collection.

12. BOTM, Oct. 17, 1980.

13. Ibid., May 15, 1982.

14. PR, 1981–82, 1.

15. AdvC minutes, Feb. 19, 1983.

16. BOTM, Oct. 16, 1982.

17. "Kate Macy Ladd" (biographical sketch prepared by Kate Macy Ladd Convalescent Home, Far Hills, N.J.), n.d., BCA. Kate Macy Ladd file, Office of Advancement, Berry College. The convalescent home used Ladd's diary to compile the sketch of her life.

18. BOTM, Oct. 16, 1982.

19. Joe Walton, conversation with Ouida Dickey, June 10, 2003; John Lipscomb, telephone conversation with Ouida Dickey, Oct. 25, 2004.

20. PR, 1982–83, 13.

21. BOTM, Feb. 15, 1992.

22. GS, "Comments to Board of Trustees," Oct. 15, 1983, HH.

23. Board of Trustees Finance and Budget Committee Minutes, Oct. 10, 1983, HH.

24. BOTM, Oct. 15, 1983.

25. ExCM, Feb. 3, 1984.

26. Ibid., Aug. 29, 1984.

27. PR, 1983–84, 8–9.

28. JRB to GS, Dec. 10, 1984, JRB Series.

29. AdvC minutes, Sept. 19, 1984.

30. BOTM, Feb. 16, 1985.

31. Ibid., Oct. 19, 1985; "Five Years of Progress," PR, 1984–85, 2.

32. Board of Trustees Oak Hill Committee Minutes, Feb. 15, 1986, HH.

33. Ibid., Feb. 21, 1987; BOTM, Feb. 20, 1988.

34. BOTM, Oct. 15, 1988.

35. Ibid., Oct. 19, 1985, Feb. 15, Apr. 25, 1986.

36. Ibid., Oct. 18, 1986.

37. Ibid., Feb. 21, 1987; funding campaigns vertical file, "Berry Works," BCA.

38. BOTM, May 21, 1988.

39. ExCM, September 12, 1989.

40. AdvC minutes, Feb. 16, 1990; O. Dickey and Higgins, *Berry Trails,* 17.

41. "Trees Fall to Boost Budget," *CC,* Feb. 12, 1988, 1; "Authorities Disagree on Clear Cutting's Effects," *CC,* Feb. 19, 1988, 1–2; ExCM, June 29, 1988; BOTM, Feb. 18, 1989, Oct. 20, 1990, Oct. 19, 1991.

42. AdvC minutes, Jan. 31, 1991.

43. BOTM, Oct. 19, 1991.

44. Ibid., May 16, 1992.

45. ExCM, Aug. 12, 1993, February 1, 1994.

46. BOTM, Feb. 19, 1994.

47. BOTM, May 18, 1994; ExCM, September 22, 1994.

48. BOTM, Feb. 10, 1996.

49. AdvC minutes, Apr. 24, 1996.

50. Ibid., May 7, 1997.

51. Ibid., Feb. 21, 1998.

52. Ibid., Oct. 8, 1997.

53. ExCM, Feb. 8, 1980.

54. PR, 1981–82, 1.

55. "Taps for R.O.T.C. Program," *CC,* Apr. 18, 1991, 1.

56. PR, 1980–81, 4.

57. Ibid., 1981–82, 3; Cooperative Institutional Research Program, 2002, Institutional Research Office, Berry College.

58. BOTM, Feb. 16, 1985.

59. "Five Years of Progress: 1980–1985," PR, 1984–85, 2; Bill Fron, telephone conversation with Ouida Dickey, Feb. 17, 2005.

60. BOTM, Apr. 25, 1986.

61. President's report to the Board of Trustees, Oct. 18, 1986, HH.

62. BOTM, May 16, 1987.

63. AcAffC minutes, Feb. 20, 1988.

64. President's report to the Board of Trustees, Oct. 18, 1986, HH.

65. BOTM, Oct. 16, 1982.

66. Mike King, telephone conversation with Ouida Dickey, June 11, 2003.

67. BOTM, Oct. 17, 1987.

68. Bandy, *Viking Tradition,* 99–100.

69. Janna Johnson to Ouida Dickey (e-mail), Feb. 16, 2005.

70. See PR, 1990–91 through 1997–98, for these and other activities and accomplishments mentioned in succeeding paragraphs unless otherwise noted.

71. Randy Richardson, "Forensic Program Benefits," spring 2003, in possession of the authors.

72. PR, 1992–93, 12; *BCC,* 1993–95, 48.

73. *Berry Dispatch,* Sept. 2, 1992, BCA.

74. http://www.terry.uga.edu/hope/gahope.html; "Berry College Basic Data 2004–2005."

75. AcAffC minutes, Feb. 18, 1995.

76. BOTM, Feb. 15, 1980.

77. Ibid., Feb. 19, 1983.

78. PR, 1982–83, 7; president's report to the Board of Trustees, Oct. 18, 1986, HH.

79. BOTM, Feb. 18, 1989.

80. *New York Times,* June 18, 1989, 35.

81. AcAffC minutes, Oct. 16, 1982.

82. BOTM, Feb. 16, 1985.

83. "Five Years of Progress, 1980–1985," PR, 1984–85, 2.

84. PR, 1984–85, 5.

85. BOTM, Oct. 18, 1986.

86. ExCM, May 19, 1990.

87. PR, 1992–93, 2.

88. AdvC minutes, Apr. 24, 1996.

89. ExCM, Jan. 30, 1997.

90. Ibid., Feb. 18, 1983.

91. Bill Fron, telephone conversation with Ouida Dickey, Feb. 17, 2005.

92. ExCM, Jan. 9, 1984; PR, 1983–84, 6.

93. ExCM, Sept. 9, 1987.

94. Ibid., June 9, 1986, Oct. 18, 1986.

95. Ibid., Feb. 5, 1988; O. Dickey and Higgins, *Berry Trails,* 62.

96. BOTM, May 18, 1985.

97. President's report to the Board of Trustees, Oct. 18, 1986, HH.

98. BOTM, May 18, 1985; AdvC minutes, May 10, 1989.

99. "The History of the Berry College Library," document hanging in BCA.

100. O. Dickey and Higgins, *Berry Trails,* 53.

101. Ibid., 24.

102. PR, 1990–91, 3.

103. Ibid., 1991–92, 5.

104. ExCM, Sept. 12, 1991.

105. Ibid., Sept. 25, 1996.

106. Ibid., Apr. 30, 1997.

107. "Land Resources," 1981, GS Series.

108. PR, 1983–84, 7.

109. Board of Trustees Oak Hill Committee Minutes, Dec. 8, 1984, HH.

110. BOTM, Oct. 6, 1984, Feb. 16, 1985; ExCM, Jan. 8, 1985; Frank George to Ouida Dickey (e-mail), Feb. 16, 2005.

111. ExCM, Dec. 7, 1987, Feb. 5, 1988, Feb. 9, 1989, Sept. 12, 1989.

112. Ibid., Sept. 25, 1996, Feb. 6, Apr. 20, 1998; Frank George to Ouida Dickey (e-mail), Feb. 15, 2005.

113. BOTM, Feb. 16, 1991, May 16, 1992, Feb. 1, 1994; ExCM, Apr. 29, 1992, May 13, Sept. 9, 1993, Apr. 26, Sept. 22, 1994, Apr. 20, 1998.

114. "Awards and Publications Listing Berry College," June 10, 2003, Public Relations Office, Berry College.

115. "100 Most Powerful and Influential Georgians," *Georgia Trend,* Jan. 1996, 52.

116. "A Tribute to Gloria Shatto" (program), vertical file, BCA.

117. *CC,* Aug. 19, 1999, 1; BOTM, Oct. 16, 1999.

1. H. G. Pattillo, Berry College press release, Feb. 23, 1998, BCA.

2. *Berry Chronicle,* summer 1998, 1.

3. PR, 1999–2000, 1.

4. BOTM, Feb. 17, 2001.

5. *CC,* Sept. 9, 1999, 7, Apr. 21, 2000, 3, Mar. 20, 2000, 1.

6. *Berry Magazine,* summer 2003, 3, BCA.

7. BOTM, Oct. 21, 2000.

8. Ibid., Feb. 16, 2002.

9. *Berry Chronicle,* spring 2002, 1; *BCC,* 2003–5, vii.

10. *Berry Chronicle,* spring 2002, 1.

11. Ibid.

12. BOTM, May 9, 2002. See https://www.berry.edu /plan/goals/keyind.asp.

13. BOTM, Oct. 19, 2002.

14. Ibid., 3.

15. *Berry Chronicle,* winter 2002–3, 1.

16. *Basic Data,* 1997–98, 2002–3.

17. BOTM, Feb. 20, 1999.

18. Ibid., Oct. 16, 1999.

19. Bob Frank, conversation with Ouida Dickey, Oct. 30, 2003.

20. *CC,* Sept. 14, 2000, 3.

21. BOTM, Feb. 17, 2001.

22. PR, 1999–2000, 4.

23. *Berry College, A Foundation for Life* (Century Campaign brochure, 2001), 10, BCA.

24. *Berry Chronicle,* fall 2002, 1.

25. PR, 1999–2000, 4, 2001–2, 14, 2002–3, 10–11.

26. "Ford Donation to Aid in Renovations," *CC,* Jan. 25, 2001, 1; *Berry Chronicle,* spring 2001, 1.

27. *Berry Chronicle,* winter 2001–2, 6.

28. BOTM, Feb. 17, 2001.

29. *Berry Magazine,* spring 2003, 3.

30. *Berry Chronicle,* fall 2001, 3.

31. Ibid., summer 2001, 3.

32. Ibid.

33. Ibid., fall 2002, 5.

34. Ibid., summer 2001, 1.

35. *BCC,* 2001–3, 37–38; *Berry College Graduate Catalog,* 2000–2002, 1.

36. *Berry Magazine,* fall 2003, 2, BCA.

37. Thomas Dasher to faculty, staff, and students (e-mail), Apr. 26, 2002.

38. PR, 1998–99, 4.

39. Ibid.

40. *BCC,* 2003–5, 124; PR, 2000–2001, 5.

41. *BCC,* 1999–2001, 79–80.

42. Ibid., 2001–3, 79–80.

43. PR, 1998–99, 3.

44. Ibid., 2000–2001, 10.

45. Ibid., 1999–2000, 5.

46. Ibid.

47. "Symposium to Honor Scholarship," *CC,* Apr. 12, 2001, 1.

48. Lara Whelan, telephone conversation with Ouida Dickey, Aug. 24, 2004.

49. Martha Van Cise, conversation with Ouida Dickey, Aug. 24, 2004.

50. PR, 2002–3, 4.

51. *BCC,* 2003–5, 49.

52. BOTM, Oct. 19, 2002; Scott Colley to students, faculty, and staff, Dec. 2, 2002.

53. PR, 1998–99, 11.

54. Jeff Gable to students, faculty, and staff, Oct. 23, 2002.

55. William Frech to Ouida Dickey, Sept. 8, 2003.

56. PR, 2001–2, 12, 2002–3, 7.

57. "Berry College Establishes Bonner Center for Community Service," press release, Sept. 18, 2003, available at http://www.berry.edu/pr/news/pressdetail-pf.asp.

58. *Renewing Our Mission: Berry College Strategic Plan, 2002–2012,* BCA.

59. Ouida Dickey, "Evolution of Electronic Computing and Information Systems," Feb. 2003, 6, BCA.

60. PR, 1998–99, 14.

61. For a discussion of Progressivism and American higher education, see Frederick Rudolph, *The American College and University: A History* (Athens: University of Georgia Press, 1990), 355–72.

62. Burton Clark, *The Distinctive College* (New Bruns-

wick, N.J.: Transaction, 1922); John R. Thelin, *A History of American Higher Education* (Baltimore: Johns Hopkins University Press, 2004), xx.

63. William S. Longstreth, "Lamps in the Mountains: American Liberal Arts Colleges with on-Campus Mandatory Student Work Programs" (Ph.D. diss., Claremont Graduate University, 1990).

64. Randall V. Bass, "A Study of Student Work Programs at Selected Colleges Traditionally Emphasizing Student Work" (Ph.D. diss., University of Georgia, 1984).

65. See http://www.workcolleges.org.

66. PR, 2000–2001, 17.

67. Jeff Gable to faculty and staff (e-mail), July 2, 2003.

68. These essays are published in *Berry College Centennial Essay Contest* (Mount Berry: Berry College, 2002).

69. Scott Breithaupt and Kathleen Ray, "Celebrating a Century," Berry College Centennial, Council for Advancement and Support of Education entry, Mar. 2003.

70. Scott Colley to faculty and staff (e-mail), Jan. 9, 2003.

71. While the trends identified and changes predicted by Harold Hodgkinson in *Institutions in Transition* (New York: McGraw-Hill, 1971), xiv–xv, 277–81 (see also commentary by Stanley Heywood, 286–88), have had an impact on Berry College, many to a less degree than at other institutions, especially public ones, Berry has reexamined its mission and purposes at each stage of its growth or transition in governance. While becoming more diverse and stronger in all its constituencies and while strengthening its academic offerings to meet the challenges of the time, Berry has continued to strengthen aspects of its purpose—the heart and the hands—and its mission of service, all a part of its hallmark since the beginning.

72. "Remarks by Mrs. Bush, College Board National Forum 2002, Fri., Nov. 1, 2002," BCA.

BIBLIOGRAPHY

Martha Berry, the Berry Schools, and Berry College

Berry College Archives, Memorial Library, Berry College

ARCHIVAL MATERIALS

RG 1: Martha Berry Collection
RG 1.1: Office of the Director
    M. Gordon Keown Series
RG 2: Office of the Principal
    G. Leland Green Series
RG 3: Office of the Dean of Women
    Sophie Payne Alston Series
RG 4: Office of the President
    William J. Baird Series
    John R. Bertrand Series
    G. Leland Green Series
    James Armour Lindsay Series
    Gloria M. Shatto Series
RG 5: Office of the Executive Assistant to the President
RG 6: Office of the Comptroller/Business and Finance
    E. H. Hoge Series
RG 7: Office of Admissions
RG 8: Board of Trustees
    Berry Charters
    Executive Committee Meetings
    William McChesney Martin Jr. Series
    Minutes (including minutes of Academic Affairs
      Committee and Advancement Committee)
      Reports

RG 9: Berry Faculty and Staff
    Jorge González Series
RG 12: Office of the Dean of Academic Services
    Ouida Dickey Series
    Reports and Handbooks Series
RG 31: Councils and Committees
    Academic Council Series
    Berry Schools Executive Committee Minutes
    Berry Schools Executive Committee Series
Renewing Our Mission, Berry College Strategic Plan, 2002–2012

PERIODICALS

Basic Data (information folder), 1974–75–
Berry Alumni Quarterly, 1914–66, 1973–80
Berry Alumni Quarterly/Southern Highlander, 1966–73
Berry Chronicle, 1995–2003
Berry College Catalog, 1973–
Berry College Graduate Catalog, 1972–
Berry Dispatch, 1985–
Berry Magazine, 2003–
Berry News, 1921–24
Berry Quarterly, 1980–85
Berry School News, 1912–21
Berry College Bulletin, 1964–73
Berry School Catalog, 1908–9
Berry Schools Bulletin, 1910–63
Boys Industrial School Advance, 1904–6

Boys Industrial School Catalog, 1902–8

Cabin Log, 1935–

Campus Carrier, 1960–

Information Weekly, 1969–85

Mount Berry News, 1924–60

President's reports/newsletters (published under various titles), 1960–

Southern Highlander, 1907–66

The Torch, 1950–83

Viking Code, 1977–

Other Sources

"100 Georgians Who Shaped Who We Are." *Georgia Trend,* Jan. 2000, 50.

Abbott, Lawrence F., ed. *The Letters of Archie Butt,* 267–69. Garden City, N.Y.: Doubleday, Page, 1924.

The American People's Encyclopedia, 3:3–4. Chicago: Spencer, 1948.

Armes, Ethel. "Roosevelt's Trail." *Atlanta Sunday Constitution Magazine,* May 3, 1925, 3, 16.

Asbury, Susan. "The Berry Family: An Evolution of a Southern Family Living in the Reconstruction and New South Eras." Unpublished paper. 1997.

———. "Demystifying the Past: Martha Berry's Problematical Identity." Paper presented at the National Council on Public History Conference, April 26, 2003, Houston.

———. "Far up from the Hills: Rethinking Oak Hill, Martha Berry's Home." Master's thesis, University of South Carolina, 2000.

———. "History of the Oak Hill Home: Historic Analysis for a Planned Historic Structure Report." Unpublished paper, 1997.

———. "Mr. Ford's Car and Martha Berry's Buggy." Unpublished paper, 2001.

Atkins, Jonathan M. "Philanthropy in the Mountains: Martha Berry and the Early Years of the Berry Schools." *Georgia Historical Quarterly* 82 (winter 1998): 856–76.

Ayers, Mary Frances. "Martha Berry: Her Heritage and Her Achievements, Part I." *Georgia Journal 3* (Aug.–Sept. 1983): 37–38.

———. "Martha Berry: Her Heritage and Her Achievements, Part II." *Georgia Journal 3* (Oct.–Nov. 1983): 26.

Bandy, Susan J. *The Viking Tradition: 100 Years of Sport at Berry College.* College History Series. Charleston, S.C.: Arcadia, 2002.

Bartlett, Robert Merrill. *Builders of a New World,* 145–46. New York: Friendship, 1933.

———. *They Dared to Live,* 7–10. New York: Association Press, 1937.

Basso, Hamilton. "About the Berry Schools: An Open Letter to Miss Martha Berry." *New Republic,* Apr. 4, 1934, 206–8.

Bellamy, Francis R. "Martha Berry." *Good Housekeeping,* Oct. 1921, 21–22, 109–10, 112–14.

Berry, Martha. Address. *National Education Association Addresses and Proceedings* (1929): 337–40.

———. "Berry School's Loss." *New York Times,* May 10, 1926, 20.

———. "Berry Schools Need Help." *New York Times,* May 1, 1926, sec. 2, p. 8.

———. "Corner Stone in Child Training." *Junior Home for Parent and Child,* Aug. 1932, 6–7.

———. "The Evolution of a Sunday School." *Charities and the Commons,* Nov. 1906, 195–200.

———. "Growth of the Berry School Idea." *Survey,* Dec. 16, 1911, 1382–85.

———. *I Wish't You'd of Come Sooner.* Mount Berry: Berry Schools, 1935.

———. "A Mountain School." *New York Times,* Dec. 30, 1915, 12.

———. "A School in the Woods." *Outlook,* Aug. 6, 1904, 838–41.

———. "The Story of the Berry School." *Southern Highlander,* Dec. 1915, 176–86, Apr. 1916, 3–21, June 1916, 53–71.

———. "To 1934 Graduates." *Progressive Farmer,* May 1934, 31.

———. "Uplifting Backwoods Boys in Georgia." *World's Work,* July 1904, 4986–92.

"The Berry Schools." *Dixie Highway,* Sept. 1917, 8.

Biographical Dictionary of American Educators, 1:119–20. Westport, Conn.: Greenwood, 1978.

Blackburn, Joyce. *Martha Berry: A Woman of Courageous Spirit and Bold Dreams.* Nashville: Rutledge Hill, 1986.

———. *Martha Berry: Little Woman with a Big Dream.* New York: Lippincott, 1968.

Booth, Alice. "America's Twelve Greatest Women." *Literary Digest,* Sept. 5, 1931, 21–22.

———. "America's Twelve Greatest Women: Martha Berry." *Good Housekeeping,* Aug. 1931, 50–51, 159–61.

Boyce, Faith. "Berry—The Living School." *Woman Citizen,* Mar. 21, 1925, 11–12, 25.

Brewster, Elizabeth. "Beginning of the Berry School." *Southern Highlander,* Jan. 1911, 7–16.

———. "Chronicles of a Flatwoods School." *Boys Industrial School Advance,* Oct. 6, 1906, 5–7, Nov. 1, 1906, 5–13; *Southern Highlander,* Jan. 1907, 19–24.

———. "Martha Berry: An Intimate Character Sketch." *Southern Highlander,* Jan.–Feb. 1912, 13.

———. "Why and How the Berry School Was Begun." *Southern Highlander,* Jan.–Feb. 1912, 20.

Byers, Tracy. "The Berry Schools of Georgia." *Missionary Review of the World,* Jan. 1933, 33–36.

———. *For the Glory of Young Manhood and Womanhood—Yesterday, Today and Tomorrow.* 2 vols. Mount Berry: Berry Schools, 1963–64.

———. *Martha Berry, the Sunday Lady of Possum Trot.* New York: Putnam's, 1932.

———. *Martha Berry's Living Glory.* Mount Berry: Berry College, 1967.

"Chase to Be Berry Speaker." *New York Times,* Dec. 2, 1936, 10.

Childers, James Saxon. "The Sunday Lady of Possum Trot." *Reader's Digest,* July 1954, 55–58.

———. "The Sunday Lady of Possum Trot." *Town and Country,* July 1954, 68–69, 96.

Compton's Pictured Encyclopedia, 2:144–45. Chicago: Compton, 1960.

Cook, S. H. *Half Century at Berry.* Mount Berry: Berry College, 1961.

"Coolidge Presents Roosevelt Medals." *New York Times,* May 16, 1925, 23.

Cooney, Loraine M. *Garden History of Georgia,*

1722–1933: Georgia Bicentennial Edition, 447–52. Ed. Hattie C. Rainwater. Atlanta: Peachtree Garden Club, 1933.

Cooper, Walter G. *Notable Constructive Work,* 8–11. Atlanta: Georgia College Placement Office, 1925.

———. "The Wonderful Work of Miss Martha Berry." *City Builder,* May 1925, 8–9, 52–54.

Crawford, W. A. "Berry Schools, Near Rome, Georgia, Unique Educational Institution." *Central of Georgia Magazine,* June 1931, 6–7.

Current Biography, 80–81. New York: Wilson, 1940.

Current Biography, 79. New York: Wilson, 1942.

Davis, Lloyd D. "Concerning the Berry Schools." *New York Times,* Jan. 1, 1916, 10.

Dean, Vera T. "The Dream of Martha Berry." *North Georgia Journal of History* 1 (1989): 56–61.

Dickey, Charles H. "Martha Berry." *Christian Herald,* June 1934. Clipping in BCA.

Dickey, Ouida. *A Brief History of the Berry Alumni Association, 1908–2002.* Mount Berry: Berry College, 2002.

Dickey, Ouida, and Herman Higgins, eds. *Berry Trails: An Historic and Contemporary Guide to Berry College.* Centennial ed. Mount Berry: Berry College, 2001.

Dictionary of American Biography, supp. 3, 62–64. New York: Scribner's, 1941–45.

"Died." *Time,* Mar. 9, 1942, 42.

"A Distinguished Citizen of Georgia." *School and Society,* Sept. 5, 1931, 314–15.

Doremus, Harnette V. A. "The Gate of Opportunity." *Young People's Friend,* Jan. 29, 1939, 1.

Dowdle, Lois P. "Martha Berry and Her Schools." *Progressive Farmer,* Mar. 1933, 5.

"Dr. Berry Honored by Kappa Delta Pi: Woman Founder of Georgia School Made Fraternity Member—28 Others Also Inducted." *New York Times,* Dec. 6, 1936, 50.

Edmonds, Richard Woods. "The Berry Schools." *Manufacturer's Record,* July 7, 1927, 77–81.

"Educators Study School in Georgia." *New York Times,* Nov. 11, 1956, 130.

Edwards, Harry Stillwell. "Epic of the Berry Schools." *Atlanta Journal,* January 14, 1932. Clipping in BCA.

Encyclopedia of American Biography, 2:150–51. New York: American Historical Society, 1934.

Fenner, Mildred Sandison, and Eleanor C. Fishburn. *Pioneer American Educators,* 145–52. Washington, D.C.: National Education Association, 1944.

Forsee, Alyesa. *Women Who Reached for Tomorrow,* 178–202. Philadelphia: Macrae Smith, 1960.

Gardner, Maude. "Martha Berry's Labor of Love." *School Arts Magazine,* May 1926, 519–26.

Gaston, Joel. "Centennial for Lady of Possum Trot." *Atlanta Journal and Constitution Magazine,* Oct. 2, 1966, 24–28, 133.

Glover, Katherine. "Working for an Education in a Southern School." *Craftsman,* Mar. 1909, 707–17.

Goldman, R. L. "The Sunday Lady." *Shrine Magazine,* June 1926, 7–11, 76, July 1926, 20–23, 65–66.

Guthrie, Carol Anne. "Education and the Evolution of the South: A History of the Berry Schools, 1902–1970." Ph.D. diss., University of Tennessee, 1994.

Hagedorn, Hermann. "A Pilgrimage to the Berry Schools." *Outlook,* June 10, 1925, 214–16.

Hammack, William. "The College That Grew from a Cabin." *Ford Times,* Oct. 1962, 10–14.

"Have You Named Your Great Women?" *Good Housekeeping,* Dec. 1930, 82–83.

Hay, James, Jr. "Lifters, Not Leaners." *American Motorist,* Sept. 1929, 13.

Heck, W. H. "Educational Uplift in the South." *World's Work,* June 1904, 5026.

Henry, Inez. "Famous Georgia Women: Martha Berry." *Georgia Life,* autumn 1979, 30–32.

Herringshaw's American Blue Book of Biography, 110. Chicago: American Publishers Association, 1915.

Hill, W. C. "What One Woman Has Done." *Inspiration News,* May 1930, 83–87.

Hillinger, Charles. *Charles Hillinger's America: People and Places in All 50 States,* 89–93. Santa Barbara: Capra, 1996.

Hoehler, Fred K. "Martha Berry—Her School and Her Forest." *American Forests,* July 1925, 400–401, 412.

———. "Sunday Lady of Possum Trot." *Success,* Nov. 1923, 54–58.

Howard, Annie H. "Home of Martha Berry." In *Georgia Homes and Landmarks,* 97–98. Atlanta: Southern Features Syndicate, 1929.

Howell, Clark. *History of Georgia,* 2:408–13. Atlanta: Clarke, 1926.

Huff, Warren, and Edna Lenore Webb Huff, eds. *Famous Americans,* 2d ser., 41–52. Los Angeles: Webb, 1941.

Hunt, Frazier. "Martha Berry." *College Humor,* Oct. 1932, 32–33, 68.

"In Tune with Our Times." *Red Book Magazine,* Oct. 1956, 44–52.

Kane, Harnett T., and Inez Henry. *Miracle in the Mountains.* Garden City, N.Y.: Doubleday, 1956.

Kelly, Florence Finch. "The Founder of the Berry Schools." Rev. of *Martha Berry: The Sunday Lady of Possum Trot,* by Tracy Byers. *New York Times,* May 8, 1932, sec. 4, p. 11.

Kelly, Fred, and Ella Ratcliffe. *College Projects for Aiding Students,* 49–53. Washington, D.C.: U.S. Government Printing Office, 1938.

King, Barrington. "To Walk in the Light." *American Forests,* July 1961, 16–19.

Klingelhoffer, George H. "Berry School Methods in Carpentry and Construction." *Manual Training,* Nov. 1915, 184–89.

Knight, Lucien Lamar. *Georgia's Bi-Centennial Memoirs and Memories,* 2:62–91. Atlanta: Knight, 1932.

———. *Georgia's Landmarks, Memorials, and Legends,* 1:250–61. Atlanta: Byrd, 1913.

———. *A Standard History of Georgia and Georgians,* 2:1034. Chicago: Lewis, 1917.

Kulkin, Mary-Ellen. *Her Way: Biographies of Women for Young People,* 33–34, 322, 352. Chicago: American Library Association, 1976.

Leaders in Education, 2:78. New York: Science Press, 1941.

"Left Family Home to Berry Schools." *New York Times,* Mar. 6, 1942, 14.

Leipold, L. E. *Famous American Teachers,* 51–58. Minneapolis: Denison, 1972.

Lewis, Ann E. "Martha Berry—Her Heirs and Legacies." *Georgia Magazine,* Oct.–Nov. 1966, 18–20.

"Long Running Ford." *Rome News Tribune,* January 25, 2001, 4.

Lord, Russell. "In Quest of Another Lincoln." *Country Home,* Jan. 1933, 14–15.

MacDonald, Victoria-Maria. "Martha McChesney Berry." *American National Biography,* 2:689–90. New York: Oxford University Press, 1999.

Main, Mildred Miles, and Samuel H. Thompson. *Footprints,* 218–26. Austin: Steck-Vaughn, 1957.

Marks, Paul. "Berry College Intercollegiate Athletics: A History from 1946." Unpublished paper. 1993.

"Martha Berry Asks Aid for Berry Schools in Training Poor." *New York Times,* Nov. 19, 1930, 23.

"Martha Berry Gets Patriotism Medal." *New York Times,* Feb. 24, 1933, 14.

"Martha Berry Gets Town Hall Medal." *New York Times,* Nov. 20, 1931, 25.

"Martha Berry Opened a Gate to Opportunity." *Southern Living,* Oct. 1985, 4, 6–7.

"Martha Berry Portrait." *Spur,* Aug. 1934, 42.

"Martha Berry Wins Town Hall Medal." *New York Times,* May 14, 1931, 2.

"Martha Berry's Vision." *Rome News-Tribune,* Jan. 23, 2001, 4.

"Martha McC. Berry." *Survey,* Mar. 7, 1942, 81.

"Martha M'C. Berry, Educator, Is Dead." *New York Times,* Feb. 27, 1942, 17.

"Martha McChesney Berry." *School and Society,* Mar. 2, 1940, 274.

"Martha McChesney Berry." *School and Society,* Mar. 7, 1942, 269.

Mathis, Doyle, and Ouida Dickey, eds. *Martha Berry, Sketches of Her Schools and College.* Atlanta: Wings, 2001.

Matthews, John L. "The Sunday Lady of Possum Trot." *Everybody's Magazine,* Dec. 1908, 723–32.

Mears, Louise Wilhelmina. *They Come and Go,* 51–53. Boston: Christopher, 1955.

"Miss Berry and Her School." *New York Times,* Nov. 2, 1928, 24.

"Miss Berry Chosen '39 Humanitarian." *New York Times,* Feb. 18, 1940, 5.

"Miss Berry Honored by 850 at Dinner." *New York Times,* Nov. 27, 1935, 18.

"Miss Berry's School." *New York Times,* Jan. 1, 1912, 12.

"Miss Earhart Gets Oglethorpe Degree: Flier Is Honored with Eleven Other Outstanding Women by Georgia University." *New York Times,* May 27, 1935, 10.

"Miss Martha Berry." *High School Quarterly,* Oct. 1928, 3.

"Miss Martha McChesney Berry." *Etude,* Apr. 1942, 220.

"More Roosevelt Medalists." *New York Times,* Apr. 20, 1925, 16.

Morgan, Angela. *Angela Morgan's Recitals,* 79–81. Philadelphia: Penn, 1913.

———. *Silver Clothes,* 144–45. New York: Dodd, Mead, 1926.

"Most Worthy Institution." *Rome Tribune,* Jan. 12, 1902, 12.

Mullett, Mary B. "21 Years of Begging—For Other People." *American Magazine,* Apr. 1923, 68–69.

Myers, Elisabeth P. *Angel of Appalachia: Martha Berry.* New York: Messner, 1968.

The National Cyclopedia of American Biography, C:49–50. New York: White, 1930.

Nevin, James B., ed. *Prominent Women of Georgia,* 14–15. Atlanta: National Biographical, 1928.

Nevins, Allan, and Frank Ernest Hill. *Ford Expansion and Challenge, 1915–1933,* 497–98, 506, 664. New York: Scribner's, 1957.

The New Century Cyclopedia of Names, 1:483. New York: Appleton-Century-Crofts, 1954.

"New Honors Come to Martha Berry for Her Heroic Work for Rural Mountain Children." *Southern Cultivator,* Nov. 15, 1928, 4.

Newton, Louie D. "Making Dreams Come True." *City Builder,* Aug. 1924, 10–13, 35–39.

North, Eleanor B. "Martha Berry . . . Pioneer in 'Different' Education." *Delta Kappa Gamma Bulletin,* n.d., 13–19.

Notable American Women, 1607–1950, 1:137–38. Cambridge: Belknap, 1971.

"Obituary." *School and Society,* Apr. 1942, 269.

"One Woman's Vision." *American Forests,* Feb. 1954, 14–15.

Parkhurst, Genevieve. "The Sunday Lady of Possum Trot." *Pictorial Review,* Jan. 1929, 14–15, 64, 75.

Parton, Mary Field. "We-uns Has Come. Larn Us." *World Review,* May 13, 1929, 218–19.

Pendley, Evelyn Hoge. *Education for Service: The Berry Schools, 1902–1979* (includes part III, final quarter of Bertrand presidency, 1973–79). Mount Berry: Berry College, 1985.

———. *A Lady I Loved.* Mount Berry: Berry College, 1966.

———. *Sixty Years of Education for Service: An Account of the Administrations of Berry College and Mount Berry School for Boys.* Mount Berry: Berry College, 1963.

———. *Sixty Years of Education for Service (1902–1962): Part II More Years of Education for Service (1962–1963–1972–1973): A Continuing Account of the Administrations of Berry College and Berry Academy.* Mount Berry: Berry College, 1977.

———. *The Vision Victorious: Sketches of the Life of Martha Berry.* Mount Berry: Berry College, 1944.

Peterson, Charles E. "Dr. Martha Berry: An Investigation into the Academic Honors Bestowed on a Remarkable Woman." Unpublished paper, 1997.

Phelan, Mary K. *Martha Berry.* New York: Crowell, 1972.

Pirkle, Willis Nathaniel. "Lectures and Historical Perspectives of the Berry Schools." Unpublished paper, 1992.

Pope, Virginia. "Bringing Light to the Mountaineer." *New York Times Magazine,* Mar. 10, 1925, 4–5.

———. "Bringing Light to the Mountains." *New York Times,* May 10, 1925, sec. 4, p. 4.

Proceedings of the Ninth Conference for Education in the South, 82–91. Richmond, Va.: Executive Committee of the Conference, 1906.

Reese, J. C. "Martha Berry." *American Magazine,* Dec. 1910, 182–85.

Roberts, Harvey. "The Berry Schools of Georgia." *Georgia Review,* summer 1955, 179–89.

Roberts, Sarah Elizabeth. "The Berry Schools." *Saint Nicholas,* Sept. 1925, 1140–43.

"Roosevelt Holds, People Back Him." *New York Times,* Nov. 24, 1933, 1.

"Roosevelt Medal for Three Pioneers." *New York Times,* Apr. 20, 1925, 19.

"The Roosevelt Medals." *Outlook,* Apr. 29, 1925, 640.

Ross, Ishbell. "Opportunity Gate on the Dixie Highway." *New York Herald-Tribune Magazine,* May 10, 1925, 5.

"Schools for the Mountains." *New Republic,* Apr. 4, 1934, 202–3.

"Schools Founder Feted: Miss Martha Berry Honor Guest at Reception in Quebec." *New York Times,* Aug. 10, 1933, 14.

Scott, Anne Firor. "Martha McChesney Berry." In *World Book Encyclopedia,* 2:272. Chicago: World Book, 1994.

"Seeks $1,000,000 for Hill Children." *New York Times,* Sept. 16, 1928, sec. 2, p. 2.

Senate Journal of the Georgia General Assembly, 214. Atlanta: Stein, 1924.

Shaw, Albert. "Martha Berry and Her Patriotic Work." *American Review of Reviews,* June 1925, 593–97.

"Southern Editors Adopt Ethics Code." *New York Times,* July 8, 1925, 5.

"Southern Educator." *Christian Science Monitor,* Feb. 19, 1940, sec. A, p. 15.

Springer, Lois. "Some Illustrious Bell Collectors: Martha Berry's Bells." *Hobbies,* Apr. 1955, 34–35.

Steed, Hal. *Georgia: Unfinished State,* 242–53. New York: Knopf, 1942.

Stidger, William L. *The Human Side of Greatness,* 162–175. New York: Harper, 1940.

The Story of Berry Schools. Mount Berry: Berry Schools, 1925.

Strawhorn, John C. *Returning to South Carolina: Growing Up in the Rural South in the Early Twentieth Century,* 171–234. Fredericksburg, Va.: BookCrafters, 1998.

Stuart, Jim. "From the Kentucky Hills." *New Republic,* Jan. 3, 1934, 228.

" 'Sunday Lady' Honored: Variety Clubs Award Plaque

to Berry Schools' Founder." *Newsweek,* Apr. 22, 1940, 37–38.

"The Sunshine Lady." *National Education Association Journal,* Apr. 1942, A54, 156.

"Supersalesman." *Entrepreneur Spirit,* Aug. 1, 1974, 49–52.

Tally, Alma. "Floyd Woman Devotes Life, Wealth to Education of Southern Mountain Folk at Berry Schools." *Rome News-Tribune,* Nov. 26, 1930, 4.

Tarbell, Ida M. "When Roosevelt Was Here." *Red Cross Magazine,* Oct. 1920, 15–20.

Tate, W. K. "A Visit to the Berry School." *Journal of Education,* Apr. 8, 1915, 375–81.

"Thanks for Miss Berry." *Life,* Oct. 24, 1955, 91–92, 94.

"Three Get Medals in Social Sciences." *New York Times,* May 11, 1939, 25.

"To Be Honored for 'Service to Humanity.'" *New York Times,* May 7, 1939, sec. 3, p. 5.

"Topics of the Times: Georgia Public Schools." *New York Times,* Mar. 4, 1942, 18, Nov. 19, 1930, 23.

"Twelve Women Declared Nation's Greatest." *New York Times,* Feb. 24, 1931, 18.

Van Ness, James. "Martha Berry and Her Mountain School." *The Mentor,* Aug. 1928, 18–20.

Wakefield, Dara. "Maintaining a Christian Institutional Identity while Embracing Religious Diversity." *Religion and Education* 29 (fall 2002): 90–102.

Webster's Biographical Dictionary, 145. Springfield, Mass.: Merriam, 1943.

West, Don. "Sweatshops in the Schools." *New Republic,* Oct. 4, 1933, 216.

Who Was Who, 1941–1950, 4:94. London: Black, 1941–50.

Who Was Who in America, 1943–1950, 2:94. 4th ed. Chicago: Marquis, 1963.

Who's Who 1935, 258. London: Black, 1935.

Who's Who 1937, 260. London: Black, 1937.

Who's Who 1941, 245. London: Black, 1941.

Who's Who in America, 11:240. Chicago: Marquis, 1920–21.

Who's Who in America, 22:313. Chicago: Marquis, 1942–43.

Wiggins, Sam P. *The Desegregation Era in Higher Education,* 50. Berkeley, Calif.: McCutchan, 1966.

Wingo, Alice Logan. "Four and Twenty Years with Martha Berry." *Southern Highlander,* spring–summer 1943, 20–25, autumn 1943, 14–17, winter 1943–44, 14–17, fall–winter 1944, 16–18.

Woman's Who's Who of America, 97. New York: American Commonwealth, 1914–15.

Index

Page numbers in italics refer to photographs.